GENDER AND THE GLOBAL LAND GRAB

FRONTIERS OF GLOBAL GOVERNANCE

How does global governance work? How do complex webs of institutions, processes, actors, and practices effectively address or anticipate global challenges such as pandemics, climate change, migration, and the internet? When do they succeed, why do they fail, and how can they be improved?

Books in the Frontiers of Global Governance series answer these questions by analyzing global governance as a distinct object of study or by applying a global governance lens to complex political, economic, and social issues. The series pushes forward theoretical, empirical, methodological, and policy debates about global challenges and their solutions. It promotes research that asks intriguing questions about global governance, and it offers compelling answers that have important implications for the practice of global governance or for the way research is conducted in the field. The editors encourage submissions that offer novel arguments and perspectives, that adopt multidisciplinary approaches, and that use innovative methodologies. Above all, Frontiers of Global Governance is a cutting-edge and accessible outlet for research by the growing number of scholars of global governance.

1 *Gender and the Global Land Grab*
A Feminist Global Governance Approach
Andrea M. Collins

GENDER AND THE GLOBAL LAND GRAB

A Feminist Global Governance Approach

ANDREA M. COLLINS

McGill-Queen's University Press

Montreal & Kingston | London | Chicago

ISBN 978-0-2280-2113-1 (cloth)
ISBN 978-0-2280-2114-8 (paper)
ISBN 978-0-2280-2169-8 (ePDF)
ISBN 978-0-2280-2170-4 (ePUB)

Legal deposit second quarter 2024
Bibliothèque nationale du Québec

Printed in Canada on acid-free paper that is 100% ancient forest free (100% post-consumer recycled), processed chlorine free

This book has been published with the help of a grant from the Canadian Federation for the Humanities and Social Sciences, through the Awards to Scholarly Publications Program, using funds provided by the Social Sciences and Humanities Research Council of Canada.

Funded by the Government of Canada | Financé par le gouvernement du Canada | Canada | Canada Council for the Arts | Conseil des arts du Canada

We acknowledge the support of the Canada Council for the Arts.
Nous remercions le Conseil des arts du Canada de son soutien.

McGill-Queen's University Press in Montreal is on land which long served as a site of meeting and exchange amongst Indigenous Peoples, including the Haudenosaunee and Anishinabeg nations. In Kingston it is situated on the territory of the Haudenosaunee and Anishinaabek. We acknowledge and thank the diverse Indigenous Peoples whose footsteps have marked these territories on which peoples of the world now gather.

Library and Archives Canada Cataloguing in Publication

Title: Gender and the global land grab : a feminist global governance approach / Andrea M. Collins.
Names: Collins, Andrea M., author.
Description: Series statement: Frontiers of global governance ; 1 | Includes bibliographical references and index.
Identifiers: Canadiana (print) 20230595537 | Canadiana (ebook) 20230595618 | ISBN 9780228021131 (cloth) | ISBN 9780228021148 (paper) | ISBN 9780228021704 (EPUB) | ISBN 9780228021698 (ePDF)
Subjects: LCSH: Land tenure. | LCSH: Agriculture and state. | LCSH: Land use—Planning. | LCSH: Women in agriculture.
Classification: LCC HD1251 .C65 2024 | DDC 333.3—dc23

Set in 9.75/14 Radiata with Bison
Book design & typesetting by Garet Markvoort, zijn digital

TO MY PARENTS,

for teaching me that
an education would
open new worlds of
possibility, opportu-
nity, and change.

CONTENTS

FIGURE AND TABLES

Figure

Tables

ACKNOWLEDGMENTS

This book has been many years in the making. A tremendous thank you to my editor at McGill-Queen's University Press, Khadija Coxon, for helping me to navigate the book publishing process. I also thank the two anonymous reviewers for providing thorough and helpful comments on the book. This book is much improved because of their generous and thoughtful feedback.

The foundations of this book were laid in my doctoral research. I thus owe a great debt to my doctoral advisor, Dr Margaret Little, for her advocacy, guidance, and support. I am also grateful for the advice and feedback from J. Andrew Grant, Abigail Bakan, Allison Goebel, and Jennifer Clapp as I began working toward this book.

This book also would not have been possible without the willingness of my research participants in Tanzania. I remain grateful for the warmth and kindness of everyone who opened their doors, offered their time, and said *karibu sana* ("very welcome"). I am also grateful to the Institute of Development Studies at the University of Dar es Salaam for being welcoming hosts during my time in Tanzania.

Thank you to everyone who encouraged and supported me as I worked on this book, or at very least helped to take my mind off it at one time or another. Special shout-outs to Heather Whiteside, Rachael Johnstone, Christopher Bennett, Anna Drake, and Emmett MacFarlane; Jo Van Every and the Academic Writing Studio; members of the Bummer Book Club and the KWizzlers; and all the cats, dogs, and babies in my orbit. Thank you to Mom, Dad, Mike, Alicia, Therese, and Jon for keeping things real.

Finally, thank you to Aaron Ettinger for the pep talks and long walks. This book would not have happened without you.

ABBREVIATIONS

AIDS	Acquired Immunodeficiency Syndrome
BEST	Business Environment Strengthening for Tanzania
CAADP	Comprehensive African Agriculture Development Programme
CCRO	Certificate of Customary Right of Occupancy
CEDAW	Convention on the Elimination of All Forms of Discrimination against Women
CFS	Committee on World Food Security
CSIPM	Civil Society and Indigenous Peoples' Mechanism for Relations with the UN Committee on World Food Security
CSM	Civil Society Mechanism for Relations with the UN Committee on World Food Security
CSO	Civil Society Organization
CVL	Certificate of Village Land
FAO	Food and Agriculture Organization of the United Nations
FOEI	Friends of the Earth International
FPIC	Free, prior, and informed consent
G20	Group of Twenty
G8	Group of Eight
GAD	Gender and Development
HIV	Human immunodeficiency virus
ICARRD	International Conference on Agrarian Reform and Rural Development
IFAD	International Fund for Agricultural Development
ILC	International Land Coalition
IMF	International Monetary Fund
INGO	International Non-governmental Organization
ITR	Individualization, Titling, and Registration

LDCs	Least Developed Countries
LHRC	Legal and Human Rights Centre
NGO	Non-governmental organization
PAN AP	Pesticide Action Network Asia Pacific
PRAI	Principles for Responsible Agricultural Investment
Rai	Responsible Agricultural Investment
SAGCOT	Southern Agricultural Growth Corridor of Tanzania
SAP	Structural Adjustment Program
SPILL	Strategic Plan for the Implementation of the Land Laws
TAMWA	Tanzania Media Women's Association
TANU	Tanzania African National Union
TIC	Tanzania Investment Centre
TNC	Transnational corporation
UN	United Nations
UNCTAD	United Nations Conference on Trade and Development
UNFCCC	United Nations Framework Convention on Climate Change
URT	United Republic of Tanzania
VGGT	Voluntary Guidelines on the Responsible Governance of Tenure of Land, Fisheries and Forests in the Context of National Food Security
WFP	World Food Programme
WHO	World Health Organization
WID	Women in Development
WLAC	Women's Legal Aid Clinic

GENDER AND THE GLOBAL LAND GRAB

1 A NEW FRAMEWORK FOR ANALYZING GENDER AND GLOBAL LAND GOVERNANCE

In the years following the global food crisis of 2007–08, global interest in food and agriculture spiked. With agricultural commodity prices hitting new highs, arable farmland became especially attractive for investment (Brondo 2013, Hall 2013a). Expanding national economies such as China and Saudi Arabia planned for more food-secure futures through securing large-scale investments in land in foreign countries (Pearce 2012b). At the same time, agricultural firms, sovereign wealth funds, and private investors sought to profit from anticipated surges in food prices. The result was renewed interest in large-scale foreign agricultural investment in states with large amounts of supposedly unused or underused arable land – for some, a veritable land rush or "farms race" (Hall 2011). Around the world, there were competing interests in land, with new pressures applied to rural peoples and peasant populations who relied on access to arable land.

This race to acquire fertile agricultural lands led to calls to stop the so-called global land grab or large-scale land acquisitions,[1] and to recognize the potential threats to rural livelihoods. Arable lands in much of the world are not vacant or unused, but are often used by communities for small-scale production and reproduction, pastoral farming, medicine, subsistence, water, and for spiritual or religious practices (Cotula et al. 2009; Vermeulen and Cotula 2010b). Large-scale land acquisitions were accused of threatening food sovereignty, depriving local communities of access to land, disrupting access to local resources, or drastically changing the landscape through irrigation, deforestation, or the introduction of new fertilizers, pesticides, and foreign crop species (Agarwal 2014). Activists argued that land must be regarded as more than a return on investment: considering land strictly for its economic value fails to recognize the community usage of land for foraging, water access, and spiritual practices.

Moreover, these land issues also have complex gendered dynamics. Gender relations structure our interactions with each other and with our environments, such as through gendered divisions of labour. Responsibilities for water, food, subsistence farming, and the gathering of fuel fall to women in many parts of the world. Gender relations also shape who gets to make decisions over land use, ownership, access, and control (Davison 1988a; Mackenzie 1990, 1993; Agarwal 1994; Walker 2005; Jacobs 2010; Razavi 2009a). Patriarchal and patrilineal customary practices around the world often mean that women access land and resources only through their relations with men, whether through marriage or a male relative. Where women are excluded from decision-making over land, their rights, interests, and expertise are often overlooked. In the context of land deals, this might mean valuable information about community needs are overlooked, or that women are excluded from decision-making or compensation (Behrman, Meinzen-Dick, and Quisumbing 2012). It also means that the ability to fulfill responsibilities can come under threat when access to resources changes or is denied, potentially leaving individuals, families, and communities vulnerable.

In response to these threats and the concerns raised by activists and social movements, global institutions began organizing policy responses to respond to agricultural investment and the global land grab. The Principles for Responsible Agricultural Investment (PRAI), developed by the World Bank in partnership with the Food and Agriculture Organization of the United Nations (FAO), the International Fund for Agricultural Development (IFAD), and the United Nations Conference on Trade and Development (UNCTAD), encouraged states to pursue land titling as a key to better agricultural development. Yet critics, like Olivier De Schutter, the former United Nations Special Rapporteur on the Right to Food, argued that the PRAI assumed that all states have the institutional and governance capacity to ensure that foreign investments will benefit local communities (De Schutter 2011). In contrast, the United Nations Committee on World Food Security (CFS), refused to adopt the PRAI, but instead created the Voluntary Guidelines on the Responsible Governance of Tenure of Land, Fisheries and Forests in the Context of National Food Security (VGGT), adopted in 2012, and its own set of Responsible Agricultural Investment Principles (CFS-Rai Principles). Both emphasize the need for both public and private investment in agriculture, but the VGGT, in particular, laid out plans to establish better land governance and tenure guidelines to be implemented worldwide. With attention to the rights of Indigenous peoples and women, it was widely celebrated as an important global measure to protect land rights in the face of land deals.

These global land and agricultural governance initiatives offer policy advice for the governance of land, as well as the recognition of customary tenure and gender inequality. However, as we will see in this book, there are key tensions and shortcomings in these policy frameworks and recommendations. Land governance is shaped by gendered power relations, but the full scope of gender issues in land politics are not often well articulated in policy at multiple levels of governance. The above-mentioned guidelines and recommendations from transnational bodies to improve land governance and mitigate the negative effects of large-scale land acquisitions refer to women's empowerment or gender equality. However, it is important to ensure that policies appreciate and understand the complexity of gender relations in the context of local land governance. Thus, considering efforts to govern large-scale land acquisitions through global-level recommendations for improved governance, there are questions to be asked surrounding the gendered politics of land, and how these politics are perceived and interpreted at the global level, if at all.

This book details the multi-level gendered politics of land governance and assesses the extent to which these global-level initiatives do or do not consider gendered power relations in the governance of land. While recommendations from international institutions stress the need for local and global monitoring, stronger governance at all levels, and community consultation, there is often a failure to detail how gendered dynamics shape agricultural land governance at community and family levels and what the implications are for land politics and governance more broadly.

Understanding the role of gender relations in land use and governance is critical for the development and delivery of global land policy guidelines. Land governance practices around the world are diverse, rooted in various institutional, political, and social structures. But efforts to introduce global guidelines or recommendations often overlook the complexity of gender as a set of relations. Because land governance is tied to identity, place, culture, tradition, and religion, while also governed by state law and situated within global investment and trade flows, it marks a critical intersection between modes of formal and informal governance. Moreover, gender is a relevant consideration across all these levels of authority. This book examines these gendered politics of land, considering the local *and* global dynamics of land governance, and the multi-level dimensions of land and agricultural politics in between. In doing so, it emphasizes the critical importance of gender-based analysis in the design of global policy.

This chapter elaborates on the key concepts of land deals, global governance, and a feminist approach to the study of global governance. From there, it builds a feminist global governance framework to conceptualize the multi-level governance of land. The chapter then concludes by introducing the remaining chapters of the book and how this framework will be applied to better understand the gendered dynamics of land governance.

What Is the "Global Land Grab"?

As used here, global land grab is the politically charged term employed by some activists, academics, and non-governmental organizations (NGOs) to describe this phenomenon of foreign large-scale land acquisitions. International non-governmental organizations (INGOs) that oppose these large-scale deals suggest that new land grabbers are perpetuating colonialism (GRAIN 2008). The sentiment associated with the phrase "land grabbing" is clear: Foreign investors are seen to be snatching up land by illegal or unethical means, depriving local populations of access or opportunity to use the land, either for economic development or basic subsistence. Yet, despite these sinister connotations of the term "land grab," these land deals typically operate through the *legal* acquisition of property rights in most of the regions targeted for foreign agricultural investment (Vermeulen and Cotula 2010b).

At the other end of the spectrum, large-scale agricultural investment is the term often used to reframe the issue as one of agricultural development practices that simply require better governance. For some, large-scale agricultural investment heralds economic growth and stability for least developed countries (LDCs)[2] with available farmlands. It holds the potential to develop underproductive land, create jobs, stimulate local economies, and improve terms of trade. Thus, debates have been heated. Some scholars have been critical of "shrill calls for [the] elimination" of large-scale land acquisitions and call for balance in assessing risks and challenges of "land investments" (Kugelman 2013, 6). Thus, while acknowledging these important definitional issues, this book will default to the terms "land deals" or "land acquisitions" and use these terms interchangeably.

Why Gender and Global Land Governance?

Scholars studying large-scale land acquisitions have noted the potential detrimental impacts of land deals on women, such as the marginalization of women from decision-making, the higher agricultural workloads, and the loss of land and water access (Cotula et al 2009; Vermeulen and Cotula 2010; Deininger et al. 2011). Behrman, Meinzen-Dick, and Quisumbing (2012) analyzed the various gendered implications of land deals by examining both the processes surrounding legal land deals, but also the broader social context and potential outcomes. They note the importance of understanding the pre-existing legal structure at the time that land deals are struck and the consultative processes in which deals are negotiated directly with, or at least with reference to, local communities (Behrman, Meinzen-Dick, and Quisumbing 2012). And beyond these formal processes, there also needs to be attention to the ways in which social dynamics – including gender identity, race, class, and ethnicity – further shape the processes of land deals: "Of utmost importance is the issue of who in the community has land rights and how gender, age, marital status, ethnicity, or other distinguishing factors may influence these rights" (Behrman, Meinzen-Dick, and Quisumbing 2012, 52). Moreover, we need to consider the distinction between formal ownership and customary rights of land use, which often operate alongside each other in many contexts, including in many post-independence states.

The gendered implications of land transactions and land rights underscore how broader gendered power relations shape the land acquisition process, specifically, who gets to participate in land transactions or decision-making. As we will see throughout this book, gender-equitable land reforms are not likely to be achieved through changes to legal codes and structures alone. Rather, legal structures are embedded in broader social relationships and inequality. Systematic inequality in terms of political status, land ownership, and educational attainment frequently lead to the exclusion of the rural poor, particularly rural women, from positions where they may have a say in land deals or land governance more broadly. In this sense, the pre-existing legal structure, as well as the structures of gendered rights and relations, shape who gets to participate in land governance and land deals. Thus, understanding the processes of land deals and the potential gender implications therein requires an assessment of broader socio-political contexts, and the various modes of governance at work.

Recent feminist scholarship has deepened our understanding of the importance of social embeddedness when considering the legal and political processes around land use, possession, and control. Lanz (2022), for instance, offers an in-depth anthropological examination of a land deal in Ghana and highlights interactions between customary authorities and the government, as well as how rights are mediated through family relations. Brondo (2013) shows how neo-liberal agrarian reforms and economic development have marginalized women in Honduras, including those in matrilineal societies, in favour of foreign investment. These studies highlight the social impacts of changing patterns of economic development and control of land, dynamics that connect various levels of economic, legal, and political activity. In addition, many scholars also examine gender and land rights under legal pluralism: systems wherein there are multiple sources of legal authority (e.g., Dancer 2015; Berry 2021; Lanz 2022). As post-independence governments have sought to recognize customary practices and authorities under statutory legal systems, they often create complex judicial and political processes for the acquisition of land and the pursuit of dispute resolution. And as documented by scholars like Dancer (2015) and Chigbu (2021), legal structures do not stand apart from these complex dynamics: gendered social relations and norms continue to shape how both statutory and customary legal systems operate. When considered in the context of gender inequality, these studies reveal the importance of knowing how customary and statutory law interact, as well as how they interact within the context of gendered social expectations.

Yet despite this research, this book illustrates that there remains a gap between the actual practices of local land governance and the kind of policy recommendations advanced at the global level and enacted across state-level institutions. Prompted by the complexities of global land deals and their gender-differentiated impacts, this book uses a feminist lens to a) highlight the multi-level ways in which land is governed in practice, and b) consider the prospects of multi-lateral initiatives to address questions of gender inequality in the governance of land. By approaching the question of land governance with a feminist global governance lens, I illustrate that solving the challenge of gender inequality in land access, ownership, and decision-making requires an appreciation of gender and land politics at various levels of activity, as well as a multi-dimensional understanding of governance. To meet these objectives, global policies need to have a fuller appreciation of the challenges of gender inequality in land politics. Below, I briefly describe this analytical approach and its contributions to our understanding of global land governance.

Feminist Perspectives in Global Governance

Rather than viewing gender politics as a strictly local phenomenon, this book shows how discussions of gender at the global level – or the lack thereof – can obscure the serious and deeply political structures of gender inequality. Global policy discourses of gender and land tend to overlook the difficulties of overcoming social, political, and economic obstacles to gender equality, particularly since land governance is often shaped by both statutory legal rules and social norms and conventions about land control, ownership, and access. To evaluate the content of global policy guidance and recommendations for land governance being advanced by intergovernmental organizations and partnerships, it is also necessary to appreciate the policy interlinkages across levels of governance activity. Global governance scholarship is useful here because of its orientation toward issues in world politics that include a multi-level or "glocal" appreciation of policy (Collins, Grant, and Ackah-Baidoo 2019), critical assessments of global institutions and policy ideas, and the broader work of feminist scholarship in this field, as elaborated further below.

Specifically, I approach global governance as an analytical *perspective* through which to "understand and describe the structures, mechanisms and processes through which collective decisions are made in contemporary world politics" (Griffin 2010b, 88). This approach entails understanding various processes and actors, without the assumption that these processes are devoid of hierarchy and inequality. Rather, global governance as a perspective allows us to study myriad authorities, including "systems of rule at all levels of human activity – from the *family* to the international organization" (Rosenau 1995, 13, emphasis added). Taking seriously the idea that families and communities *are* sites of analysis in global governance – insofar as governance at these sites has transnational implications – aligns with feminist work on power and governance, as explained below. Understanding global governance as a perspective also permits more critical reflections on the normative dimensions of global governance projects, such as the reproduction of neo-liberal capitalism by international organizations and institutions (Hoffmann and Ba 2005). Such criticisms are essential for understanding the differential power structures at work in the global economy, particularly within the context of transnational land deals.

The multi-level understanding of global governance also allows us to appreciate the interlinkages between various levels of policy activity: local, national, regional, and global (Dingwerth and Pattberg 2006). Building upon the understanding that processes at the local level can be understood as a constitutive component of global processes (Freeman 2001), we can examine the various links between the local and global systems of governance. Rather than looking only for the impacts of macroeconomic and national land policies on local communities in a top-down manner, we can also consider the relationship between global and local governance in practice. Here, understanding the co-constitution of governance processes reveals how these processes are intertwined. Thus, in addition to state-level formal governance, which has received much attention from land governance scholars (Deininger et al. 2011; Anseeuw et al. 2012), we must consider sub-state, customary, and community-level governance as integral components of land politics. By recognizing how these local and global processes are intertwined, we can have a better understanding of how women and other marginalized groups are part of these processes, or where they are excluded. It is vital to have a sense of how government-led land reforms interact with existing local practices, including traditional practices of land access, as well as of the influences of the global political economy, including state development policies and influence from non-state and corporate actors, donor countries, and global institutions like the IMF and World Bank.

Building on Feminist Global Governance Research

Global policy discourses and their implementation are likewise situated within gendered social relations, which also shape the contours of how policy can be enacted. To highlight this complexity, I use a feminist global governance approach to emphasize the role of gendered power relations at multiple levels of governance. Building on the work of Shirin Rai (2008), this book illustrates how the intersections of political and community governance are fundamental to understanding the gendered politics of land. By applying this analytical framing to questions of land governance, we can improve policy development at local, national, and global levels through feminist critique. This approach also unsettles the tendency in international relations and global studies that tends to dichotomize gender as a local rather than global issue (Freeman 2001; Shepherd and Ferguson 2011), and instead highlights how important it is to appreciate structures of gender relations in the study of global policy.

Critical feminist perspectives of global governance also unsettle idealistic conceptions of collective decision-making, interrogating these sites for the various inequalities that operate therein. Collectives and communities are not devoid of hierarchy or power, and feminist inquiry can illustrate how communities, collectives, and families can be spaces of both solidarity and violence or alienation. While feminist analysis is certainly not the only mode of scholarship to assess inequality or conflict within such settings, feminist analysis focuses specifically on the role of gender relations in these settings, such as through gendered divisions of labour, gender-based exclusion or discrimination in decision-making or resource control, and gender-based harassment and violence. Feminist analysis examines the nature of family dynamics and household divisions of labour to illustrate how gender oppression operates. Moreover, feminist analysis encourages an understanding of the intersection of various oppressions and the diversity of experiences within demographic groups (e.g., rural divorced women belonging to a specific ethnic group). Contemporary feminist scholarship on land politics directly addresses the inequalities that exist within communities, clans, families, and other modes of social organization. Adding feminist analysis of the constitutive parts and dynamics of global governance can expand existing debates and reveal the ways in which global policies might affect or interact with local forms of formal and informal governance, and better appreciate the diversity of local experience.

This idea of a feminist agenda for global governance is not a new one. Scholars have been discussing gender and global governance since the concept emerged as a focus of study in the 1990s. Of note, Meyer and Prügl's (1999) *Gender Politics in Global Governance* marks one of the first attempts to unite the emerging-yet-disparate gendered analyses of global governance and highlights how the studies at the time converged around three general approaches: 1) the study of how advocates for women's interests carved out niches in various international, regional, and transnational organizations, both public and private; 2) studying how women have organized themselves to engage with institutions and actors at the global level; and, 3) looking at the formal and informal rules and discursive practices at work in different issue areas (Prügl and Meyer 1999, 4–5). The first two approaches reflect the tendency of some scholars to focus on engagement with governance institutions. This tradition in the field continues, with some scholars noting the optimism with which global governance is embraced as a feminist project (Sauer and Wohl 2011).

Yet the third area of study that Prügl and Meyer identify – the study of formal and informal rules and discursive practices – still receives little attention from scholars of international relations and political economy. There is a need to pay more attention to the gendered nature of ideas and institutions: how governance processes and institutions are themselves gendered and have "institutional, discursive and structural [gender] bias" (Whitworth 1994; Rai and Waylen 2008, 2). Elson (1995; 2007), Griffin (2009; 2010b), and other feminist economists and political economists have emphasized how commonly held notions of gender and sexuality are critical in policy formation, articulation, and implementation.

Thus, in addition to different forms of engagement, these scholars call for an investigation into the embedded gender bias that is at work in global policy-making. We must also appreciate the ways in which policies are gendered "in the sense of being shaped by the system of gendered power in which they are formulated and implemented" (Elson, Grown, and van Staveren 1995, 1). This means that we need to examine assumptions about the functioning of markets and economies, of local governance, of access to courts or other forms of juridical review, and so on. We need to understand the role of gender in policy formation, institutional practices, and the study of international and transnational politics.

This appreciation for the role of gender in the formation of policy is important given the tendency for scholars, politicians, and policymakers to view macro-level policy and economic activity as gender neutral. The virtual erasure of gender as a component of social and economic dimensions of global politics and policy development has become a central focus for several feminist scholars. Economic planning has earned increased scrutiny for the supposed gender-neutral formation of global policies, particularly economic-development policies, and scholars have called for incorporating a consideration of structural gender inequalities into macroeconomic planning (Elson 1995; Seguino 2007; Razavi 2009b). Feminist scholars have been unsettling the accepted knowledge(s) of global organizations and other governance institutions by highlighting the realities and the effects of gender-neutral policy development that tends to focus on men, assumes heterosexual, two-parent households to be the norm, and does not consider power dynamics within households or families (Manji 2003; Griffin 2010b). This includes an appreciation of how gender is considered – or not considered – in the formation of macroeconomic policies and the pervasiveness of these gender constructs when economic concepts are institutionalized in practice.

Why do we need a feminist analysis in global governance? Feminist analyses such as these provide essential insights into how policies and practices are themselves gendered, and how they have gendered impacts on the ground. These governance analyses, which examine the role of formal and informal institutions in structuring, restructuring, or reinforcing social inequalities through the construction of gender relations and the implementation of policy, remain important for the field in general. This research demonstrates the usefulness of the global governance ontology, so long as it also takes seriously the interactions between various levels and forms of governance, particularly the importance of local, community, and family governance.

Formal and Informal Governance: Polities and Communities

To create a fuller understanding of the gendered quality of multi-level governance dynamics, we must consider where formal and informal modes of governance intersect. Beyond considerations of how legal reforms and economic demands influence change, we must also investigate the less formal modes of governance that discipline behaviours and restrict change. Rai (2008) argues that we can understand the interactions of formal and informal rules through studying governance along two different axes. The first is the *governance of polities*, which includes the regulation of "economic and political life at local, national, and international levels and roles of different actors at different levels," including state and non-state actors, market actors, epistemic communities, and social movements at all these levels (Rai 2008, 38). This type of analysis falls in line with existing global governance analyses noted above, focusing on formal political authorities, networks of policy experts, and the role of civil society organizations. These actors and forums are the typical focus of global governance analysis within which we must integrate a more complex understanding of gender and governance.

The second axis Rai proposes for analysis is *the governance of communities*. This axis considers how the regulation of the community occurs "through both formal and informal institutions, systems, and discourses – caste, clan, religious and ethnic local governing councils, modes of communication and excommunication," but also the state, as it can defend "dominant social norms through constitutional, legal and policy frameworks" and policy implementation (Rai 2008, 39). As such, the governance of communities through community languages and traditions, including but not limited to those of sexism, racism, and homophobia, prevent the expression of alternative visions of community and belonging, including gender roles (Rai 2008, 38). Thus, understanding the governance of communities requires more than a technical analysis of policy frameworks and economic policy and their impacts, but an understanding of socio-cultural control and division through discourses and practices. It demands that scholars consider these modes of governance alongside the conventional study of polities to fully capture the dynamics of global governance and the power wielded within economic, political, and social relations.

Rai (2008) argues that the study of these intersections could be used to guide feminist global governance research on the ways in which these two axes intersect, influence each other, and change over time. Rai's intent is to bring feminist theory into the study of global governance, highlighting the ways in which these intersections might be used to guide feminist interrogations of neo-liberalism's effects on the welfare state and to question the assumptions of institutional language in global institutions. While not fully elaborated upon by Rai, both examples of how these axes might be used show how attention to language in these realms might offer new areas of analysis in the study of global governance.

I operationalize this central premise to illustrate how the intersection of these two axes provides new grounds for analysis of global land governance and land reforms. Rai argues that we need to examine how the governance of polities intersects with the governance of communities, particularly how the two axes complement each other and restrict alternative conceptions of community and economic organization. I argue that we can use this understanding of the governance of politics and communities to better understand the limits and possibilities for land reform and land governance across multiple levels of activity. For example, where communities have strongly held views about the inappropriateness of women holding land rights, this can make recognizing women's rights to hold land or participate in decision-making difficult to achieve. As the next chapter demonstrates, understanding these relationships is essential for understanding the governance of land, as traditions of inheritance and ownership interact with national legal rules, as well as domestic and global economic pressures.

Trends in land governance also point to the ways in which the lines of political and community-based governance intersect. While it may be tempting to characterize customary land governance as strictly a community-based form of governance, in practice customary governance stems from long-standing traditions and procedures. While customary governance may not have a written record, oral traditions nonetheless still create rules and guidelines to govern local political life. As Dancer (2015) argues, legal pluralist approaches should consider customary practice alongside statutory law, particularly where state law requires that customary governance be considered in the adjudication of land disputes. For this reason, I consider customary rules and decision-making bodies around land control and access to be more accurately characterized as the governance of polities, although they are clearly socially embedded and reflect community practice. While Rai (2008) mentions local governing councils only in her discussion of the governance of communities, they are often an important example of the intersection of community and political governance. Depending on the constitutional and historical context, traditional governing authorities may exert power as an extension of state or colonial power or may exercise power contrary to statutory law. Customary authorities may also enforce community-based norms in contradiction to state rules or broader state expectations. As we will see in subsequent chapters, the functioning of local customary governance is critical to understanding land governance.

A multi-level understanding of governance helps us to further understand the interlinkages between different local community practices and national land laws, while a feminist approach allows us to see both as socially embedded in gendered relations. Both customary and statutory law are shaped by assumptions about gender roles and relations and the reproduction of these roles and relations by communities and the languages that they use. Thus, rules-based systems – whether customary or statutory – are still influenced by societal assumptions about gender and the appropriate place of women and other marginalized groups in society. It is understanding the governance of communities that enables us to better understand the ways in which biases, exclusion, threats of violence, and so on shape the actual enjoyment of land rights, even if statutory law seems written in an equitable way.

Finally, this new approach invites scholars of global governance to consider the intersection of political and community governance at multiple levels, including communities, states, and international institutions. As we will see, land governance takes place at each of these scales, and all approaches require an appreciation of both the formal rules as well as the underlying assumptions or ideas about how gender roles and relations should operate. However, beyond just a scalar, level-by-level analysis of how governance operates, this approach also illustrates the interconnections between levels of governance. To understand the functions of national land governance requires attention to both local practices and implementation, as well as global economic pressures. Together, the recognition that global land governance is gendered, multi-level, and manifested in the intersections of both political and community-based governance, prompts important questions. Specifically, these dynamic characteristics highlight the complexity of land governance and the need to rethink global policy-making. Below, I briefly highlight how this framework leads to new conceptualizations of land governance as gendered, multi-level, mutually constituted, formal, and informal.

Land Governance: From the "Local" to the "Global"

In a broad sense, there are four levels at which we can consider land to be governed – transnationally, nationally, locally, and within the family – and at each level we can consider how the governance of polities and communities intersect, specifically regarding gendered assumptions and frameworks that operate at each level. However, the mechanisms of governance are also tied to each other across these nominally spatial divides. In a sense, delineating between transnational, national, local, and familial is somewhat artificial, because all of them operate at once, shaped by the power exercised by local officials, the design of legal frameworks, and global drivers and pressures on land and agricultural markets. Yet, at the same time, each level of analysis entails consideration of different actors, gendered power dynamics, and modes of governance. Thus, these levels help to illustrate how governance structures are interrelated and intersecting, creating unique local contexts for how land is governed and how communities experience and participate in land markets, whether liberalized or vernacular markets (Chimhowu and Woodhouse 2006).[3] As a result, although I briefly consider these levels independently, they should be understood as intimately interconnected, particularly in terms of how individuals, families, and communities experience their effects.

This section briefly considers the roles of various modes of land governance and governance actors: international institutions, foreign investors, national regulation and land reform, local councils, community, and familial or kinship ties. How land governance operates across various levels of political activity ultimately shapes land use in the most immediate local contexts, including those who live on the land. Integrating analysis of these levels promises a more complex understanding of land governance and underscores the importance of gender-based analysis that emphasizes connections between the formal and the informal, the global and the local.

Global Land Governance and Actors

Even at the global level, the efforts to govern land and land markets are complex and gendered, though not often explicitly so. As noted above, the very institutions that constitute the conventional political axis of governance are gendered and affect development of land governance policies and their outcomes. Here I use "global" or "transnational" to capture in a broad sense those forces beyond and across state governments that influence the governance of land. This includes policy-making in international organizations, such as the Rome-based food agencies of the United Nations system[4] and financial institutions like the World Bank, regional bodies such as the European Union and the African Union, and the institutionalization of international conventions, treaties, norms, and global codes of conduct. For instance, the World Bank and the UN system are critical for setting the expectations of foreign donors that support low-income countries (Toulmin and Quan 2000). For this reason, assessing voluntary global initiatives with broad transnational support is critical when considering their influence not only on states that might implement policy changes at the national level, but also for those who exert influence through development projects.

An appreciation of global governance should also account for the roles of non-state actors in shaping global policies, discourses, and norms. These actors include epistemic communities, experts, policy-analysts, policy-makers, and intellectuals with specialized knowledge; global civil society organizations (CSOs); and multinational corporations. These non-state actors need to be considered based on the influence they wield over governance processes, the negotiation and contestation of land deals, and the subsequent restructuring of productive and reproductive relations. In the context of new modes of multilateral global governance like the UN Committee on World Food Security (CFS), experts, civil society, and private organizations are also now active participants in the shaping of global land and agricultural policies (McKeon 2015). These global non-state actors play several important roles in shaping land and agricultural governance, both within and outside of formal processes.

However, the rules or recommendations that are created and shaped by these institutions and actors are underpinned by gender-based assumptions. Gendered assumptions inform policy-making across international institutions, including assumptions of the household as a unitary actor, of heterosexual single-family units, and of the centrality of heterosexual behaviour (O'Brien et al. 2000; Bedford 2009; Griffin 2010b; Bergeron 2011). In terms of land governance, many global initiatives reflect an efficiency imperative in promoting gender equality – that there are productive benefits in recognizing women as equal to men – rather than an intrinsic value to recognizing women's rights (Bedford 2007). During the 1990s, the World Bank and the FAO actively engaged in funding initiatives related to land policy, specifically land titling and land registries "with the principal aim of creating dynamic, free and transparent land markets" (Zoomers 2010, 431). These initiatives often focused on creating markets as efficiently as possible, rather than considering equities or inequities in accessing land.

Yet these strategies were not broadly successful and have subsequently resulted in policy revisions. As reflected in the 2003 Policy Research Report *Land Policies for Growth and Poverty Reduction* (Deininger 2003), the World Bank's previous focus on individualized land titles was revised to recognize the potential efficiency gains in recognizing customary tenure. However, this raises new questions about the assumed efficiency gains of customary land tenure. For instance, efficiencies in the customary land tenure model assumes – indeed, depends on – the presence of family, or non-contractible, labour to replace wage labour and reduce supervision costs (Manji 2003). Manji (2003) notes that the real efficiency gains in customary tenure lie in the non-remuneration of household labourers, typically women and youth labourers. As a result, these policy ideas rely on the often-invisible labour provided by women and youth and erases the gender-differentiated impacts that exist in practice.

These international institutions and the policies, rules, recommendations, and guidelines they produce thus need to be interrogated for the ways in which they perpetuate gender inequality or exclude consideration of gender-differentiated impacts. Analysis of gendered assumptions or the erasure of gender in various policy areas needs to be documented and assessed. As later chapters will demonstrate, several contemporary land and agricultural initiatives articulate policies with varying levels of attention to the complexity of gender relations in land and agriculture.

National Legal Frameworks and Development Strategies

The capacity of states to govern land is repeatedly cited as one of the drivers for attempting to establish global standards for agricultural investment. The so-called problem of weak governance is predominately associated with low-income countries that lack either the capacity or interest to regulate foreign agricultural investments or redistribute the gains from investment among affected communities (Anseeuw et al. 2012; Deininger, Selod, and Burns, 2012). Yet state land governance frameworks – legal, administrative, and market-based – are key to understanding how land deals will be struck, how land is transferred, who will be formally involved in consultations and negotiations, and the long-term effects of the deal. Despite previous assumptions that liberalized land markets would be an inevitable outcome as states become more fully integrated into the global economy, various hybrid land governance frameworks exist across states targeted for agricultural investment (Deininger 2003). These frameworks, in conjunction with a state government's desired development or investment strategy, combine to create unique local circumstances. These circumstances can also exacerbate existing gender, racial, or ethnic vulnerabilities.

National land reforms take many forms: redistribution and/or expansion of land rights to individuals or communities; the recognition of customary modes of land governance; the liberalization of land markets; and various other combinations of new rules for the management of land. Expanding formal land rights to women has been fairly common, though as this book will demonstrate, the widespread implementation and actual enjoyment of such rights are rare (McAuslan 2010). The recognition of customary modes of land governance have been celebrated as efficient modes of land organization, as well as critical for the recognition of the rights of Indigenous peoples. The liberalization of land markets has likewise been sought on the presumption that it will bring efficiency and productivity gains, as well as act as a key mechanism for facilitating investment in land and expanding employment.

Yet all these modes of reform shift and shape gendered patterns of land ownership and access, for better or worse. While national land governance models that recognize customary forms of tenure are sometimes viewed as democratic and progressive and can provide real benefits to women (Koda 2000; Whitehead and Tsikata 2009; Jacobs 2009; Alden Wily 2011a), devolution to such customary authorities also provides cause for concern among advocates of gender equality who are concerned by local structures of inequality that shape customary governance (Agarwal 1994). Both World Bank officials and women's-rights activists have argued that the implementation of statutory land rights alongside gender-equality provisions provide significant protections and advantages for women that are not available under customary systems (Agarwal 1994; Tripp 2004; Yngstrom 2002). With protection for individual statutory land rights, some scholars argue that women can enter land markets on more equitable terms and are better able to gain access to credit to further small-business endeavours or support their families (Agarwal 2003; Deininger 2003).

Others take issue with such claims, noting the hazards of promoting gender equality via market mechanisms and the advantages of flexible and negotiable customary systems of rule (Jackson 2003; Manji 2003; Razavi 2007). Moreover, individual-rights frameworks frequently discount or ignore the challenges of overcoming gendered patterns of production, reproduction, and social organization (Ferguson 2013). The implementation of a statutory land titling system or individual land rights does not erase the social inequalities that came before it or immediately reform existing social attitudes or practices. In fact, it may reinforce existing gender inequalities and favour those who are already capable of making formal claims to land (Razavi 2003; Peters 2010). As we will see in later chapters, both gender-neutral policy and male bias in policy design and implementation all come into play when examining state-level policy. The failure to consider gender relations – say, through failing to account for male bias in marital or property law – end up creating gender-differentiated outcomes. Moreover, even where the rules may be written to enhance gender equality, the role of front-line officials and staff are also critical. If key officials are not equipped with sufficient training or operate according to gender stereotypes and assumptions, written rules may not have a significant impact in practice.

As the following chapter will demonstrate in more detail, variations in land governance across states and regions create different processes for how land acquisition occurs, with further differences in how communities are affected, and gendered inequalities therein. Given that the majority of large-scale agricultural land deals are legal, the legal framework of land ownership and acquisition in host states remains important. At the same time, disparities in legal knowledge and access to legal recourse among the rural poor affect who will, and who will not be, participants in land deal processes – especially women (Behrman, Meinzen-Dick, and Quisumbing 2012). Assumptions about who gets to be a rights-holder matters.

Understanding state strategies for development or investment in addition to the role of foreign investors highlights the role of states in the governance of land and the facilitation of land deals. This is an important reminder when it may be tempting to focus more attention on the role of foreign states or companies. The recipient or host state plays a critical role in determining the classifications of land, which may determine the placement of agricultural projects (Lavers 2012). These views about the proper use of land can lead to the appropriation of land under continued use by pastoral communities, leaving already-marginalized communities further disadvantaged. In this way, the power of the state to shape land deals, either in collaboration with or as a means to attract investors, needs to be analyzed.

While acknowledging the overarching power of the state, the pluralist nature of land governance also requires that attention be paid to the councils and authorities that exercise power at the local level, whether with or without state support. However, even where states have not formally devolved authority to local councils, the role of local authorities in the governance of land remains critical in how land is used and, in the case of land deals, transferred.

Local Authorities in Land Governance

The decision-making power wielded by local authorities is fundamental to understanding how people control and transfer land. State withdrawal of social-service provision has fragmented governance and authority "among a multitude of governmental and nongovernmental actors to increase efficiency and effectiveness" (Krahmann 2003, 327). Rankin (2001) notes that such liberalization is not the "hollowing out" of the state, as some scholars have argued, but the "re-scaling" of state power from a central authority to sub-national authorities. In the case of liberalizing land markets, state power is often rescaled to local authorities in a way that fuses global economic pressures with locally based authority structures. State-led land reforms often mediate between global pressures and local economic and political structures, which are embedded in unequal social relations at the village level.

Yet this dynamic does not hold across all countries. For instance, in the context of many sub-Saharan African countries, the devolution of responsibility to new authorities and the implementation of new governance structures can also represent the exertion of state authority where little or none had existed before (Pedersen 2012). Importantly, this decentralization demonstrates the blurring of authority between the state and local councils. This devolution of state power to the village, "where ordinary, often unpaid citizens are expected to control administrative processes ... leaves room for local customs and local control" (Pedersen 2012, 277). Thus, the authority vested in local councils is shaped not only by state land policies, but by long-standing local practices. We must pay attention to the ways in which local norms and customs influence the practices of local governance. This is particularly important as international institutions recommend recognition of informal rights to land.

This devolution of authority also opens opportunities for other actors to intervene in land deal processes. Struggles for domination occur in multiple forums, not solely in the "commanding heights" of the state executive (Migdal 2001, 121). So-called "middlemen" can be important actors in the land deal process (Sud 2014; Fairbairn 2013). Representatives of national political parties have also been known to interfere with local politics and decisions over land: incitements to violence over land by politicians has been one dimension of Kenyan national politics from the 1980s through to the present day (Boone 2014).

The reliance on customary local practices, combined with the opportunities for elites to intervene in land governance practices, results in serious challenges for those seeking to democratize governance and improve gender equality. Importantly, reliance on local customs and authorities might exist in tension with notions of gender equality advocated by both global and national civil society groups. Community attitudes about the proper roles of men and women in governance and adjudication bodies often prove to be obstacles in the effective implementation of land reforms intended to address gender inequality. Where national law mandates gender equality in governance – such as in the form of gender quotas – it may lead to support for women representatives who will ultimately help maintain the political status quo, rather than have any meaningful effect on gender inequality more broadly.

Sub-state authorities also need to be considered as part of the broader picture of the social dimensions of land tenure and governance. In addition to their position in political structures, these actors may also enforce or reproduce social expectations about the role of women in public consultations or decision-making. Some forums may limit the extent to which women are able to actively contribute to public discourses and participate in consultations. These gendered and classed socio-political dynamics exist alongside, and will inevitably interact with, land tenure frameworks, ongoing titling processes, consultation processes, compensation, and contract negotiations, all of which are involved with land deals (Behrman, Meinzen-Dick, and Quisumbing 2012). Moreover, "gender disparities in human capital," largely in the form of educational attainment, may limit women's knowledge of legal frameworks, political structures, or available resources (Behrman, Meinzen-Dick, and Quisumbing 2012, 53). This site of analysis illustrates the blurring of lines of authority between the state and village authorities, customary and religious authorities, and the ways in which customs shape land governance practices. However, acknowledging how local customs can influence the governance process at the village level also needs to be coupled with a consideration of how customs also govern through the role of kinship relations in the regulation of land tenure.

Kinship, Community, and Family Governance

Community norms and customs are often very tightly linked to various forms of kinship or familial governance. These forms of governance should not be understood solely as governance within a household unit, but as part of the recognized kinship ties that determine land ownership and inheritance. These patterns of land ownership operate both within the family and within the broader communities that recognize and reinforce such rights to access or ownership. Consequently, they are often very closely tied to customary land tenure governance for the broader community. As a result, we need to examine how kinship relations facilitate or restrict land access for certain identity groups or age cohorts, and how these dynamics are affected by large-scale land deals.

The assumptions made by many advocates of liberalized land markets and stronger legal land rights for individuals is that customary forms of land tenure, especially those that are hereditary or transferred through kinship relations, are disadvantageous for women (Agarwal 2003; Deininger 2003). In some cases, kinship requirements to land access do appear restrictive. For instance, in some patrilineal societies, a woman's access to land may be tied to her marital status or position within her or her partner's family (Razavi 2007). Patrilineal and patrilocal practices can create significant barriers to women's ownership or co-ownership of family land. In communities where patrilineal inheritance is the primary means to access land, women can face tremendous barriers to securing land independent of relationships with men.

Advocates for liberalized land markets and large-scale agricultural investments also often argue that women engaged in household farm labour will be able to transition into local labour markets (Deininger 2003; FAO et al. 2010). Yet the assumption of such a transition needs to be examined alongside how many women actually participate in formal labour markets and what familial or community needs and expectations might prevent them from doing so (Freeman 2001). Community or familial expectations of women can also dictate land use and ownership, such as the perceived appropriateness of a woman using land for subsistence versus using land to produce goods for sale (Mackenzie 2010; Amanor 2010).

Given instances of gender norms restricting women's independent access to land or their ability to reap the potential benefits of large-scale agricultural production, establishing women's individual land rights is often perceived by feminist advocates as a means of providing a bulwark for women's rights against discriminatory community practices (Agarwal 1994). However, in many cases, men's structural advantages over women – particularly as the recognized owners of existing assets – can result in strengthening men's land claims under statutory reforms. At the same time, such reforms can have a limited effect on women's land claims. The transition from customary claims on land to statutory claims on land may also deprive some women of powerful counterclaims on land or block certain practices that have gained acceptance in the realm of land ownership, such as a widowed woman taking on a "female husband" who can provide labour and bear children in the deceased husband's name (Mackenzie 1993; Tsikata 2003). Such practices speak to the ways in which local communities might accommodate the changing needs of women through their community relationships. Indeed, there is a concern that greater liberalization of land markets undermines these practices (Koda 2000).

In short, the impact of kinship and community governance will remain regardless of the broader structures that exist to govern land ownership or use. Scholars have debated the merits and shortcomings of customary governance that relies on familial ties, especially in the context of land titling, yet few dispute the lasting influences of customary tenure (Whitehead and Tsikata 2003; Englert 2008; Nyamu-Musembi 2008). Understanding the contextually specific ways in which kinship and community norms shape land ownership, access, and use is critical if investors want to acquire land *and* mitigate any negative social impacts. Doing so requires attention to gender imbalances in both the statutory and customary forms of land governance, especially where gender norms might prevent women from participating in consultations, possessing land titles, or entering land or labour markets. Thus, understanding how various forms of formal and informal governance intersect will be key to understanding the complex social and political context into which foreign investors are entering.

Conclusion

The governance of land is mediated and influenced by multiple levels of governance, and it is also gendered and context specific. These gender relations may be shaped by local, familial, and religious traditions, agricultural practices and gendered divisions of labour, local politics, legal and customary rules, economic exchange, and broader global politics. The analytical framework (figure 1.1) laid out in this chapter shows the importance of taking a multi-level approach to understanding the politics of land governance while also appreciating the ways in which these politics are embedded in gendered social relations. The ways in which assumptions or expectations about gender roles or the exclusion of gender relations altogether shape the governance of land have important implications for resolving inequities in the access to and control over land. As a result, serious efforts to reform the power dynamics around land governance need to understand gender inequality and have strategies for addressing inequality at multiple levels of authority. The development and implementation of land governance reform policy needs to have a full appreciation of the ways in which gender relations structure access to land.

To demonstrate the interlinkages between gender relations and land policy across levels of governance, the remainder of the book proceeds as follows. Chapter 2 reviews common trends related to gender and land reform policy around the world, and then specifically examines the challenges of gender equity and land reform across several post-independence sub-Saharan African countries that have been targeted for agricultural investment. This chapter also provides further detail on the need for diverse strategies to address gendered power imbalances. Chapter 3 offers a specific case study of these dynamics in Tanzania,

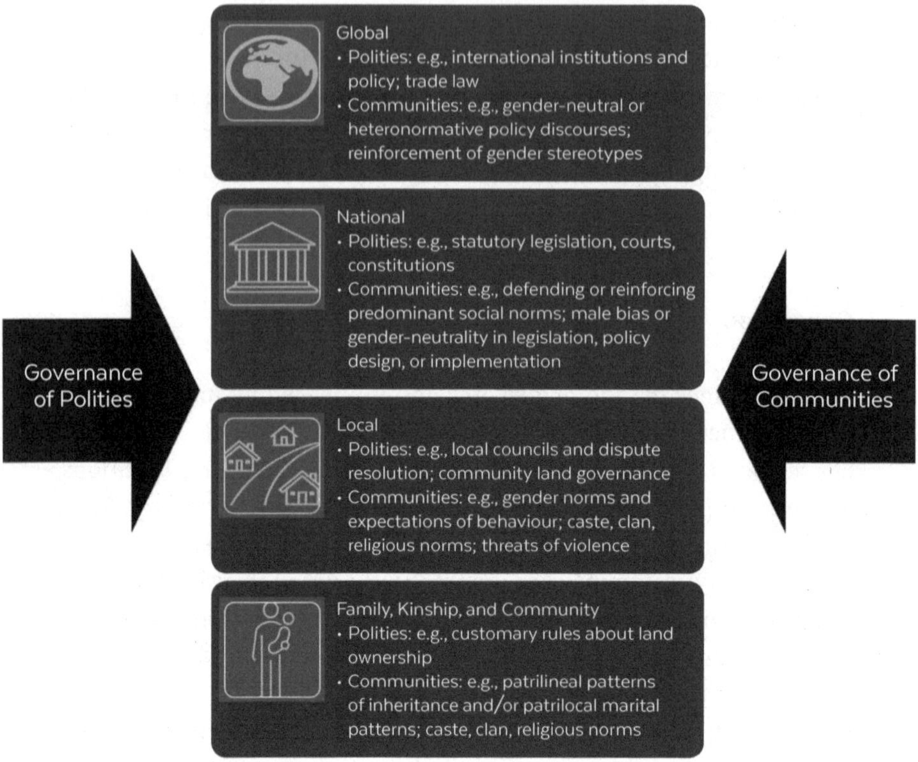

Figure 1.1 Feminist analytical framework for multi-level governance

employing the analytical framework to study gender and multi-level land governance nationally, locally, and within family, kinship groups, and communities. Tanzania is chosen in particular because of its longer history of efforts to integrate local customary governance into state structures of land governance, while incorporating gender-equity in local land governance. Tanzania is thus presented as a "most-likely case," wherein these reforms hold significant promise to recognize local custom, and yet have still struggled to resolve issues of inequality. Together, these two chapters detail the various ways in which land governance and land deals have complex gender-differentiated effects and present important considerations for land policy reform.

Using this understanding as a base, the remaining chapters assess the extent to which various global land and agricultural governance initiatives have addressed gender issues. Chapter 4 considers how gender has been incorporated into responsible agricultural investment principles, which were developed in response to concerns about how land acquisitions in the post-2008 period affected small-scale farmers. Chapter 5 examines how gender has been addressed within the United Nations Committee on World Food Security (CFS), a body that has both incorporated gender into key land governance documents and has recognized "the importance of mainstreaming gender equality, women's and girls' rights and women's empowerment ... in all CFS work streams, products and documents" (CFS 2017, 10). Finally, given some of the promising elements of these global initiatives, chapter 6 takes stock of the prospects of feminist global land governance within the context of competing pressures on states to both recognize land rights and accommodate large-scale foreign agricultural investment. By understanding the immense challenge of effective gender-equitable land reform and the commitments required of states and non-governmental organizations, it is clear that such change is expensive and complex, but is still a worthwhile endeavour on a global level.

Through this examination of global efforts to govern land acquisition, we can see that the complexity of gender-inequality issues warrants more critical attention from policy-makers at all levels. Bringing gender and land scholarship into conversation with studies of multilevel governance highlights the gaps in both global and domestic policy development, and the challenges of equitable land governance reform. Feminist scholarship on land and resources expands our understanding of global governance by highlighting the gaps between policy and practice and expanding how we conceptualize gender issues in global governance. There is a need to provide the resources that can facilitate change through both conventional state mechanisms and meaningful engagement with local, non-state actors. Yet these answers will not be universal and require that decision-makers pay attention to formal and informal modes of land governance that exist, understand how they intersect, and work with the people whose lives and livelihoods depend on land to find lasting, equitable solutions.

2 LOCAL OBSTACLES, GLOBAL TRENDS: GENDER AND LAND GOVERNANCE IN AFRICA

The gendered norms and behaviours that shape our day-to-day interactions may be invisible to us. When I first began research on land and gender in Tanzania, I was struck by the experiences of development workers who noted that, although rural Tanzanian women were paid less and faced more precarious work situations, they often said that they felt they were treated the same as men. It was not until these practitioners asked more pointed questions about pregnancy, menstruation, physical ability, land ownership, and local politics that women and men began to discuss their different gendered experiences in agricultural land governance and management. Only in discussing personal daily experiences were gendered patterns in agriculture more evident. And indeed, such discussions revealed how treating everyone equally might ultimately result in treatment that discriminates based on gender or sex. Being paid by the piece instead of by the hour might mean that women who cannot carry as much as men would be paid less for the same time and effort spent at work. Women who must take time from work due to pregnancy face lost wages and may ultimately have no job to which they can return.

Efforts to treat everyone the same can also have limitations when it comes to how we conceptualize gender and land issues at the global level. Trying to develop broad policies and principles of land governance that can be enacted everywhere is a laudable goal, and one that attempts to overcome the challenges associated with large-scale land acquisitions. However, when these efforts approach gender the same way in every context and do not consider the specificities of gender inequality or how gender can interact with other forms of social exclusion, they risk overlooking important context-specific differences. When we start to understand patterns of gender relations as they relate to land governance and land grabbing, we see that, although there are common themes related to gender and land use or ownership – such as marital status, inheritance patterns, domestic divisions of labour, and women's mobility – the specific ways in which these function within different communities, countries, and regions all manifest in different ways. Moreover, different political rules, customs, traditions, and norms combine in distinct ways, which open some doors for change but may also keep others closed.

Importantly, there are connections between patterns of local gender relations and the broader global processes that shape land use that also need to be examined. These connections may or may not support greater gender equality or processes of women's empowerment. Socially embedded gender relations shape the local outcomes of global processes in context-specific ways. As a result, claims that local customary practices are uniformly discriminatory fall flat, as do claims that individualized land rights are the only mode of land governance that can protect women's rights (Collins 2019). Both modes of land governance are shaped by broader patterns of gendered social relations and expectations that may or may not facilitate equitable access to or control of land. The "return" to customary governance to meet the needs to land users has been widely embraced by policy-makers, with many African countries upgrading the legal position of customary tenure in their constitutions (Whitehead and Tsikata 2003; Alden Wily 2021). Yet scholars note the need to consider the impacts on women in patriarchal communities when "returning" to customary practice (Whitehead and Tsikata 2003; Chigbu 2019; Chigbu 2021).

At the same time, individualized land rights for women have also had limited impacts because of gender-based discrimination in the administration of the law, gender inequalities in education and representation, and women's relative lack of income and resources. Chimhowu (2019) observes that pushes for individual land rights in the African context has led to the neo-liberalization of customary tenure, in which women's access to land is still mediated by patriarchal practices, but also by markets. Thus, neither approach to land governance has been fully satisfactory in addressing gender inequality. Both customary and statutory land governance need to be examined for the extent to which they can protect land in the context of the global dynamics of agricultural investment.

As explained in the previous chapter, the intersections of formal political governance and informal community governance occur at many levels of political activity. The structures of power that shape land governance manifest in different places, from the immediacy of the household and family, through communities, villages, districts, markets, states, and beyond state borders (Razavi 2003). This chapter further elaborates on the gendered dynamics of land politics that are created by these intersections of governance. Specifically, this chapter answers the question of what does domestic land governance look like when refracted through the lens of gender politics? The answer to this question lies in understanding the ways in which political and community governance intersect to create specific social, political, and economic dynamics that frequently create gender-differentiated outcomes. Understanding these dynamics and outcomes is critical for the development of better policy.

Below, I briefly recap the analytical framework from the previous chapter. I then summarize key insights from existing feminist scholarship on land governance before focusing specifically on land governance in three sub-Saharan African countries. This review confirms both the importance of feminist scholarship on land, but also highlights the diversity of practices that exist. Feminist scholarship indicates the ways in which marital status, parenthood, age, birth order, and so on are relevant to land access and decision-making, even though these will all look different in specific times and places based on the broader history, political context, and structures of customary and statutory law.

The goal here is to develop an understanding of the complexity of gender relations and land politics. Understanding how gender is relevant across these various levels of governance provides a clearer sense of how policies should be designed and redesigned to respond to complex local realities. It is imperative that those who design policy have a clear sense of the gendered dimensions of land politics at multiple levels.

Outlining the Analytical Framework

This chapter uses the analytical framework established in chapter 1 to analyze the national legal land laws and frameworks, national development policies, sub-national institutional and implementation challenges, and community and family practices, including cultural and social obstacles to gender-equitable land governance.[1] But in addition to these levels of analysis, we also must pay attention to the intersection of the governance of polities and the governance of communities, where both formal and informal rules intersect to shape access to land and decision-making based on gender. For example, statutory legal obstacles to gender-equitable land governance include the design of national land laws, the ways in which they are implemented, and prohibitions or prescriptions on who can own or sell land. It is estimated that 40 per cent of countries have at least one legal rule that constrains women's property ownership (World Bank 2018). Yet even where there are few or even no legal restrictions that explicitly prohibit women's land or property ownership, there are cases in which other laws – such as laws that prioritize patriarchal customary rules – undermine gender-equality provisions in law. As we will see below, new provisions in land laws on the African continent vary in their commitments to gender equity, and gaps regarding property ownership, inheritance, and decision-making persist despite most constitutions directly promoting women's rights (Alden Wily 2021).

Similarly, although legal land frameworks in some countries may be progressive, there can be significant gaps in how land laws are implemented or a general failure to change how laws are implemented. Administrative or technical personnel might prevent the implementation of more progressive rules. As Ravnborg et al. (2016) explain, this draws our attention to institutions that employ men and are also oriented toward providing services to men. These institutions can be political in nature, but also entail the delivery of important services, such as land registration or extension services. These are services that women often do not receive. These obstacles can occur at various levels of governance – national, sub-national, or local – and illustrate the importance of considering not just the rules as written, but obstacles to implementation and how the assumptions and biases of front-line implementers can shape the actual practice of rules.

Yet, beyond the state, we also need to consider community-level dynamics and governance practices. Like the obstacles in policy implementation, the role of local councils or community leaders in the governance and management of land may be essential, particularly where traditional practices may be favoured over statutory law. Many local communities govern themselves according to local traditions and values, whether with or without state endorsement or protection of such practices. In the absence of dedicated implementation of land law reform, this can make legal changes slow or ineffective. Social, cultural, and religious norms often discipline claims on land or participation in land governance and dictate who does and does not participate in land governance. These norms commonly include expectations about women's and men's respective roles in society, including who participates in public life and decision-making.

These social, cultural, and religious norms are also important features of understanding how family and kinship relations shape land governance. In addition to influencing expectations about who participates in public life, these norms also shape household and familial decision-making, resource management, and agricultural roles. Perhaps most influential are the roles of gendered inheritance practices and expectations, patterns of marital residence, and clan or tribal control of land. All these features affect gendered control of land, as well as the gendered control of material wealth and resources. These rules can have tremendous impact on the extent to which people participate in land or labour markets, and, as we will see in later chapters, many international institutions see women's further inclusion in land and labour markets as key to women's economic empowerment. However, there are many obstacles to women's full and equal participation in these markets, even where they have land titles. Understanding these obstacles to equal participation requires deeper attention to social norms around physical mobility and resource control, as well as predominant public and private gendered divisions of labour. As we will see, these different patterns and practices intersect in interesting and sometimes divergent ways.

When we examine all these dimensions in more detail in different regional contexts, we can see how both political and community governance intersect to create complex environments for gender-equitable land reform. The variations in land politics, social practices, and economic conditions around the world tend to make specific prescriptions for reform unfeasible. However, global guidelines and codes of conduct that can reflect these complex dynamics stand a better chance at success.

Key Themes in Gender and Land Governance Scholarship

Marital status, inheritance practices, economic inequality, and other factors can all shape land governance issues, but the specific practices and intersections of various factors all create unique, locally specific, outcomes. As Agarwal's landmark (1994) book demonstrates, it is the interactive effects of economic factors, cultural norms, gender ideologies, and politics that shape women's access to land rights as well as the amenability of communities to change. Here, I summarize several key findings from feminist land governance scholarship that are used to structure the cases that follow.

Gendered Legacies of Colonization in Contemporary Land Governance

Scholarship from across South Asia, Latin America, and sub-Saharan Africa illustrates the impacts of colonization on land governance, including the shaping of gender relations. For instance, prior to British colonization, many South Asian communities allocated portions of land for communal use (Agarwal 1994). However, these common lands are now in rapid decline, driven by increased privatization since British colonization. Today, the few remaining commons resources – both land and water – remain under threat due to industrialization and ecological change, often with their own gendered effects (Nayak and Berkes 2010; Khan et al. 2018). Spanish colonization in Latin America also resulted in the enforcement of patriarchal values that presumed that women were subordinate to their husbands and deemed women's participation in leadership or governance as unbecoming (Deere and León 2001a). In the nineteenth century, several Latin American states adopted portions of the Napoleonic Code of 1804, enshrining male control over household resources and diminishing women's legal rights. Indeed, the practice of *postetad marital* – meaning all the legal rights that husbands have over both their wives and their property – became the norm (Deere and León 2001a). While these colonial practices are no longer codified in law, the legacies of these assumptions remain in many places, and continue to influence gender norms around property ownership. Colonial legacies thus extend beyond the influence on legal structures, shaping contemporary gendered norms and practices as well.

Male Bias in Post-Independence Land Policy Design and Implementation

Male bias and heteronormative assumptions about divisions of labour influence the design and implementation of policy. And beyond the role of the state, familial practices and social norms around marital residence and inheritance also shape statutory and customary land access and ownership. The practices of both communities and administrators are influenced by patriarchal legacies in laws that favour men. For instance, the tendency to view men as heads of households often translates into policy-making that views households as unitary, rather than as a site of potential disagreement or as a site housing different needs and interests. The result is that policy-makers may presume that households will have a male breadwinner who will receive redistributive benefits or land claims, and that household members will share in those benefits equally (Razavi 2003). Of course, this is often not the case.

The privatization of land had the effect of concentrating land control and decision-making in the hands of men in South Asia (Agarwal 1994). Then, following independence in many formerly colonized states, new national policies and governance schemes tended to reinforce the same rules that prioritized men over women. Redistributive state-led land reforms in the 1950s in India, Pakistan, and Sri Lanka, and in the 1970s in Bangladesh, were largely modelled on the notion of a unitary male-headed household, with land titles being granted only to men (Agarwal 1994). This male bias was also replicated in resettlement schemes in Sri Lanka, even though customary inheritance in the country was predominately bilateral or matrilineal. As a result, the assumption that men are household breadwinners who represent the harmonized interests of the family was built into redistributive land reforms (Agarwal 1994).

In contrast, however, there are many states wherein land reforms were undertaken with more attention to gender inequality. Many Latin American countries have enshrined principles of equality in land ownership and property. For example, several states support bilateral – that is, gender equal – inheritance: "all Latin American civil codes provide for equal inheritance among all children, irrespective of sex," or of age (Deere and León 2001a, 7). In the Latin American countries that have full common property regimes in marriage, the property obtained in common between two spouses is considered to belong to both, and subject to equal division in cases of divorce.

Still, even with such legal provisions, joint titling frequently encounters obstacles in implementation, including legal obstacles in the form of civil codes; institutional shortcomings in implementation and policy design; administrators' attitudes about who typically owns rural land and who does agricultural work; awareness of different forms of property owned by a single household; and gender gaps in literacy and legal awareness (Deere and León 2001b). The pushes to individualize and title land in Latin America in the 1980s and 1990s often overlooked the gendered dimensions of land ownership, even in instances where governments undertook specific actions to include women. As a result, when many Latin American governments undertook processes of individualization, titling, and registration (ITR) of lands, which in some cases meant a turn away from communal land ownership, women's land rights were not necessarily protected.

In addition to male bias in policy design, one of the most cited obstacles to gender-equal land policy is the role of male bias in *implementation*. When administrators of land policy favour men in the control of resources, their own biases and assumptions about who should have control of those resources may shape the actual outcomes of law in practice. For instance, the presumption of a male breadwinner or household head may be evident even if it is not written formally into policy. In India, as the government displaced and resettled population in favour of development projects, Levien (2017) finds that those implementing policy considered women to be represented by male heads of household. Even in cases where women had their own land rights, "governments registered compensation plots in the names of their husbands," which ultimately erased those rights (Levien 2017, 10). Land titling projects in some Latin American states have tended to overlook the gendered dimensions of household land ownership, presuming that the male household head owns all the property, although a single household may hold several plots of property that belong to the husband, the wife, and to the couple jointly. But instead of recognizing that land might belong to different members of the household, those implementing land registration often assume that the entire property belongs to the male household head (Deere and León 2001b). And even though some countries have enacted laws that recognize common property regimes in marriage, under actual land titling and registration practices undertaken by administrators, land may be titled only in the name of the husband instead of both partners. This practice undermines the legal provisions designed to protect both partners in cases of divorce. Deere and León (2001a) also note that, where a double signature is required for the sale of common property, officials may not enforce the need for the wife's signature, thus undermining common property protections that exist in law.

These examples illustrate the ways in which state implementation of land policy can work to undermine the rules in practice. Informal rules or assumptions about gender roles can limit the effectiveness or implementation of formal measures designed to address gender equality, again marking the intersection of political governance and community governance. The gaps between written rules and their actual implementation can be driven by many context-specific factors, but often include the lack of training and/or capacity for administrators, lack of clarity in procedure, lack of funds from state sources to support training and implementation, and the broader social and cultural context. Indeed, as we will see below, despite progressive land ownership rules, cultural practices that favour some children over others are rooted in family traditions and expectations and can be very difficult to challenge in practice.

Patriarchal Traditions of Land Ownership and Inheritance

Many societies favour men in inheritance and the control of resources, which can lead to the reproduction of patriarchal values in the ownership, access to, and control of land, even under gender-equal state land policies. This is reflected in patterns of land ownership all over the world. Although there are gaps in the data, FAO (2018) estimates that women make up less than 15 per cent of landholders worldwide. In many places, practices of patrilineality and patrilocality reinforce men's control of land. In her study of South Asia, Agarwal (1994) argued that patrilocal residence is one of the primary factors restricting the exercise of women's legal rights. For some, access to land through male lineage is considered essential to preserving family lands and peasant practices.

However, more than gender identity shapes patterns of inheritance. Land claims are also situated within other social relations, including religion, caste, kinship, and class. Agarwal also finds variation in Muslim inheritance practices across the region: although the Koran allows women's inheritance rights – though not on the same terms as sons – in practice, the custom varies from the textual rules. In parts of southwest India and Sri Lanka's eastern province that practice matrilineal inheritance, Muslim women are likely to inherit land, but in many other places in South Asia, Muslims seem to carry out inheritance practices that are more similar to Hindu traditions, which favour male inheritance (Agarwal 1994). Bilateral inheritance is largely the norm in many parts of Latin America, with roots in both colonial histories and the customs of several pre-Columbian civilizations (Deere and León 2001a). Yet in practice, land inheritance is not mediated just by gender, but by age as well. This results in cases where families defy statutory legal requirements for gender-equal inheritance, and instead allocate land according to tradition. For example, in Peru, the youngest in the family is expected to provide care for elderly parents, which earns them a larger share of inherited wealth. As a result, families in several villages defy the notary public by registering wills that comply with the law, but then return home to carry out inheritance rules consistent with traditional practice (Deere and León 2001a). Thus, despite legal requirements for gender-equal inheritance, families may register equal inheritance formally, but go home to divide property as they see fit, including practices in which fathers favour sons, mothers favour daughters, and parents favour the youngest child.

Economic and demographic pressures may also drive changes in the way that land is apportioned to both men and women. For example, increasing pressures on land and the resulting land scarcity can drive new gendered patterns of inheritance, but these patterns clearly vary based on local needs and preferences. In an Aymara community in Bolivia, daughters used to inherit land, but in the context of land scarcity, women are now favoured. Yet, in other parts of Bolivia, land scarcity and increased male out-migration have instead led to the decline of peasant agriculture but more gender-equitable inheritance patterns (Deere and León 2001a). In Mexico, declining agriculture and increased out-migration have reshaped inheritance patterns in different ways: in some cases, the family members who send the most remittances are favoured in inheritance, or, in others, the youngest daughters who are increasingly taking on elder care are favoured (Deere and León 2001a). In short, generalizing about the potential impacts of economic or demographic changes is difficult, as adaptation can be unpredictable. The combination of these economic pressures, combined with local preferences and gender norms, may lead to various outcomes.

Gender bias also shapes the ways in which land markets operate in Latin America. Presumptions about women's productivity, their ability to repay loans, and the absence of additional material support all undermine the equal participation of women in land markets (Deere and León 2001a). At the same time, rural women are interested in participating in markets and will save for years to purchase land. These women are aware of the bargaining power they have in households when they have their own plots of land. Thus, although land markets will not be free from gender bias or discrimination, they still prove to be potential sites for women's empowerment, as suggested by scholars like Nancy Fraser (2013a). But it is critical for policy-makers to see how these social and cultural gender biases can shape policy outcomes, including those that are in demand from women.

The gender gap in land ownership may also be perpetuated by gender stereotyping that fails to recognize women's contributions to agriculture or questions their productivity. In Latin America, this undermining of women's contributions occurs despite evidence indicating the increasing feminization of agriculture (Deere 2009). The resistance to acknowledging Latin American women's contributions to agriculture and farming belies the pervasiveness of gender norms: despite shifting economic fortunes that see women increasingly heading rural households and farms while men take on paid labour, there is still a strong bias against recognizing women's contributions to the sector.

The scholarship on gender and land rights over the past few decades has highlighted the diversity of local practices and cautioned against blanket policies to address gender inequality. Rather, scholars have identified key themes that are relevant to understanding the challenges around land governance from a gendered perspective. Consistent with Behrman, Meinzen-Dick, and Quisumbing's (2012) advice around examining the gendered dimensions of land deals, scholarship on gender and land governance point to the need to consider the statutory legal structures, but also who has rights within a community. These factors influence who can lay claim to land, but also influence who gets to participate in land governance.

Understanding local specificities in land governance is imperative to understanding the gendered power relations around land, not just at the family or community level, but at the national level as well. There are clear socio-cultural obstacles to change that are exhibited in several different ways. For instance, government policy and practices are often imbued with male bias. Even though most governments permit women's land ownership, in practice these policies typically do not promote the exercise or recognition of these rights. Efforts to register land have often assumed that households will have a male breadwinner that reflects household interests. This results in a failure to jointly recognize land rights or to redistribute land rights to women. This lack of awareness about how male bias operates in the development and/or implementation of land policies has had the effect of concentrating land rights in the hands of men.

As a result, we must be keenly aware of the importance and diversity in socio-cultural norms and practices, but also the ways in which institutions reproduce structural gender biases. Again, we see the importance of understanding the interplay between formal political governance (the governance of polities) and informal modes of governance and discipline (the governance of communities). Here, both state-led reforms and customary practices can be seen to favour men or perpetuate male bias. But, interestingly enough, both state-led reforms and customary practices are likewise seen as being possible instruments of change. As we might expect, new policies could be enacted to promote joint titling of lands or the pursuit of women's land rights. Yet there are likely additional ways to promote equity by understanding how flexible customary practices can foster women's rights as well.

Gender and Land Governance in Sub-Saharan Africa

These same themes – colonial legacies, the role of male bias in both policy-making and implementation, and patriarchal traditions in land ownership and inheritance – are also evident in gender and land governance across several sub-Saharan African countries. These concepts from the existing literature are useful for understanding the broad trends around how gender relations shape land access across levels of activity and the potential obstacles to gender-equal land access. However, the diversity of cases – both within and across these state contexts – further illustrates the need for place-based and specific policy for combatting land insecurity. Indeed, as scholars of gender and land governance have long found, there are important variations in local practices and dynamics. As a result, there is no one-size land policy that will fit all.

Below, I examine several cases in sub-Saharan Africa to illustrate how their different historical, political, cultural, and religious dynamics combine to create locally specific modes of land governance. As the analysis demonstrates, these case studies are to be viewed as examples of the diversity of land governance practices rather than as direct comparisons.[2] Existing systematic comparative analyses of gender and land governance likewise find diversity, even within regional contexts. While such a systematic analysis of sub-Saharan Africa would be worthwhile, such a project is beyond the scope of the present study. Here, the analysis establishes how both legal and customary traditions work to shape contemporary land politics, and the ways in which gender relations can enable or restrict gender-equitable land governance. The cases of these three sub-Saharan African countries – Kenya, Uganda, and Ghana – all highlight the importance of taking a long view of land governance that includes both the colonial and post-independence periods.

The analyses below – and the case study of Tanzania in the next chapter – demonstrate the importance of considering how the governance of polities and the governance of communities intersect. These intersections reveal the difficulty of implementing land governance reforms without paying due attention to the social, political, cultural, and economic contexts in which they occur and the multiple ways in which gender is relevant. In examining these multi-level dimensions – specifically the enactment of national laws and land policies and the nature of customary, traditional, and religious practices governing land situated in the broader history of colonialism and post-independence development policy – this chapter highlights the importance of taking a nuanced approach to questions of gender and land governance. These two chapters provides a basis on which we can assess global guidelines and principles of land governance in chapters 4 and 5. Moreover, the discussion illustrates the complexity of these issues across various regions and contexts. Understanding the diversity in the ways in which modes of community and political governance intersect in the governance of land, and the ways in which some modes and practices support or inhibit inclusivity, highlights just how important this analysis is. By highlighting complexity and diversity in these practices, we can better understand the difficult work of designing and implementing equitable land governance reforms.

Sub-Saharan African countries have long been targets for foreign investment in agricultural land. Indeed, by the best estimates available, African land still accounts for approximately 22 per cent of foreign interest in land worldwide, even after peaking in the mid-2010s (Land Matrix 2023). This land rush on the continent has been driven by food and fuel price crises, but also has deeper roots in the economic and political reforms under structural adjustment programs in the 1980s. The withdrawal of extension services for farmers and the opening of agricultural commodity markets and land markets has created new socio-economic vulnerabilities for some of Africa's small-scale farmers. The increase of commercial interest in land across sub-Saharan Africa has created new tensions in land governance, and new economic pressures may undermine the potential for more progressive land governance practices designed to protect the rights of rural peoples.

Often lost in these discussions is the acknowledgment of the gender gap in land ownership in sub-Saharan Africa. Although African women are estimated to do 60 to 70 per cent of all agricultural labour, they are estimated to have legal control of less than 20 per cent of the land across the continent (FAO 2010). This ownership gap exposes women's livelihoods to risk under shifting economic and climatic conditions, risks that are further exacerbated when women are shut out of political and community discussions over land use planning, sale, and management. The social and cultural obstacles that women face in political forums are thus vital to understanding the realities of land governance. As we will see, even where several countries have enacted legal changes to expand women's role in politics, such efforts might not be matched with consistent political will to enforce or implement them. Recent scholarship from the African continent demonstrates that, despite the efforts to enshrine women's rights to land in law, the implementation of such rights in practice remains a significant challenge (Quan et al 2021; Caron 2021).

The local social context, including the gendered organization of society, is a key factor in determining the extent to which gender-equal rules are devised and enacted. Laws and rules may change, but there are issues with implementation and societal practices that still get in the way. These findings further highlight the need to think about the governance of communities – those social norms and expectations that govern human interactions – when we consider land governance.

Patterns of land governance in several African countries illustrate these dynamics and their implications for the broader politics of land acquisition. Though countries like Kenya, Uganda, Ghana, and Tanzania share some similar political, historical, and topographical traits – they all have diverse ethnic populations; were subjected to colonial rule by European states, including the British; have made post-independence political transitions; and have significant arable land attracting foreign interest – we will see that the experiences in land governance across these African countries are different. Specifically, they all employ distinct land governance frameworks with varying effects on local populations and investors, both foreign and local. There are unique conflicts and debates over land and land reform in each country, all of which interact with complex gendered social relations and inequalities. Together, these African countries provide useful examples for understanding political and community governance, the ways in which gender relations shape multiple levels of governance, and the gendered politics of customary and individual land rights. All of these have implications for better policy design.

Kenya

Colonial Legacies and Legal Reform for Land Security

African governments have attempted to manage the challenges of legal pluralism in different ways. Often, these efforts to manage land have roots in colonial histories, with post-independence state governments still favouring significant parts of colonial governance.[3] For instance, rather than dismantling statutory systems imposed by British, French, or German colonizers, several African countries enacted land reforms to further promote individualization, titling, and registration (ITR) of land. Yet these efforts to individualize or privatize land tenure often conflict with customary and traditional modes of governance. Although feminist scholars have long debated the prospects of gender equality under both ITR and customary forms of tenure, both types of systems need to be evaluated using a gendered lens (Whitehead and Tsikata 2003; Collins 2014a). The complexities of legal pluralism in land governance illustrate how these various systems of rule interact, even in cases where ITR has been the dominant rule.

Kenya's shift to ITR began in the 1950s, while the country was under colonial rule, and was maintained through independence and to the present day. Following colonial thinking that endorsed a shift to individual titling as more efficient than customary practices, the Swynnerton Plan was enacted in 1954 by colonial authorities. This plan was intended to encourage a shift from collective to individual ownership and to end customary practices in rural Kenya. From the outset, ITR largely benefited men as heads of households, and customary law continued to govern women's access to land through kinship relations (Davison 1988b; Mackenzie 1990).

Despite these efforts, the Kenyan government neither fully replaced the practice of customary law across the country, nor did it secure citizens' land from land grabbing by Kenya's political elites (Mackenzie 1990; Klopp 2000). As a result, the introduction of ITR law still coexisted with customary practices in many rural parts of the country. Formal land titling in Kenya has also historically excluded pastoralist communities from the legal protections and economic benefits that have been afforded sedentary farmers. And, as noted below, government efforts to commercialize pastoral farming and privatize communal land have their own challenges. Throughout the 1990s and 2000s, academics and legal experts debated the merits of statutory and customary tenure, including through a gender lens. Only recently, with the passing of the 2016 Community Land Act, did the Kenyan government take steps toward the formal recognition of customary tenure.

Male Bias in Policy Implementation

The introduction of individualized tenure in Kenya had the effect of centralizing the control of land in the hands of men. Although ITR is sometimes thought to facilitate market-led agrarian reform and provide greater economic opportunities for women, broader shifts in agricultural production and women's limited off-farm activity and income prevented women from accumulating the capital required to purchase land in rural Kenya (Davison 1988b; Mackenzie 1990; Nyamu-Musembi 2007). It has been well-documented that the ITR process in Kenya ended up primarily registering men as the heads of households and resulted in "a gendered pattern of exclusion" (Nyamu-Musembi 2007, 1472). As argued by scholars like Nyamu-Musembi (2007), grappling with gendered patterns of exclusion and the realities of gender inequality within families is essential for understanding property rights. As she puts it, discussions that equate formalization with secure rights without reckoning with gender inequality lack credibility (Nyamu-Musembi 2007, 1472). Though the law itself may appear equal, the bias in favour of men and broader family and community dynamics means that the implementation of formal land tenure has had gender-differentiated outcomes in practice.

Moreover, government efforts to manage pastoral livestock farmers have also exhibited bias in favour of men, with lasting gendered effects. In the 1960s, following decades of colonial policies that displaced Maasai pastoralist communities, the post-independence Kenyan government established "group ranches" for Maasai populations (Archambault 2015). The group ranches granted a collective title to members, and membership was restricted to adult male residents, meaning that women had no ownership or control. When these group ranches failed in the 1980s, the government privatized the land, subdividing the ranchlands among the male members, giving men individual control of the plots of land. In the decades since, there have been concerns about the negative effects of land privatization on Maasai livelihoods and calls to return to customary tenure. But as Archambault (2015) argues, these debates about the privatization of land and the return to custom have largely ignored the expertise and experiences of women in pastoralist communities. She notes that her own survey research of women in the Maasai community of Elangata Wuas found that women, on average, were less favourable toward land privatization than men, more likely to note how it had increased the potential for conflict, and more likely to indicate that it had impacted their ability to undertake pastoral farming (Archambault 2015, 205). Specifically, women noted that, given polygamous practices in their community, wives had less access to land because of privatization.

Rather than having more access to communal space, private ownership of land created issues with inheritance and women's ability to undertake their own farming responsibilities. Here, the failure of policy design to consider the broader social relations associated with inheritance and gender roles demonstrates a key problem with male bias: when gendered divisions of labour and patterns of marital relations do not factor into policy planning, it can have lasting detrimental impacts on well-being. Women's lack of independent land ownership in Kenya also further increases their vulnerability in the land markets that titling and registration create. This economic inequality, which is closely connected to social exclusion, is not likely to be remedied by economic governance initiatives alone.

In 2010, Kenyans voted to alter the constitution to include several new provisions regarding land rights, promising the right to own property to "every person" and equitable access to land and security of land rights. These provisions do not explicitly mention women, but the Constitution does commit to eliminating gender discrimination in the law, customs, and practices related to land and property (Republic of Kenya, Sec. 60.1f). It remains to be seen whether these constitutional changes will translate into long-term social change; in 2018 it was reported that women accounted for only 2 per cent of title deeds issued between 2013 and 2017 (Mwanza 2018). Moreover, Po and Hickey (2018) report that their community-based research shows that Kamba women are reluctant to pursue land resources through both customary and institutional means, preferring to maintain the status quo of gendered household relations. As described further below, practices related to family dynamics, gendered divisions of labour, and family traditions also shape land access and security.

Patriarchal Traditions and Socio-cultural Obstacles to Gender Equality

Even though customary tenure may not be recognized by law in Kenya, norms and customs nonetheless shape land access, political engagement, and access to justice. Many Kenyan women, specifically poorer, rural women, face systemic discrimination regarding access to and ownership of land, in spite of the legal protections and guarantees that exist. Kenyan women's contemporary access to and control of land is shaped by marital relations, gender roles, and expectations (Mackenzie 1990; Yngstrom 2002). Chronicles of property grabbing – wherein victims, largely female widows, are forcibly evicted from their homes by family members, traditional leaders, or neighbours – suggests how deeply ingrained women's social exclusion can be and the persistence of customary practices (Izumi 2007). Pervasive gender-based socio-political exclusion can limit women's participation in local decision-making, as well as decision-making at multiple levels. The exclusion of women from community discussions can result in a lack of attention to women's land usage or the potential impacts of land projects on women's productive and reproductive activities (Daley 2011).

Given that Kenya is home to dozens of ethnic groups, it is beyond the scope of this short section to describe the traditions of each group. However, existing research on the practices of dominant ethnic groups in rural areas illustrates the ways in which traditional practice and customs can influence how women access land under both customary and statutory law. Kamba women's experiences with land access illustrates how gendered relations – such as women's positions as daughters, sisters, wives, mothers, divorcees, widows, etc. – are key to understanding women's access to land (Po and Hickey 2018). Women report social and relational reasons for not pursuing registration of their own land: mothers claiming their own land would run afoul of patrilineal inheritance practices and the security of land for their sons (if any). For this reason, women are likely to register land in their sons' names to maintain social relations and still retain access to land through relations with their sons (Po and Hickey 2018). These choices made by women in their management of land suggests just some of the reasons why women would choose to continue the practices of registering land in the names of husbands and sons to maintain their position in the family and preserve the status quo.

But as noted by Alden Wily (2011), it is also critical that we do not perceive customary systems as archaic or static: norms can be and are reinterpreted based on local needs. Women have gained access to land through creative reinterpretations of custom. For instance, as mentioned earlier, in some Kenyan communities, widowed women or women without male heirs have protected their claims to land by marrying a female husband, who may bear children that can claim land inheritances (Tsikata 2003; Po and Hickey 2018). While such practices do still involve access to resources if a bride-wealth or bride-price must be paid, such practices speak to the flexibility of custom. Even though the general trend since the colonial era has been away from this flexibility and toward more rigid statutory land laws, the influence of customary practices remains strong and, in some cases, progressive and protective of women's rights and interests (Mackenzie 1993; Mbilinyi 1991, Odgaard 2002; Tsikata 2003). These practices illustrate the potential for flexibility and agency within customary practices.

In the Kenyan case, there has been a focus on registering and individualizing land tenure in line with colonial received practices of law. However, as reviewed above, Kenya remained a pluralist system, with enduring community-based practices of land ownership. The recent recognition of women's rights to land under the 2010 Constitution and the recognition of customary tenure as legitimate in 2016 raises new questions about the future of land access and legal pluralism in Kenya. These questions are beyond the scope of this book, but they are similar to those in other debates in sub-Saharan Africa and elsewhere about how to grapple with gender equality under various modes of land tenure. Importantly, however, these challenges speak to the need to consider the legacies of colonialism and the role of legal pluralism – even in a state that only recently moved to recognize pluralism under the law. Questions of gender and land control are threaded throughout this history and will continue to be relevant in the future.

Uganda

Colonial Legacies and Contemporary Land Reforms

In contrast, countries like Uganda, also subject to British colonial rule, have charted different contemporary approaches to land governance, but have addressed issues of legal pluralism through the recognition of different modes of land tenure. Uganda, similar to countries such as Ghana (discussed below) and Tanzania (see chapter 3), has enacted land reforms that try to recognize customary land tenure and individual land titles. Like these and other African countries, Uganda's current land structure originates from the colonial period. In the pre-colonial era, many customary land tenure practices in Uganda were patriarchal, but women were still able to receive supports through communal structures. However, the colonial push to focus on cash crops undermined these practices (Ezeuduji et al. 2022). According to Tripp (2004, 8), British colonists initially left many local family and community issues under the jurisdiction of customary rules and modes of governance. However, when these arrangements conflicted with the British priorities of export-oriented economic growth, colonial authorities introduced individual land ownership. It is in this context that women saw their rights to land undermined: "By titling and registering land, colonial governments eliminated the importance of secondary rights of women to access land and men increased their control over land" (Tripp 2004, 8). Moreover, the changes in land use and a shift to export-oriented cash-crop production also undervalued women's labour contributions to agriculture and further marginalized them (Tripp 2004).

Uganda introduced land reforms in the 1990s, including a progressive model of land reform that recognizes customary tenure (Okoth-Ogendo 2000; Alden Wily 2011). Uganda's 1995 Constitution recognizes four different forms of land tenure – freehold tenure, leasehold tenure, *mailo* land tenure, and customary tenure – and declares that the land of Uganda belongs to the people of Uganda (Coldham 2000). Freehold tenure functions most similarly to individual land titles in Kenya and other statutory land systems, where the landholder has full ownership rights. Leasehold tenure is held for the tenure of a lease. *Mailo* tenure has its origins in the Land Law of 1908, in which freehold titles were given to about four thousand individuals and is still subject to clan approval (Tripp 2004). Finally, customary tenure in Uganda is regulated by community-based rules and is often administered by clan leaders (Tripp 2004; Andersson Djurfeldt 2020). Since 1995, all four categories of land have equal legal footing – customary land is regarded the same as the rest (Hannay and Scalise 2015).

Ugandan policy-makers have been aware of the challenges of land registration in Kenya, specifically the marginalization of family and community members as land became registered under individualized tenure (Coldham 2000). To avoid this marginalization, the Land Act of 1998 requires the Land Committee to record third-party rights over customary land to safeguard the rights of women, people with disabilities, minors, and absent people (Coldham 2000). Yet, as we will see below, these efforts have not fully resolved these matters of exclusion.

Male Bias in Policy Design

Despite measures in Uganda to recognize marginalized groups, especially women, other measures radically undermined their rights (Tripp 2004). The 1995 Constitution lays out some rights for women, specifically, the equal rights of men and women, the rights of all people to own property, and the prohibition of customary laws that are gender discriminatory. The subsequent 1998 Land Act requires spousal consent for property sales, a policy designed to protect women from land dispossession (Hannay and Scalise 2015). There are also progressive elements in the design of Uganda's succession laws, in that they don't make distinctions between sons and daughters in terms of inheritance, meaning that women can inherit familial property (Hannay and Scalise 2015).

However, as noted by Hannay and Scalise (2015), many these rules are of limited usefulness in practice because of their explicit and implicit male biases. They note that the spousal-consent rule in the 1998 Land Act has many flaws in its design that do not consider the realities of gendered relations in Uganda. For instance, the law applies only to legally married women, though many people live together in cohabitation arrangements that are not formalized by legal marriage. Moreover, few women are familiar with the law or their rights, and the strength of community and family relationships mean that women often have limited ability to speak out against male relatives, such as husbands or fathers. Finally, the consent obligation falls on the person who is trying make a transaction. As Hannay and Scalise put it: "'consent' is not a right held by the person who must give consent ... leaving the decision to obtain consent to the male who already holds power in the relation" (Hannay and Scalise 2015, 257). Moreover, they also identify male bias in the succession laws, both in terms of direct, stated bias in favour of men over women as legal heirs, and indirect biases, such as deferring to the selection of customary heirs. And, as above, because of the use of the term wife, the law applies only to those who are legally married.

While the Land Act of 1998 included some provisions for women's rights, other initiatives to improve land rights later faced stiff opposition. Of note is the ultimate defeat of a proposed clause to the Land Act that would have required the co-registration of spouses on land certificates (Tripp 2004). Tripp quotes President Museveni's admission that he pulled the clause: "'When I learnt that the Bill was empowering the newly married women to share the properties of the husbands, I smelt a disaster and advised for slow and careful analysis of the property sharing issue'" (Tripp, quoting Museveni, 2004, 7). Museveni's hesitations reflect widely held beliefs about gender roles and land ownership, not only in Uganda, but also more broadly across several regions in sub-Saharan Africa. As Kabumbuli (2016) notes, subsequent attempts to introduce spousal co-ownership and protections for both spouses under property law included the Domestic Relations Bill (2003) and the Marriage and Divorce Bill (2009), neither of which were successful. For some, the opposition to spousal co-ownership is so strong that "the prevailing view among scholars and practitioners is that a spousal co-ownership provision is a lost cause in Uganda" (Hannay and Scalise 2015, 258). In Uganda, "women are frequently prevented from holding property by the justification that they *are* property" (Andersson Djurfeldt 2020, 6).

Patriarchal Traditions and Socio-cultural Obstacles to Gender

The discussion of male bias in Uganda's land laws is difficult to disentangle from the broader influence of patriarchal traditions and customs, as well as broader social attitudes about women's position in society. For instance, the high-profile opposition to the proposed spousal co-ownership provision indicates the ways in which gendered norms and expectations undermined and defeated efforts at legal reform. But gendered norms and expectations also affect the ways in which legal protections for women's rights to land that have been passed into law are – or are not – enforced. As in other countries with plural legal traditions, Uganda's efforts to recognize both gender-equal land rights *and* customary land tenure creates a legal tension in which customs and traditions rely on patrilineal patterns of inheritance and patrilocal residence. The challenge to recognize women's rights while also respecting long-standing customary tradition presents a clear legal challenge. As Hannay and Scalise (2015, 251) put it, women have rights in law, but these aren't seen as "culturally legitimate." Although the Constitution states that state law should overrule discriminatory customary practice, the reality is that customary rules are still often the ones that are followed (Andersson Djurfeldt 2020).

Some scholars have tried to document these tensions through assessing people's thoughts on joint land ownership. For instance, Kabumbuli (2016) profiles two communities' opinions on the prospects of joint ownership of family land in Uganda. Although Kabumbuli (2016) finds some support for joint ownership among these populations, with 60 per cent of respondents supporting the idea, that number obscures a gender divide, with women far more likely than men to support the concept. Patriarchal values remain strong when it comes to land ownership, with deeply held convictions about the importance of male inheritance to protect family land (Kabumbuli 2016). This is evident in conversations about spousal death or divorce, and the perceived risks associated with women remarrying. "Beliefs such as 'land is for men' are anchored in strong cultural convictions about male superiority … Since joint ownership opens up possibilities for the family land to pass on to another lineage if the wife outlives the husband and marries someone else, it is not likely to be wholly embraced in patriarchal societies such as Uganda" (Kabumbuli 2016, 79).

This idea that women are not permanent members of a family or a community is echoed in other patriarchal traditions in Uganda as well. Under Acholi customary practices in northern Uganda, men are always head of household, with wife and children only having use rights to land. The payment of a bride-price makes women property and "property can't own property" (Hannay and Scalise 2015, 258). The examination of the unmarried women's position in Acholi society reveals the ways in which women are regarded as being in "transition": women who have not been married are expected to marry into another family; women who are unmarried but already have children are regarded as a burden, with male children excluded from inheritance in their mother's clan; and women or girls who are widowed, divorced, or abandoned are all also regarded as being in transition (Hannay and Scalise 2015). While some customs may allow for some land security for women, they also come at a cost. For instance, a widow may become head of household, but Acholi clan members may also choose an inheritor for her to marry (Hannay and Scalise 2015).

Any changes in either customary or statutory land law ultimately rest on the broader socio-cultural attitudes about gender roles and expectations. Despite the advocates who have pushed for joint ownership of land in various pieces of legislation, as well as local reforms to customary practices, and gendered norms about land ownership – the conviction that "land is for men," as Kabumbuli (2016, 79) puts it – remains powerful. The negative reactions among national politicians and the people alike suggest how deep-rooted gender norms continue to shape what is possible in both customary and statutory legal practices. Moreover, customary traditions are also viewed as part of social cohesion and relations: "The persistence of informal, communal norms can therefore be understood as a way of maintaining male power but also social harmony in concrete, village level contexts" (Andersson Djurfeldt 2020, 6).

The combination of statutory law, customary law, and gendered expectations and practices in Uganda creates gender-specific vulnerabilities regarding land, vulnerabilities that are further exacerbated by the pressures of large-scale land acquisitions. As Doss et al. (2013) find, Ugandans surveyed largely feel secure in their land ownership, even in the absence of joint-ownership provisions or formal titles, with both men and women expecting to maintain land access, ownership, or use rights for the foreseeable future (i.e., within the next five years). However, this sense of security may not align with the realities of large-scale land acquisition: "there are serious questions about whether such rights will be robust enough to withstand challenges from powerful outside interests seeking to acquire land – or to negotiate favorable terms for the transfer of land to investors, if they seek to do so" (Doss et al. 2013, 94). Such vulnerabilities might be particularly pronounced for women, if the complexities of local customary practices are not taken into consideration when land deals are negotiated.

Ghana

Colonial Legacies and Contemporary Land Reforms

Ghana, located in West Africa, has also experienced challenges in reforming land tenure while facing pressure from investors in agricultural land. Like Kenya, Uganda, and Tanzania in East Africa, Ghana has several different land rights and tenure systems based on different regimes. Constitutional and statutory legal reforms since independence have tried to exert more state control into land governance, while also recognizing and protecting the role of customary authorities. As a result, land is governed by a plural legal system like these other countries. Arguably, however, Ghana's chiefs and heads of families exercise even more control over land, in some places having control of allodial title to land. In the Ghanian legal context, allodial title refers to having the highest authority over land and can be derived from customary practices. In Ghana, chiefs' control of allodial title has led to conflict over land, as well as concerns about the ways in which land is managed when there are significant rents to be extracted (Collins and Mitchell 2018; Spichiger and Stacey 2014). The presence of some matrilineal inheritance practices in Ghana, the constitutional recognition of gender equality, and the recognition of women's rights to purchase and own land do create opportunities for women to own land, perhaps more so than some other sub-Saharan African countries (Spichiger and Stacey 2014). However, the dominance of chiefly authorities and clan rule in rural parts of Ghana may undermine pushes for more equal land rights.

An estimated 80 per cent of land in Ghana is governed under customary modes of tenure – with land controlled by the clan, stool, skin, or head of the local community, and individual access mediated through family relations – with the remainder controlled by the state (Lanz 2022; Ackah-Baidoo, Collins, and Grant 2022). The roots of this practice go back to the colonial era wherein colonial authorities granted control of land to "traditional rulers who had already been co-opted into the colonial administration" (Collins and Mitchell 2018, 7). This solidified chiefs' control of land at a key point in Ghana's colonial era, when the expansion of cash crops such as cocoa also led chiefly authorities to maximize rents from these resources and manipulate customary practices (Collins and Mitchell 2018).

The balance between state control of land and empowering chiefly control of land is a common theme in Ghana's land reform experiences in the twentieth century. Following independence in 1957, the Ghanaian government under President Kwame Nkrumah passed legislation designed to exert state control over customary lands. These included the 1962 Administration of Lands Act, the 1962 State Lands Act, the 1962 Concessions Act, the 1963 Lands Act, and the 1965 Public Conveyancing Act. Some of these reforms also "empowered chiefs to appropriate land on behalf of the state" (Ackah-Baidoo, Collins, and Grant 2022,

104). However, there was still widespread resistance to these state efforts from chiefs, and after the Nkrumah government was overthrown in a military coup, subsequent regimes would expand chiefly authority (Lanz 2022).

Later reforms expanded chiefs' control of land through the 1979 Constitution, the 1992 Constitution, and the 1999 National Land Policy (Berry 2009; Collins and Mitchell 2018). These revisions affirmed the role of chiefly authorities in land management, while still also attempting to retain state control over land. These efforts show the ways in which the Ghanaian government attempted to improve transparency in land management, while still reinforcing the customary roles of chiefs.

Lanz (2022) demonstrates the interactions between customary authorities and the government in the Ghanaian context. In many parts of rural Ghana, the power of customary authorities like chieftaincies allows them to allocate lands to investors, without going through government authorities. The various powers possessed by local chiefs and other elites thus enable some potential buyers to approach different local authorities in order to find and acquire lands while also sidestepping certain land claims from local populations.

Male Bias in Policy Design

The dominance of chiefly authority in land governance has been supported by these legal reforms made since Ghana's independence. At the same time, there have been efforts to codify gender equality in the 1992 Constitution and through several legal statutes. Yet the protection of customary and chiefly authority, while attempting to promote legal gender equality, has created legal contradictions. Ghana's 1992 Constitution protects the equal rights of women, while at the same time protecting customary systems and recognizing legal pluralism. In doing so, the Constitution allows for discriminatory customary practices to continue, even where it otherwise prohibits gender-based discrimination.

The failure to consider gender equality in the governance of land is evident in land reform efforts in the twenty-first century. As noted above, the 1999 National Land Policy was introduced to expand land registration and titling in rural areas, though it affirmed the roles of chiefs in the process. However, the National Land Policy was silent on women's-rights issues. From the perspective of women's-rights advocates, this was a major misstep. By failing to consider women and gender inequality in this policy, the government overlooked major obstacles to realizing women's rights to land. For instance, the fact that women have lower incomes and less control of resources meant that they are less likely to be able to afford the titling process and less likely to be able to purchase land after it has been titled: "The increased value of the land after it is titled may render it inaccessible for women, who are most often hindered by their socio-economic position" (Spichiger and Stacey 2014, 23). In addition, even in cases where women applied for title registration, many still allowed the land to be registered in their husband's name (Spichiger and Stacey 2014). Beyond these obstacles, the failure to consider gender inequality in this policy also overlooked other elements of women's lower socio-economic status, such as their inability to navigate formal institutions, their lower literacy rates, their lack of financial resources – or even time – and the gender roles that inhibit women's abilities to seek out legal recourse or remedy for land issues.

In addition, the 1999 National Land Policy's affirmation of the role of customary and chiefly authorities, without consideration of gender inequality or patriarchal traditions, further undermines women's position on land. Because customary tenure is tied to community or family membership, customary rules about who are the rightful heirs to land govern who gains and maintains access to land. While there are some communities that practice matrilineal inheritance in Ghana, many practices are patrilineal, and even matrilineal lines of inheritance may favour men. Marital status is often a critical consideration in whether women can gain access to customary land. Community-based rights also limit the rights of migrants or settlers, including communities of herders that may not stay in one place. Ethnic and group identities thus layer additional vulnerabilities and obstacles onto the secure ownership of land (Spichiger and Stacey 2014).

As a result, the governance of land by chiefs, family, and clans in Ghana are critical for understanding the ways in which land is controlled and managed. In some parts of the country, chiefs have the allodial title over land, allowing them to parcel out land and govern it as they see fit. In others, family or clan heads have this decision-making control. As Lanz (2022, 30) explains, because of the importance of ancestry, tradition, and family membership, "land rights of individuals are embedded in their membership in a particular family." This focus on ancestry and tradition means that migrants and women are typically at a disadvantage (Lanz 2022). The specificities of how land would be inherited vary from one location and community to another: for instance, depending on the clan, a woman marrying within her own clan might have usufruct rights, with the ability to pass land on to children. A woman marrying outside her clan would lose all those rights (Lanz 2022, 42).

These tensions between centralized control and customary practices are further evident in the subsequent 2003 Land Administration Project (LAP). Despite not having any reference to gender inequality, the National Land Policy guided the design and implementation of the LAP. The multi-million-dollar project funded by the World Bank aimed to create a decentralized land governance system in Ghana that was more transparent, and would register land claims and manage disputes (Spichiger and Stacey 2014). However, the LAP has failed to address the roles of chiefs, "including checks on the power of chiefs" (Ackah-Baidoo, Collins and Grant 2022, 105). The LAP was to decentralize control to Customary Land Secretariats (CLS) with the idea that these institutions would ensure more equitable land access, protect the rights of landowners, ensure fair compensation, and resolve issues around speculation and land disputes (Obeng-Odoom 2016).

However, it would take six years before gender was even incorporated into efforts to implement the LAP (Spichiger and Stacey 2014). Thus, in addition to broader concerns about the LAP working to bring traditional land systems into Western logics of land ownership (Obeng-Odoom 2016), the program was also not designed to address key gender inequalities in land access and ownership. Moreover, even where women may control an asset, they do not have the same control over land or property as men: women may lack the authority to bequeath it or sell it according to community practices (Spichiger and Stacey 2014). Similarly, in some communities, women will have use rights, but lack full ownership or inheritance rights of land (Tsikata and Yaro 2014).

Patriarchal Traditions and Socio-cultural Obstacles to Gender

Both statutory and customary law in Ghana typically favour men's control over land at the expense of women's land rights. Despite some statutory legal provisions to promote gender equality, the broader socio-cultural context, as well as the lack of implementation or enforcement, undermine them in practice. Indeed, it is difficult to disentangle these features: as in other countries, the lack of enforcement or political will to implement laws may stem from broader socio-cultural biases against women's rights. Yet in addition to these challenges, Ghana's land reform efforts stand apart because of the very strong position of chiefly and clan authorities in the country. Constitutional and legislative support for customary authorities means that customary law is critical for understanding women's access to and control over land. Scholars have documented the implications of this control for various resource sectors, such as cocoa, as well as the implications for land deals in the Ghanaian context (Collins and Mitchell 2018; Tsikata and Yaro 2014; Lanz 2022). For instance, Tsikata and Yaro (2014) note how, despite differences between northern and southern regions of Ghana, the commercialization of land has the effect of undermining kinship ties and the land access that women may have traditionally held under customary practice.

The dominance of patriarchal values in Ghana limits the realization of women's land rights under both statutory and customary law. As noted above, there are constitutional and legislative protections for women's rights, however they have not been widely implemented in practice or are difficult to enforce. For instance, Ghana has legal provisions that establish that, if a spouse dies without a will, the surviving spouse and children receive two-thirds of the estate. However, even though this is celebrated as progressive, the reality is that the law is not enforced, since it contradicts traditions around inheritance (Ravnborg et al. 2016). Ghana's Matrimonial Causes Act specifies that women must prove their contributions to household property to lay claim to it in the event of divorce. However, this is very difficult to establish, and there is not wide recognition of non-monetary contributions to household well-being, meaning that divorce can severely undermine women's access to property (Ravnborg et al. 2016).

The dominance of chiefly authorities and customary tenure in Ghana makes challenges to gender inequality difficult. Most women in Ghana access land through kinship relations, whether through their own familial lineage or through marriage (Lanz, Prügl, and Gerber 2019).

Even in this context, however, women's land rights are typically usufruct rights, meaning that they have access and use rights, but not ownership or control over land. Men may also deny their wives access to customary land, and so even these use rights might not be guaranteed (Tsikata and Yaro 2014). Chiefly and clan-based decision-making tends to concentrate decision-making in the hands of men, leading to the exclusion of women's knowledge and expertise.

But beyond the enforcement of customary law and traditions, social norms, economic divisions of labour, and other gendered expectations also influence land governance and resource use. Tsikata and Yaro (2014) explain how economic responsibilities marginalize women's contributions in Ghana's Northern Region. There, men are seen as the providers for families, while wives and children support their productive work. In this division of labour, women still take on extensive reproductive, or household provisioning and care, work to support their families and communities, such as meal preparation. However, women must negotiate for access to the male-controlled resources that they need (Tsikata and Yaro 2014, 208). These broader socio-cultural norms and divisions of labour matter for understanding gendered patterns of land control and resource use and speak to the broader socio-cultural obstacles to realized women's land rights. As Spichiger and Stacey (2014, 29) argue, "embedded cultural values concerning the role of men and women constrain potential change."

Conclusion

Across these three countries and elsewhere on the African continent, there is demand for and evidence of greater gender equality in politics and land governance. Many countries have made legal changes designed to address gender inequality in land ownership, and in politics and governance more generally. At the same time, many countries – such as Uganda and Ghana, and as the next chapter will describe, Tanzania – have made important achievements in recognizing the rights of rural and Indigenous peoples by enshrining some modes of customary land governance in statutory and constitutional law. And although colonial authorities and several post-independence Kenyan governments attempted to move to an ITR system, customary rules still dominate land governance in rural areas. Thus, we see similar, though also distinct, challenges in the intersections of political and community land governance in these African countries.

There are clear themes that emerge across these regions that point to how gendered power relations shape land governance. These include gender bias, most commonly male bias, in the design and implementation of statutory law, as well as in customary governance practices; women's systematic exclusion from land control and ownership; the uneven implementation of legal reforms; unequal resource access based on gender; the importance of kinship relations, inheritance, and marital status; gendered norms and expectations; and both customary and political modes of gender discrimination. This is not an exhaustive list of all the ways in which gender shapes land governance, but it does serve to illustrate the multi-level quality of both land governance and the influence of gender bias. The study of social and cultural norms is imperative here: not only do gender roles and norms shape daily lives and practices within households, as is quite commonly understood, but they may also limit participation in decision-making over land and access to resources, thus restricting the application of otherwise progressive policies.

Yet there remain critical differences. It is not enough just to understand the respective legal frameworks to assess the gendered dimensions of land governance; one must look more closely at local practices and the broader set of gendered social relations within which all systems of rule are embedded. This is imperative in order to appreciate the nuances and differences in customary governance and understand the opportunities to address inequality. As we have seen in the cases outlined above, understanding the many ways in which gender shapes land governance requires attention to the national level of statutory and constitutional law, practices of customary governance that operate at regional and community levels, familial patterns of inheritance and land control, and the socio-cultural norms and expectations that shape governance at all these levels. As we can see from just these few brief cases, socio-cultural expectations shape everything, from whose name ends up on registered land to whether or not new gender-equal measures are enacted into law and enforced. The governance of polities and the governance of communities collide to create gender-unequal outcomes.

Development scholars and practitioners have long debated the relative merits of both individual land rights systems and customary systems in sub-Saharan Africa in protecting the rights of women (Whitehead and Tsikata 2003). As these cases illustrate, there are no clear answers, and care must be taken to appreciate the diversity of legal frameworks and customary practices across the continent. Given the increased economic pressures and demands on arable land, understanding the complexity of governance and the interactions between local and global polities and communities is as important as ever. Regardless of the mode of political governance – legal or customary – these modes are embedded within a broader context of gendered norms, expectations, and divisions of labour that also govern societies. Understanding how these modes of community governance interact with political governance allows us to assess the potential of various proposed reforms to improve gender equity in land rights, especially in the context of transnational interest in land acquisition.

In order to take a closer look at these dynamics at work – and see the ways in which community and political governance intersect across multiple levels of political activity – the next chapter examines Tanzania's experiences with land grabbing and land reform in closer detail. The colonial era imposed rules and dynamics that have influenced land governance since. Tanzania's post-independence land reform efforts involved a combination of individualized land rights as well as customary land rights, determined by local authorities. But these local authorities also need to have elected representatives and gender balance. Local governance is designed to be inclusive and participatory, including on questions of land. Yet, as we will see, these political institutions interact with community norms and family practices. The result is that, despite having a widely celebrated and progressive land governance framework, Tanzania still experienced controversial land dispossessions and faces gender discrimination in the governance of land. This closer look at one case allows us to see the specifics of how land governance operates and what truly effective land governance reforms might look like.

3 GENDER AND MULTI-LEVEL LAND GOVERNANCE: TANZANIA IN FOCUS

Both gender relations and land governance are inherently political. As we saw in the previous chapter, gender relations pervade land politics and decision-making at various levels of political activity and shape family dynamics around the control of land. At the same time, land governance is likewise shaped by political histories and reforms and is embedded in contemporary resource politics and the global political economy. As a result, understanding gender and the governance of land requires a fuller appreciation of how gendered power relations intersect with political rules and governance processes at work. If land governance reform is to address the negative outcomes around large-scale agricultural land deals, we need to have a clear sense of how such governance operates, and who it might be excluding. This requires attention to the ways in which community norms around gender roles and expectations intersect with how polities create and enforce rules.

To delve into the challenges of governing land in the context of global land deals, this chapter goes deeper into an analysis of land governance in Tanzania. Tanzania is an instructive example because it has undertaken significant land reform, but has also been host to several controversial foreign agricultural investments in land in the post-2008 period. In some ways, Tanzania is a most-likely case when it comes to equitable land governance (George and Bennett 2005): Tanzania's land reforms created a land governance framework designed to protect community lands and improve women's land security and participation in local land governance. Yet in the context of global land deals, critics allege that it was not able to do either. For these reasons, Tanzania is worthy of closer examination to understand the ways in which domestic land reforms have attempted to recognize women's rights and customary tenure, even prior to the recent land rush.

This chapter briefly reviews Tanzania's experiences with large-scale land deals in the post-2008 period. It then proceeds to apply the multi-level governance framework established in chapter 1 to analyze global, national, local, and family dynamics that shape land ownership, use, and governance in the Tanzanian context. In parallel with the cases in the previous chapter, we see the ways in which modes of customary and statutory governance, socio-cultural obstacles, and kinship relations all shape land governance. This analysis reveals that, although Tanzania has a progressive land governance framework that *could* ensure rural peoples – including women – have a strong position vis-à-vis investors, several complications interfere with successful governance. There are failures in implementing key reforms; tensions between protecting customary practices and promoting gender equality; and a mismatch between the slower pace of social change and the quicker pace of agricultural investment. Overall, the Tanzanian case highlights the limitations of political reforms that don't simultaneously consider the governance of communities that stems from gendered roles and norms. The governance of polities and communities intersect when it comes to land reform, and can undermine legal strategies attempting to advance gender equality. This intersection highlights the importance of considering local contexts when developing policy solutions to large-scale land acquisitions.

To develop this case study, I undertook a combination of primary and secondary research. I reviewed Tanzanian legislation, with specific attention to the 1999 Land Acts and the 2002 Courts Act, and the legislation's provisions for community-based governance. This was complemented by a review of the literature on Tanzania's land reform history, as well as the available literature on gender and land reform in the Tanzanian context. I reviewed materials from the Institute of Development Studies (IDS), University of Dar es Salaam; the Tanzania Gender Networking Programme (TGNP) Library; the Legal and Human Rights Center (LHRC) Documentation Centre; and the Women's Information Centre (WIC) at the Ministry of Community Development, Gender and Children (MCDGC). I also conducted interviews with twenty-four key informants in Dar es Salaam and Morogoro in 2013. Interviewees included NGO researchers and activists, civil society leaders, lawyers, land experts, and government officials. These interviewees were selected for their detailed and intimate knowledge of Tanzania's legal structures and land reforms, as well as their experience on the ground and in rural communities attempting to implement land reforms. Together, the existing academic literature, legislation, governmental documents, grey literature, and key informant interviews allow for the development of a detailed case study that reveals the multi-level challenges of land governance reform in the context of large-scale land acquisitions.

Land Reform in Tanzania

The Tanzanian government signed the Land Act (No. 4) and the Village Land Act (No. 5)[1] into law in 1999; both Acts came into effect in 2002. The authors of the 1999 Land Acts sought to secure the land rights of rural villagers by providing legal recognition for customary practices and customary claims on land. In parallel with the countries in the previous chapter, Tanzania sought to grapple with a long history of legal pluralism, shaped by colonial and post-colonial efforts to bring land governance under the purview of the state (Scott 1998). The Land Acts of 1999 remedied a long-term failure to recognize customary claims on land and marginalized peasant populations. These acts introduced the Certificate of Customary Right of Occupancy (CCRO), to be approved and granted by authorities at the village level. Under the law, CCROs are to be regarded as having the same legal status as a statutory individualized title. The Village Land Act authorizes village authorities to grant customary claims on land based on local practices or to consent to transfer land to outsiders/investors through the government. In addition to this recognition of custom, the Village Land Act also introduced more democratic accountability at the local level. The Village Land Act entrusted final approval on land transfers of less than 250 hectares to the Village Assembly, which is a meeting of an entire village population (United Republic of Tanzania 1999b, Sec. 4.6a). Land transfers greater than 250 hectares still require advisement from the Village Assembly, Village Council, and the District Council, but also require ministerial approval (United Republic of Tanzania 1999b, Sec. 4.6b; Collins, Grant, and Ackah-Baidoo 2019). With these approval processes, the Acts attempted to balance customary practice with democratic principles and community participation and engagement.

In addition to new recognition for customary land rights, the Acts also seek to advance gender equality in several ways: addressing women's land rights (United Republic of Tanzania 1999b, Sec. 23.2c); spousal co-registration of land ownership (United Republic of Tanzania 1999a, Sec. 159); and a declaration that, where customary laws violate principles of gender equality, the Land Acts would override customary practice (United Republic of Tanzania 1999b, Section 20.2). In addition to women's land rights, the Acts also created mandatory gender quotas in Village Land Councils (United Republic of Tanzania 1999b, Section 60). The subsequent 2002 Courts (Land Disputes Settlements) Act also mandates minimum representation of women on Ward Tribunals and District Land and Housing Tribunals (United Republic of Tanzania 2002, sec. 5.1, sec. 11, sec. 14.1, sec. 26.1). The locally based adjudication authorities are instructed by the Courts Act to mediate and promote harmony based on local customary practices.

On paper, Tanzania's 1999 Land Acts appear fairly robust. They enshrine the rights of communities to make decisions over land and to govern as they see fit. This progressive land governance framework could ensure rural peoples – including women and other marginalized groups – have a strong position vis-à-vis investors. As discussed below, the Land Acts and other governance reforms include minimum standards for gender representation in some bodies, require community consultation, and promote local customary control and decision-making over land. Yet, once a community decides to transfer land to other users, they abdicate control of community lands. As a result, ensuring that land governance is undertaken fairly and with full participation from communities – including their informed consent – is essential. Community-based decision-making and customary land rights *may* be key to protecting community interests in land under the present constitutional framework.

Despite these important legal changes, observers that once celebrated the Tanzanian Land Acts as monumental reforms are disappointed by the lack of implementation and administrative support and critical of the ways in which foreign investors have been able to acquire land in Tanzania. Though there are many dynamics at work here, key obstacles include gaps in the state's governance frameworks and the ways in which policy implementation is envisioned and executed. For instance, the 1999 Land Acts did not address how the Radical (or allodial) Title is still in the hands of the President, meaning that the state may still expropriate land as it sees fit.

But of particular interest to the current study are the ways in which gender roles shape governance outcomes. As we will see below, an understanding of the challenges of implementation reveals that, despite strong legal reforms in favour of women's rights, the local realities of community norms, individual needs, and relationships of dependency are critical to analyzing governance processes. By strengthening customary modes of governance without likewise supporting gender equity, the implementation of the 1999 Land Acts has undermined efforts to improve gender equality. By confirming certain traditions and not highlighting where these practices are in tension with gender-progressive laws outlawing discrimination, the implementation of the Acts has not resulted in widespread recognition of the land rights of rural peasant women. The Acts have also not undermined hierarchies associated with village governance nor encouraged broad public consultation and discussion over land use. These dynamics are critical as investors seek land in Tanzania. Thus, despite efforts to secure land for rural communities, elect more women to decision-making positions, and extend land rights to women, the people have still lost lands to foreign investment and women are still underrepresented in land governance and ownership.

Land Deals in Tanzania

Tanzania is one of many African countries targeted for agricultural investment and land acquisitions over the past couple of decades, and the Tanzanian government has continued efforts to attract foreign agricultural investment. These deals, several of which are described below, involved thousands of hectares of land, and although these lands were sometimes framed as uninhabited or unused, they were nonetheless critical for supporting local livelihoods and traditions. What many of these deals have in common is that they did involve negotiations with local landholders. As stated in chapter 1, most land deals are legal under state law. Yet, despite these negotiations, people still faced displacement and lost access to key resources, including food, medicine, and water sources.

However, in Tanzania, the specifics of land governance structures are significant for understanding the impacts of land deals. In Tanzania, land that has been transferred from local communities for sale to an investor is transferred not to the investors, but first to the state. Because the President of Tanzania holds the Radical Title to all land – a holdover policy from the colonial era – if a community or a family decides to transfer control of customary land to an investor, the deal is not strictly between two parties. Rather, control of the land is transferred back to the state, which then has the authority to negotiate a lease agreement with an investor. As a result, when a land deal fails, communities do not receive their land again. Thus, in addition to not receiving whatever benefits that might have been promised by investors in the form of infrastructure, social programs, or employment, communities will also lose land control.

Yet these rules around the control and transfer of land are often not understood by local decision-makers when they decide to transfer land. Tanzanian legal advocates explained how local communities would discuss and negotiate terms with investors, often having lengthy discussions about their needs and demands. These demands might also include requests to have land returned to them under certain conditions or if the investor withdraws. However, communities would later learn that that these terms, despite being recorded locally, held no standing under statutory law. One NGO director pointed to several cases where the minutes of village meetings laid out the terms of a proposed land transfer to outside investors.[2] Village leaders would articulate demands in these minutes, requiring, for instance, that the investor provide infrastructure, compensation, medical clinics, and employment to receive land. However, when these Village Councils and Assemblies approved the transfer of land to General Land under control of the Commissioner for Lands, this allowed the investors to lease land directly from the government, with no deal required between the villagers and the investor. Moreover, since there are no provisions in the Land Acts for General Land to be converted back to Village Land, these land transfers will be permanent, regardless of a village's preferences, unless the state intervenes. According to one INGO Land Rights advisor: "[t]he assumption is that at the national level, the people will be negotiating on behalf of the villagers, but in a real sense, they don't know their needs. They're not there to know that a school is their need, or hospital is their need, or what kind of social services."[3] As a result, despite the legal reforms of the Land Acts that were designed to recognize local land governance, there are still deep vulnerabilities for rural communities as they try to navigate land acquisition.

For example, Sun Biofuels, a United Kingdom–based company, negotiated the transfer of 8,211 hectares of land in Kisarawe District, Tanzania, to grow jatropha (Sulle and Nelson 2009). At the time, the deal was scrutinized by NGOs like Friends of the Earth International (FOEI), the Oakland Institute, and Oxfam International, which claimed that villagers had not been compensated for lost access to land, water, and resources (Pearce 2012; Oakland Institute 2012). Residents had previously used the land for water, timber, bee-keeping, and traditional medicines (Wise 2014). An official with Sun Biofuels claims that the company consulted with over eleven thousand people and compensated those whose land was acquired fairly, but residents complained that promises of infrastructure and compensation were not kept (Carrington 2011; Pearce 2012). In 2011, the Sun Biofuels project went bankrupt (Oakland Institute 2012). The land lease was acquired by a new company, Mtanga Farms, which, in addition to growing jatropha, planned to raise cattle instead. According to Tim Wise (2014), despite significant shareholder overlap between Sun Biofuels and Mtanga Farms, Mtanga Farms argued that they were under no obligation to fulfill the promises made by Sun Biofuels, despite taking over the ninety-nine-year lease the company had acquired from the Tanzanian government. Here, the structures of land governance resulted in the loss of lands, jobs, and resources, despite consultations with local communities.

Similarly, one of the longest controversies over land acquisition in Tanzania involves Swedish companies SEKAB and Agro EcoEnergy, the latter of which took over many operations initiated by the former. SEKAB was criticized for acquiring the Razaba farmlands in Bagamoyo District from the Tanzanian government in 2006. The farmlands were home to an estimated six hundred people (Beyene et al. 2013; *The Citizen* 2013), but because the land acquired was not fertile farmland, there were additional ecological concerns about proposed irrigation practices using the Wami River that would affect land fertility and farming further downstream (ActionAid 2010). SEKAB later sought additional land from villagers in Rufiji District, asking for one hundred thousand hectares of land. Village authorities offered fifty thousand hectares instead, but there were reports of corruption and corporate interference with the village decision-making processes, suggesting that this offer did not have the broad support of the community (Benyene et al. 2013).

Later, SEKAB ceased operations, but controversies with Agro EcoEnergy – which acquired the lands and continued operations in 2009 – persisted. The company continued to seek land beyond the Razaba farmlands, with the support of the Tanzanian government. Yet confusion over village borders and ownership of land led to resistance on the part of residents[4] and environmental activists. Although the courts affirmed the government's right to transfer land to Agro EcoEnergy, in 2017, the Government of Tanzania revoked the land title, violating a bilateral investment treaty between Sweden and Tanzania (Agro EcoEnergy 2017). Ultimately, fifteen hundred residents will be able to remain on the lands previously acquired by the company, although the Tanzanian government was then sued by Agro EcoEnergy for violating the agreement (Makoye 2016).[5]

Gendered Effects of Land Deals in Tanzania

These new land enclosures also have important gendered effects. Although there is limited research on the specific impacts of these deals in Tanzania, there is emerging research that offers insights into how land deals in Tanzania have had distinct gender-differentiated outcomes. Chung (2017) describes the gendered effects of displacement due to land deals in the Tanzanian context, specifically the EcoEnergy deal in Bagamoyo highlighted above. In this context – where the land was under dispute for many years and land was enclosed to prevent trespassing – the imminent loss of land had gender-differentiated effects. These included material impacts, such as women being formally excluded from compensation negotiations, the failure to consider women's lost subsistence crops when calculating compensation, the loss of important commons resources, and the inefficiencies and struggles of acclimating to resettlement.

There are similar impacts where women have lost access to common resources because of large-scale land acquisitions. Examining the enclosure of land by the New Forests Company (NFC) in Kilolo District, Iringa region in Tanzania, Gmür (2019) finds that, in many cases, family or clan heads decided to transfer their land to the company without consulting women in the family. The exclusion of women from decision-making often rests on justifications around patrilineal or patrilocal practices: "it is the clan land of the husbands' clan, so the wives or sisters have no say in family land matters as they live with the families of their husbands anyway and now belong to the clan of the husband" (Gmür 2019, 310). However, the resulting enclosures and lost access to land increased women's workloads, deprived women of income-generating activities, and increased their dependency on men, particularly husbands and elders (Gmür 2019, 301). Women lost access to fruit trees that they used to feed their families, treat illness, and generate income. But because the deals were undertaken by men, only men were compensated for the land acquired, and the value of these lost resources were not accounted for.

Beyond the material impacts, Chung (2017) notes the ways in which enclosures and resettlement also disconnect people from the spaces in which they exercise autonomy – like women in their own subsistence vegetable plots – and the loss of culturally significant species, such as the *mkole* tree, which is a symbol of women's fertility and important in local rituals near Bagamoyo. The important connections between gender identity and specific environments and ecosystems have long been recognized by feminist political ecologists (Nightingale 2006).

These gendered impacts of land deals highlight the ways in which land rights are differentiated based on gender relations. While there are clear gendered after-effects of land deals, below I investigate further the issues of *governance* and decision-making around land in the Tanzanian context. As we will see in subsequent chapters, there is no shortage of policy ideas about how to improve land governance in the context of land acquisition and agricultural investment. But there is often little appreciation of how gender structures inclusion and exclusion in the governance of land. The above instances of land deals illustrate how the local control of land has significant consequences, and often still excludes women. This occurs despite the presence of statutory laws designed to protect women's land rights in this context. And so, we need to look closer to understand how community practices shape land governance.

Gender and Multi-level Land Governance in Tanzania

> You have a law that's pretty progressive and then you have customary law, which is much stronger in the traditions and in the minds of people, which makes that law kind of redundant ... If you go to the local level, you find that people are just following the customary laws because they don't really know about this law. And when they do know about that law, then you do see some changes, but it's not like everybody changes.[6]

When asked about the quality of women's land rights under the 1999 Land Acts, members of high-profile women's-rights groups – which once enthusiastically endorsed the Land Acts – express disappointment. Implementation, as highlighted in the quotation above, remains a primary concern. Feminist activists, NGO officers, and legal-aid providers point to the broader challenge of addressing discrimination in customary practices and belief systems and the implications for land governance. Though the Land Acts explicitly declare null and void customary practices that discriminate based on gender, the lack of training and awareness about the laws means that local officials are often not familiar with either the gender-equality provisions in the Land Acts or other sections relevant to land administration. The different experiences of rural women – young or old; single, married, divorced, or widowed – as village citizens, as participants in governance bodies, and as claimants of land rights highlight the gender-based challenges of land governance. Rural women, especially divorced and widowed women, face serious obstacles in trying to claim land and property rights independent from husbands or male heirs. The broader ordering of societies around gender roles impacts the ways in which people can access rights or the ways in which policies are implemented – or not.

Gender relations – and especially marital relations – are closely tied to customary land access and rights. Widowed women have long been the victims of property grabbing from their husbands' families, and high rates of HIV and AIDS in Tanzania have increased the number of households headed by single females (Kessy et al. 2008; Izumi 2007). According to the most recent census data available, approximately 15 per cent of women aged twenty to eighty in rural areas are widowed, with another 6.8 per cent divorced or separated (United Republic of Tanzania 2014). Though these rates of divorce are relatively low, the Women's Legal Aid Centre (WLAC) reports that the number of women seeking legal assistance with divorce is increasing and that land disputes, matrimonial issues, and inheritance issues are the primary reasons why women seek legal aid in their rural offices (Women's Legal Aid Centre 2013). Moreover, even where women are secure in their marital arrangements, they may nonetheless be excluded from village decision-making over land use and transfers based on gendered norms of participation.

Village governance bodies and family governance interact with each other and with national governance frameworks: the Land Acts devolve complicated governance responsibilities to local bodies. These efforts to implement land reforms that rely on both an individualized liberal-rights framework and communal customary practices bring different understandings of rights into contact with each other. Without considering the broader structures of gender relations, the various power relationships and the connections women have to their families, kinship relations, and communities, legal land reforms are unlikely to overcome long-standing practices of gender-based exclusion and discrimination. Rather, regardless of whether individualized or customary rights are sought, gender-based norms and community governance are likely to shape outcomes.

To understand these multiple levels of governance, I employ the analytical framework established in chapter 1, focusing on the national, local, and kinship-based levels of analysis and the intersections of community governance with political governance. First, I briefly review the lasting effects of colonialism on land governance in Tanzania and situate Tanzania within the contemporary global political economy. I then analyze the national political frameworks, with attention to how gender norms affect policy implementation. Local village governance is examined as a site at which devolved governance and community norms intersect to create specific outcomes. Finally, I review kinship and family patterns of land control and decision-making, specifically inheritance practices. Together, this multi-level analysis shows the ways in which the governance of polities – including legal frameworks and customary governance – and the governance of communities intersect to shape land governance and often constrain the enacting of gender-equality measures.

Colonialism and Land Governance in Tanzania

Prior to colonial rule, the area that constitutes contemporary mainland Tanzania was sparsely populated by kin groups, in some cases ruled hierarchically by chiefs or elders (Gastorn 2008). Despite differences between groups, they typically had communal land tenure for grazing and water access. Under German and British colonial rule, however, the policy of indirect rule established by colonial powers used a "reconstituted system of chiefs and headmen" (Mbilinyi 2003, 122). Under German rule, land had to be occupied to be considered owned, which resulted in grazing and fallow lands being taken from pastoralist communities. Cultivator communities were accommodated, with land rights entrusted to chiefs and some reserve lands established for pastoralists (Gastorn 2008). Control of land was granted to kin-group authorities, and Indigenous groups were punished when modes of production did not conform to the German model of land use. Similar enforcement occurred under British rule. "The interference of colonial rulers in indigenous norms concerning the use of land [in Tanzania] was usually determined by their own interests" and not out of any concern for the Indigenous population who lived there (Gastorn 2008, 32).

Efforts to codify customary law by colonial authorities typically strengthened the rights of men over women (Chanock 1989). Under both German and British rule, colonial authorities also relied on patriarchal forms of marriage and property ownership (Mbilinyi 2003). Colonial agricultural policy encouraged large-scale plantation agriculture by white settlers and foreign corporations, establishing the roots of the contemporary gendered division of labour (Mbilinyi 2003; Tsikata 2003). In general, codification of customary laws, as well as bylaws restricting divorce and movement, had the effect of formalizing what had been regarded as more fluid sets of gender relations.

In addition, land administration principles from German rule that dictated land had to be occupied to be owned are evident in local practices and national land laws (Tsikata 2003; Gastorn 2008). British authorities took advantage of customary tenure systems that allowed land to go fallow to encroach upon customary lands and establish commercial farming, wildlife reserves, and conservation schemes under the pretexts of economic efficiency (Gastorn 2008). Under British rule, the deemed rights of occupancy of native communities were treated subordinately to granted rights of occupancy by the state (Okoth-Ogendo 2000).

Customary forms of land tenure and local governance still shape how land is acquired in the post-independence era, in part through marital rituals and the practices of inheritance (Koda 2000). These practices continue to represent both obstacles and opportunities for community members and should not be viewed as archaic. Some marginalized groups have gained access to land through creative reinterpretations of custom. Koda (2000, vii) illustrates the ways in which members of the Wapare community of Msindo developed "flexible" and "open-ended" negotiations for accessing land, especially for marginalized women. At the same time, patriarchal practices in many of these communities, combined with gendered norms about political participation and roles in public life, may limit rural women's involvement.

As discussed below, the role of customary authorities in contemporary land governance is of critical importance, especially where the Land Acts devolve responsibilities to the local level. Not only are there often different sets of norms in these communities, but in Tanzania there is both cultural discrimination against pastoralist groups as well as conflicts based on these different modes of production and land access (Gastorn 2008).[7]

Post-Independence Global Influence in Tanzanian Land Governance

Tanzania's post-independence history has been marked by several periods of national land reform, beginning with villagization[8] in the 1960s under President Julius Nyerere, and followed by land, economic, and political reforms in the 1980s under the guidance of the World Bank and IMF. After decades of colonial rule that shaped the landscape of customary rule, villagization was designed to reform agricultural production and push a new state-driven development agenda. However, by the 1970s, Tanzania's economy was negatively affected by global drops in export commodity prices, increases in import prices, periods of drought, and war with Uganda. By the end of the decade, the country was experiencing a persistent foreign-exchange crisis (Tripp 1994). Tanzania's vulnerable position in the global economy led to important structural changes in land governance.

It is against this backdrop that Tanzania was pressured to restructure its economy by the World Bank, IMF, and the broader international donor community (Gastorn 2008). Facing these economic challenges, Nyerere stepped down as president in 1985, ending socialist practices and making way for IMF and World Bank Structural Adjustment Programs (SAPs) beginning in 1986. The IMF's structural adjustments included a 50- to 60-per-cent devaluation of the Tanzanian shilling, the removal of import controls, a reduction in funding for health, education, and other social services, and the removal of subsidies for key dietary staples, such as maize, and agricultural inputs, such as fertilizer (Campbell and Stein 1992; Kihacha 2002; Mshana 2003).

Under structural adjustment, Tanzania experienced an upsurge of interest in commercial farming and the number of land occupancy rights granted to wealthy, urban-based investors rose dramatically (Daley 2008). Those who had been resettled under Nyerere's villagization scheme were also permitted to return to their previous customary settlements (Kamata 2003). These shifts in policy and practice, as well as cuts to agricultural inputs and social services, resulted in a rise in the number of land struggles across the country and the creation of class polarization in rural communities (Kamata 2003; Koda 2000). The combination of privatization of land with cuts to social welfare caused poorer peasants to sell their land, because they could no longer cover their needs on farming alone (Koda 2000). Some rural people described the root cause of their income insecurity as the *soko holela* – the "chaotic market" – created by liberalization, privatization, and structural adjustment (Kihacha 2002).

Structural adjustment in Tanzania had gender-differentiated effects. The introduction of SAPs resulted in widespread unemployment and shifts to labour in the informal sector. Households increasingly shouldered responsibilities previously provided by the state, such as health care, which increased demands on women's domestic labour. With this increased need for women's labour at home and rising education costs, women and girls were further excluded from education (Mbilinyi 2003). Currency devaluation meant that women had to work longer hours on farms or in petty trade to compensate for lost income (Rusimbi 2003). Female smallholder farmers faced major barriers in the form of patriarchal social relations, family structures, and customary land tenure practices, while shouldering increased agricultural workloads (Koda 2000; Mbilinyi 2003; Rusimbi 2003). The livelihoods of younger generations were also put at greater risk: would-be inheritors were also excluded from land ownership and control as peasants were forced into land sales (Koda 2000). As a result, younger generations lacked land to cultivate and live on, driving urban migration and growth in labour markets. These patterns are consistent with the broader research on the gendered impacts of macroeconomic policies (Perrons 2021). As scholars like Mbilinyi (2017) have argued, the broader pattern of agricultural commercialization in Tanzania, including land privatization, has had clear gender- and class-differentiated impacts.

International financial institutions like the World Bank and the IMF thus had a significant impact on Tanzanian land governance. The land crises initiated by structural adjustment prompted the creation of the Shivji Commission in 1991 to review land administration, and later led to the creation of the 1999 Land Acts. However, the liberalization of the Tanzanian economy in the 1980s still has ripple effects today: the Tanzanian government continues to pursue export-oriented growth, both in agriculture and industrial development. Following the Comprehensive African Agriculture Development Programme (CAADP) model, the Tanzanian government partners with international institutions and donor countries to improve the business climate for international investors. National institutions such as the Tanzania Investment Centre (TIC) are designed to help facilitate investment from foreign countries, including the facilitation of land leases.

Tanzania's efforts under CAADP have led to partnerships with the US government, and the G8 countries, under the G8 New Alliance for Food Security and Nutrition, have initiated the development of the Southern Agricultural Growth Corridor of Tanzania (SAGCOT), and attracted several large-scale foreign agricultural investments. Despite the volatility and precariousness of foreign investments in agricultural land, the Tanzanian government continues to support foreign investment in agricultural land in line with Tanzania's national agricultural policy, Kilimo Kwanza, The Big Results Now Initiative, and CAADP (Collins et al. 2019). And it is within this context that Tanzania has attracted – and allowed – several controversial land deals. The Tanzanian government continues to attract foreign investment into SAGCOT, which pledges to assist small-scale farmers alongside larger operators in the region. Tanzania's rural landscape has become a popular target for large-scale land acquisitions since 2008–09. The International Land Coalition's (ILC) Land Matrix estimates that over seven hundred and thirty-five thousand hectares of land in Tanzania have been contracted by firms, with nearly 80 per cent coming from outside Tanzania and major acquisitions of over twenty thousand hectares each originating from the United States, Sweden, the Netherlands, and Norway (Land Matrix Global Observatory 2019). However, civil society organizations still raise concerns about the practices of large-scale agriculture in the country and the impacts on small-scale producers, including women. In particular, because of the absence of consultations with local people, and particularly women, the lands that have been targeted for agricultural investment are often regarded as idle, but are used by rural peoples.

It is at such points where drawing the connecting lines between global and national agricultural governance is critical. As we will see below, the Tanzanian domestic context illustrates the importance of considering multiple levels of land governance, both legal and economic. While the Tanzanian government opens new opportunities in the SAGCOT, the local political and legal structure matters for shaping the acquisition of land. Tanzania's national land reforms offer new legal protections for customary land users and for women, suggesting that land governance might create more transparent and inclusive land investment, with significant local input in decision-making. At the same time, however, agricultural development plans – designed for the domestic context but with input and support from international partners – highlight a policy agenda in which foreign land investment is welcomed and encouraged. Together, this might seem like a recipe for increased agricultural investment, as well as more protections for local people. However, as we will see, there are significant shortcomings in practice, and many of these affect rural Tanzanian women.

National Land Governance Frameworks

As detailed above, the state is responsible for economic growth, agricultural development, and industrialization, goals which may or may not contradict other initiatives designed to protect land rights. In the Tanzanian case, government actions to implement the 1999 Land Acts and complementary legislation illustrate the capacities that states have to extend land rights to those with customary land tenure or to promote women's legal equality. However, the effectiveness of these reforms is contingent on several factors, as described below.

Institutional Reforms

Following the aforementioned economic crises and in advance of the post-2007-08 land rush, the Republic of Tanzania passed the Land Acts in 1999. As noted above, the drafters of the Land Acts tried to formalize a dual system of tenure (McAuslan 1998). Specifically, the introduction of the Certificate of Customary Right of Occupancy (CCRO) was an important step toward the formal recognition of customary land. The Land Acts resolved the lack of recognition of customary land tenure by introducing Certificates of Village Land (CVLs) and CCROs as means by which communities could demarcate their land and apportion land parcels according to local practices and through elected bodies at the village level. Once a CVL has been issued to a Village, Village Assemblies can approve the granting of CCROs to individuals or households, with co-registration of spouses the preferred option. These CCROs are equal in law to land titles, where previously customary claims on land were dealt with only through administrative processes (United Republic of Tanzania 1994; Tsikata 2003). As a result, villages and villagers are supposed to have legally recognized claims to land, documented in local land registries, and signed by the District Land Officer (United Republic of Tanzania 1999b, sec. 21.1, Sec. 25.2d).

Though these reforms are gender progressive in many respects, there have nonetheless been setbacks in implementation (McAuslan 2013). Although the Acts prohibit gender discrimination and require gender quotas in decision-making bodies, such rules have not been enforced in practice. In addition, the process to roll out CCROs has also been slow.

Issuing CCROs relies on the establishment of the Certificate of Village Land (CVL) and the creation of a local land registry. Reliable data on the number of established CVLs and CCROs are still difficult to establish. Dancer (2015) notes that, in 2010, only four of seventy-six villages in Arusha District had land registries, and thus most could not yet issue CCROs. Biddulph and Hillbom (2020, 3) estimate that, in February 2017, only thirty-seven of ninety villages in Meru district had received a Certificate of Village Land, and only twenty had begun issuing CCROs.

Moreover, in addition to the intersection of structural inequality and access to legal remedies, legal proceedings are still influenced by customary practices and authority, as well as the gender-based expectations around land use and control. Dancer (2015) has shown that, even where women pursue legal remedy through statutory court systems, customary leaders may still exercise a great deal of influence over their cases. As will be discussed in more specific detail below, this institutional complexity has not been matched with training for front-line implementers. Social and community-based governance still shape the gendered outcomes of both statutory and customary tenure practices.

Decentralization and Capacity of Implementers

The devolution of responsibility for land administration in Tanzania has been heralded as an important step for the democratization of land governance and the recognition of customary forms of authority (Alden Wily 2011; Deininger et al. 2012). However, meeting these goals is not a simple or straightforward process. The absence of resources and public-education campaigns results in a lack of training of key officials and the tendency to default to existing patriarchal practices, as highlighted in Dancer's (2015) analysis mentioned above. By decentralizing authority to existing authority figures, the Land Acts create complicated tasks for front-line implementers at multiple levels in the state structures of land governance. Not only are implementers agents of the state, but they are *required* by state legislation to govern according to custom and local practice (Boone 2014; Dancer 2015). They are not functionaries of either state or community, but *both* (Pedersen 2012). While this incorporates local customs into state structures of land governance, its effectiveness in securing land tenure for all members of the community is contingent on the ability of front-line implementers to balance several complicated responsibilities.

Front-line implementers are expected to govern according to local custom, while at the same time ensuring that gender discrimination does not occur. Without appropriate training as to the provisions of the Land Acts, clarity about their responsibilities as governance officials, and clear instructions from central authorities, it is difficult for implementers to balance these responsibilities in a way that satisfies the complex requirements of the Land Acts. The influence of customary authorities may ultimately be the decisive factor in determining the outcomes of women's land claims before the courts because of the ways in which customary tenure is linked to marriage, separation, divorce, or the death of a male relative or spouse (Dancer 2015, 38). In this way, judicial power and social influence are enmeshed with each other and how land claims remain embedded in social relations (Dancer 2015). Furthermore, by making village land decisions democratic, effective implementation requires not only that local officials understand the rules, but that the broader public understands the rules as well. This level of policy implementation is thus a key area within which the governance of polities and the governance of communities converge in an explicit way.

In the absence of training for local officials, there is unlikely to be change in how local authorities and officials view the importance of securing land for rural smallholder farmers and families. An official in the Ministry of Lands, Housing, and Human Settlements Development acknowledged that local administrators and populations responsible for implementing the Land Acts did not value the CCROs nor view the administration of village land as a priority.[9] This attitude is confirmed by recent research: administrators are still slow to obtain Certificates of Village Land and to issue CCROs, since there are other quasi-formal options available (Biddulph and Hillbom 2020). Without appropriate training and support for land administration, front-line implementers lack the specific skills required to execute changes in the Land Acts and implement the signature change in rural land administration: the CCRO. This reinforces Pedersen's (2013) view of the "decoupling" that occurs between front-line implementers and the goals of public policy, where the mindset of the implementers does not match that of the designers of the Acts. This decoupling factors into the disconnection between the stated policy goals and the discriminatory practices at the local level. Though the Land Acts are designed to create land tenure security, there are shortcomings in equipping front-line implementers to meet the expressed goals of the legislation.

Moreover, the political context has also shifted since the Acts were designed, further undermining the likelihood of CCROs being used to secure customary lands. As Biddulph (2018) concludes, the Tanzanian government has not supported the implementation of community-governed land, favouring instead an individualization, titling, and registration approach as it further pursues commercial agricultural development.

These practical issues of implementation are influenced by culturally specific gendered norms and customs that limit the extent to which rural women and other marginalized groups can participate in local forums and claim land rights. The reinforcement of patriarchal customary land tenure practices often contradicts efforts to ensure a more gender-equitable land governance system. While the formalization of customary forms of tenure and governance may cause little disruption in local practices, the efforts to implement gender-sensitive, individual-rights-based reforms in this context face a difficult challenge. Broader gendered norms and the important influence of customary authorities over legal proceedings can prevent the realization of the gender-equity provisions in the Land Acts. Attempts to reform local governance in the name of gender equality encounter very real challenges in customary practices and predominant gendered norms, especially where local officials are tasked with implementing provisions that conflict with existing practices.

Institutional Complexity

A common concern expressed by scholars, activists, NGO workers, and legal-aid practitioners is the complexity of the Land Acts and the number of institutions now created to deal with land administration, adjudication, and governance. Despite the delineation between the two forms of land occupancy, the governance and adjudication of land and land ownership is more complicated. At the village level there are at least six different bodies involved in this governance and administration.[10] Yet only three of these bodies – the Village Council, the Village

Assembly, and the Village Land Council – fall under the auspices of the Land Act, Village Land Act, and the Courts Act. Legal-aid advocates note that this institutional complexity leads people to apply for remedy at the wrong bodies, with administrators also unclear about the scope of their authority.[11] The Courts Act (United Republic of Tanzania 2002) creates further confusion over the governance of land and adjudication of land conflicts: adjudicative bodies at different levels belong to different hierarchies of authority, and, in some cases, different ministries altogether, meaning that dispute resolution pursued at one level might not be enforced.

Tanzanian feminist legal advocates view institutional complexity as having distinctly gendered impacts. In addition to overcoming whatever social and community-based pressures there are to avoid contesting land decisions in rural villages (Koda 2000) – a consideration elaborated upon further below – women also face resource and distance constraints that dictate whether they will be able to pursue remedies in other courts. Even then, their cases may be tied up for years to come. In these instances, broader structural inequalities can shape women's access to justice through these legal measures, as the practicalities of distance, time, and financing can hamper this access. With the difficulty of obtaining legal remedy that will be enforced, marginalized people who lack the resources needed to navigate the legal system will be at a disadvantage. Moreover, the widespread confusion and lack of training in these institutions poses yet another obstacle for rural populations to overcome.

The institutional confusion created by the legal structures of the 1999 Land Acts serves as a cautionary tale for other states endeavouring to formalize pluralist land tenure systems. Thus, while the modes by which land is obtained might appear clear and direct, the methods of land adjudication and governance are myriad and complex and deny access to those who lack the monetary resources or community or family connections to pursue lengthy contestations over land rights (Dancer 2015). This complexity further entrenches class- and gender-based stratifications in the access to legal remedies over land disputes. Though various legal-aid bodies exist, many of their legal advocates reside in urban centres, with only paralegals and other resources available in some rural areas (Tanzania Women Lawyers Association 2013a; Women's Legal Aid Centre 2013a; Women's Legal Aid Centre 2013b). Access to legal recourse thus becomes tied to both class and geography in addition to gender, with wealthier, urban-based populations given easier access to legal assistance than poorer, peasant populations in rural Tanzania. These gaps in access are further compounded by structural gender inequalities that favour men over women in terms of land claims, and the customary norms that reinforce these inequalities.

Gender and Local Political Participation

Tanzania's 1999 Land Acts devolved authority to communities, such that land could be governed according to local needs. Yet patriarchal customary practices in many of Tanzania's rural communities influence the operation of village governance bodies, including those that now have significant power in decision-making over land. This community governance creates insiders and outsiders at the village level, and in some cases relies on threats of violence to discipline transgressions. Given the role women play in the maintenance of Tanzania's rural agricultural economies – 85 per cent of rural people in mainland Tanzania are engaged in agriculture, and 81 per cent of rural working women are self-employed agricultural workers (United Republic of Tanzania 2015) – their marginalization in local governance is a concern for those interested in more gender-equitable land governance. In the context of increased investment in land, decisions made at the local level can have wide-ranging consequences for entire communities. To ensure all voices are heard, more attention needs to be paid to tools to encourage more inclusive participation and to the ways in which some voices might still be silenced in spite of such tools.

Use of Gender Quotas

Quotas are often employed to help to address gender imbalances in political bodies. Tanzania's land reforms introduced gender quotas into local decision-making to help ensure that women were represented in reformed governance bodies. For instance, three of seven members on Village Councils and District Land and Housing Tribunals must be women, and a quorum of Village Land Councils requires two of four members be women. Yet, despite these reforms coming into effect in 2002, these requirements were only beginning to be met in the mid-

2010s. The Tanzania Media Women's Association (TAMWA) notes that women made up only 8 per cent of Village Council members elected in 2009, well below the legally required threshold of approximately 43 per cent on each council. Only 2 per cent of elected Village Chairpersons – arguably the most influential position at the village level – were women (Tanzania Media Women's Association n.d.).[12] There are reports that women's representation on these bodies has improved, but challenges remain. Dancer and Sulle (2015) report that quotas are increasingly being met, though it is still rare to find instances where more women are being elected than is strictly required. Other observers note that, despite the quotas being filled, women are still less likely to attend meetings, given their other care and work responsibilities (Kisambu 2016). Perhaps counter-intuitively, Chan et al. (2016) find evidence that quotas have served to *undermine* women's representation in matrilineal societies, where women's representation is lower than in bodies where there is no gender quota. Genicot and Hernandez-de-Benito (2022) report that, although in their study they find that village authorities express more progressive gender-equal views, when tools were used to measure gender bias, they find that the participants fall short of the gender-equal prescriptions of the law.

Descriptive vs Substantive Representation

Instituting quotas to push for more gender equality is an important step, but one that risks overlooking the broader challenges of structural gender inequality. The women elected to Village Councils or Village Land Councils are often not provided training on their roles or the roles of the councils in the structure of governance. This raises doubts about government-mandated efforts to improve gender equality in participation and local governance, as women may not have the training to be effective representatives. Experts cite women's lack of capacity to perform as representatives in Village Councils and Village Land Councils as a limiting factor in transformative change, and express disappointment in the lack of capacity-building for women who serve in local councils (Kisambu 2016).[13] Without additional training, the perception is that women are present only to be counted, and not to participate in a meaningful way (Chan et al. 2016). There is skepticism about how effective reforms in local governance will be and to what extent village-level decisions legitimately reflect local needs in the absence of government support for civic education and training for women.

Even where civic education and training efforts are undertaken, gender roles and expectations still tend to shape local attitudes about the appropriateness of gender-inclusive local governance. Village Councils tend to be regarded as the domain of local men, rather than democratically elected, gender-inclusive bodies (Collins and Mitchell 2018). Village Assemblies also demonstrate the limits to women's meaningful participation in local forums. Village Assemblies are supposed to include the entire adult population of the village, but meetings are often not held regularly or with appropriate notice. Furthermore, attendance is low, particularly among women: "the village meetings are called during parts of the day where it's mainly men who can attend. Women are in the field, or they're in the home, or they're in the market ... It's not done at a time when you can get women who can participate, so it ends up being older men."[14] These patterns persist in rural villages across the country, with women not being able to attend important community meetings (Kisambu 2016).

For those women who *do* attend meetings of the Village Assembly, there is the additional challenge of overcoming gendered expectations and divisions in the practices of the meetings themselves. The general quality of women's substantive participation in village politics in Tanzania has historically been low, shaped in large part by attitudes toward the position of women in society, attitudes held by both men and women (Misafi 2014; Genicot and Hernandez-de-Benito 2022). These attitudes are often manifested in the physical spaces of governance bodies. Village meetings tend to have a clear gendered order to seating, with women seated at the back. Says one INGO program director: "There's the high table where the village leaders sit, and you often have the men who sit close, youth and, right at the back, you might have the women who attend. So, the women are further [back], cut away from where the real power is."[15] This physical organization of Village Assembly meetings reinforces community attitudes about women's proper role in public forums and makes it a challenge for women to speak up for their own interests.

These dynamics also have the potential to take a more violent and threatening form when rural women attempt to challenge the status quo in public forums. When women participate or articulate their concerns publicly, they may face public discipline from the community and from within the home. An NGO director who had conducted village-level training around the Land Acts reported that "[A young man] stood up and interfered, and pointing a finger at the woman, saying, 'These are just passers-by. They are leaving and you are going to remain here and face the consequence of pointing out our weaknesses in front of these guests and visitors.'"[16] These threats, in combination with the aforementioned attitudes that regard decision-making spaces as the domain of men, create disincentives for the meaningful public participation of women. As a result, women's limited access to land and their diminished status in political forums means that they cannot participate in land decision-making with the same latitude granted to men.

Although the Land Acts attempt to address the matter of gender inequality by instituting gender quotas in village bodies, there are broader community and social norms that also need to be considered. If reforms address only matters of descriptive representation in political governance, such as adding more women to political bodies, without attention to community-based norms and practices, quotas will move only incrementally toward the full inclusion of women in political decision-making. When we consider both the norms and practices around decision-making bodies, including attitudes that restrict women's ability to speak or even attend village meetings, we can see how the governance of communities and polities intersect. In the case of Tanzania, the devolution of authority combined with customary decision-making may reinforce discriminatory practices. Indeed, many scholars note the tension between encouraging the customary governance of local land while also expecting local authorities to follow legal gender-equity provisions (Genicot and Hernandez-de-Benito 2022). It is essential to consider more than just the formal institutional reforms; there must be an understanding of the societal context. Without attention to the governance of communities, including gendered social norms, changes to political rules may have little effect.

Yet land governance expands beyond these considerations of institutional village governance and community relations into the customary and family practices that structure inheritance and ownership patterns as well. With local authorities able to govern land and adjudicate land disputes according to custom, understanding the gendered hierarchies of customary inheritance practices at the local level are essential for anticipating how customary authorities may or may not favour gender-equality provisions in the law.

Kinship and Community Relations in Land Governance

Tanzania's land governance framework explicitly links the governance of polities with that of communities. Local gendered norms in the conduct of public life influence the levels of participation in local governance. Yet because land governance under the Land Acts requires governance in accordance with local customs, political and community governance are further entwined under these reforms. These customs include intra-family dynamics and practices, particularly the intergenerational transfer of land, and community- and clan-based interests in keeping land under collective control. Kinship relations and clan-based inheritance practices are critical to understanding gendered patterns of land control and decision-making under the 1999 Land Acts. These dynamics highlight the ways in which family and community practices might constrain the gender-equitable delivery of decentralized land governance and decision-making. Indeed, understanding these dynamics demonstrates the limitations of land governance reforms that do not consider patterns of gendered land ownership and control. At the same time, analysts need to be mindful of the diversity of customary practices within Tanzania, and the opportunities to support gender equity within the context of such diverse practices.

Inheritance Practices

Inheritance under customary rules remains the primary means by which rural Tanzanians access land.[17] It is estimated that about 80 per cent of Tanzanian ethnic groups follow patriarchal customary practices in the administration of inheritance (Isinika and Mutabazi 2010; Dancer 2017). Despite the potential for negotiation and flexibility within customary governance, customary practices in mainland Tanzania often marginalize women as inheritors of land. A study by WLAC confirms that Village Land Councils tend to adhere to discriminatory customary practices in their rulings, an unexpected finding since "these organs were required to be at the forefront in disallowing traditions and customs that impinge on the rights of rural women to land ownership" (Women's Legal Aid Centre 2010, 30). Thus, even where women have claims to land under the law, they still must often overcome the traditional expectations of village authorities who adjudicate land disputes.

Under the Village Land Act, CCROs are issued in accordance with customary village practices, with land adjudication committees directed to consider challenges to proposed allocations with reference to customary law (United Republic of Tanzania 1999b, sec. 53.3d). Given the relatively open definition of "customary law" under the Interpretation of Laws and General Clauses Act, 1972, these provisions permit local communities to govern themselves according to practices accepted within the community.[18] And although there is also a provision in the law mandating that women and pastoralists be treated "not less favourably" than men or agriculturalists (United Republic of Tanzania 1999b, sec. 57.3), reconciliation of these two provisions often does not happen in practice.

The traditions of customary law thus shape land inheritance and the prospects of joint ownership of land. Patriarchal customary land governance tends to undermine joint spousal ownership of land, because clans often want to keep clan land undivided in mainland Tanzania (Pedersen and Haule 2013). The view that women are transitory within patrilocal communities – that is, that they will marry and settle within their husband's community – presents a challenge for communities concerned about the security of community or clan land. Some communities have instituted bylaws to restrict land allocated to women in order to keep clan land together (Isinika and Mutabazi 2010). Though these practices might be viewed as discriminatory, one expert noted that, in some cases, such rules were instituted to prevent outsiders from using marriage to acquire land, only to divorce women shortly thereafter. "I always tell people that if you look at that bylaw quickly, you will say that it is sexist. But really it was done to protect women of that village ... I don't know if it was correct, but in context it justified the means."[19] Regardless, this bylaw – and the attitudes around it – illustrate how women are viewed as a potential threat to clan land. In patrilineal communities such as the Sukuma of Shinyanga district, restrictive inheritance practices are also typically in place to protect the integrity of clan land. In these cases, women may have usufruct (use) rights, "but they are not allowed to transfer land through bequeathal, gifts or sale and [it] is typically owned by the clan, community or family" (Isinika and Mutabazi 2010, 140). In these cases, women are seen as "heirs of the third degree," after the eldest son and all other younger sons (Isinika and Mutabazi 2010, 140).

Patrilineal inheritance practices are not uniform across Tanzania. Isinika and Mutabazi (2010) contrast the practices of the Sukuma with those of the Bena, which they describe as more favourable toward women. In Bena culture, both young men and women are given clan land as teenagers, and women retain that land even after marriage. Children inherit the land of both parents after death, a departure from other patrilineal practices (Isinika and Mutabazi 2010). However, if a woman is childless when she dies, the land reverts back to the woman's clan rather than to her husband, which also illustrates the limits to women's bequeathal and transfer rights among the Bena (Isinika and Mutabazi 2010).

Again, such instances require attention to context-specific gendered dynamics around kinship and the control of land. As demonstrated in the previous chapter, there is diversity in gender dynamics and land control across regions and within countries. However, what remains salient across Tanzania is the need for careful attention to how inheritance practices operate. There are key differences across patrilineal societies that lead to starkly different outcomes and decisions made by communities. And indeed, this diversity further illustrates the flexibility that exists in both patrilineal and matrilineal societies. It is thus important to pay attention to inheritance practices in order to understand the potential constraints on gender-equitable decision-making, as well as the opportunities that might exist in customary practices.

Marital Status

Marital relations are women's key access point for land in rural Tanzania, but they are also a security mechanism to maintain the integrity of clan land. For married rural women in most patrilineal and patrilocal societies, their access to land typically remains stable as long as their marriage is intact. A sense of security in her marriage may undermine efforts to co-register land or register women's land in their own name. Of course, it is difficult to predict when or how a marriage may come to an end, which may leave women vulnerable. The threat of alienation from their land is high, especially after the death of the land giver and/or spouse.

There are various constraints and opportunities afforded by women's marital status. For instance, Koda's (2000) research in Msindo Village, Same District, found that married and single women in the Wapare community were more likely to pursue remedies for land and property disputes through the customary practices at the village level, while divorced and widowed women were more likely to seek remedies in primary courts, removed from the practices within the community itself. Married women receive the most respect from the broader community and may be able to navigate local customary authorities with ease. Divorced and widowed women, on the other hand, though they may seek out formal institutions for land appeals, find themselves unable to familiarize themselves with the practices of formal institutions, bound as they are by gendered attitudes about the appropriateness of women observing court proceedings during the day. "If a woman imitates men on these issues, she will be accused of being lazy and wasting time while men who do so are envied and praised by villagers" (Koda 2000, 162).

Given the nature of patriarchal customs, many women find it difficult to challenge clan authority figures or even claim property that belongs jointly or even primarily to them. Gendered ideas about land ownership within families are pervasive, making implementing the gender-equality provisions of the Land Acts a greater challenge. These gendered ideas are not limited to viewing women as a threat to land ownership but are also tied to conceptions of masculinity and pride. Wives are denied decision-making powers on clan or family land transfers on the grounds that their status cannot be compared to their husband's because a bride-wealth has been paid for them (Koda 2000). Entrenched ideas about the inappropriateness of women owning land or property in her own name influence whether women will or will not register land under their name (Collins and Mitchell 2018). The result is that women risk losing land in the event of spousal death or divorce, or if a surviving wife attempts to sell land that was jointly used, but not co-registered. Because of the associations between masculine roles and property ownership, and the lack of access to legal assistance in many rural areas, the legal provisions for spousal co-registration on CCROs thus may not remedy women's land insecurity. These practices reinforce the idea of men as the proper owners of land and, consequently, the ones to make individual and community-based decisions about land use and ownership.

The idea of women as transitory members of the community is also a factor in divorce proceedings or when a spouse dies. In patrilineal and patrilocal communities, if a woman is widowed, she may find her and her husband's land reclaimed by the husband's family.[20] If she has children, especially male children, a widowed woman may have access to the land if it is granted to her by her children or may retain custodianship of her deceased husband's land until male children can take over (Pedersen and Haule 2013). If a woman is divorced, she typically has legal recourse to claim matrimonial land, but this may need to be pursued outside the village authorities and according to statutory law, which has additional financial and social costs. Women's access to land may also be challenged or changed if her husband remarries within a polygamous arrangement, whether under Islamic or customary practice (Hilhorst 2000). The rights of senior or junior wives may or may not be recognized by community authorities under customary law and, because customary law is typically not recorded, records of decisions might not be kept for later reference or consistency in decision-making. Thus, where one senior wife won an appeal against her husband in Msindo Village, another senior wife lost her appeal, as senior clan members ruled in favour of a father's right to allocate land as he chooses (Koda 2000).

Women who are widowed or divorced are often those most likely to speak out in public forums or pursue legal challenges. These women often have little to lose by challenging conventional customs, as there is little chance that they will face retribution at home, and they have often already been stripped of rights they held previously. By contrast, a married woman who is dependent on her husband and his family, and thus needs to maintain good relationships with them, is less likely to protest family inheritance practices or participate in public fora. Single women planning to marry also often need to maintain good relationships with the broader community in order to arrange a marriage. Divorced and widowed women who have been denied access to land and property by their ex-husband or the husband's family typically lack these social constraints or dependencies, and are thus more likely to assert themselves.

Gender-based Violence

Finally, household relationships and the threat of domestic violence also shape the extent to which women can control land or participate in public decision-making. Women who challenge traditional gender norms and customs by pursuing individual land rights, observing political or judicial decision-making, or actively engaging in local politics might face domestic violence in addition to public scorn or shaming. Intimate-partner violence against women continues to be a socially acceptable form of discipline within Tanzania, which poses an additional deterrent to challenging common customary practices. The 2015 Tanzania Demographic and Health Survey estimates that 40 per cent of all women aged fifteen to forty-nine years have experienced physical violence of some kind, and 42 per cent of women who have ever been married have experienced intimate-partner violence (MoHCDGEC et al. 2016). At the same time, intimate-partner violence is widely accepted as a form of discipline in rural parts of the country: the World Bank Tanzania Gender Assessment 2022 reports that 58 per cent of women and 40 per cent of men believe "that husbands are justified in beating their wives in certain circumstances" (World Bank 2022, 54).

There are connections between the social acceptance of gender-based violence and the disciplining of women who challenge current governance practices or pursue land rights. One INGO officer shared the risks that women face from within their own household when they decide to participate in village politics:

> We were having a small mentoring session with a farmer group, and one of the members of the farmer group was a woman who was the wife of the Village Chair. So, she spoke up in the meeting, and we really encouraged her to because she was really quiet ...

> And she finally spoke up and she started talking about some of the issues in terms of the transparency in terms of income ... She got home and her husband beat her badly because he had heard that she had spoken up and she had said things that were not in the right light.[21]

These real threats of physical violence are used to maintain the boundaries of acceptable participation and governance. Though several NGO officers reported some positive improvements in local attitudes about gender-based violence in interviews, threats of violence still have a silencing effect on rural women's political participation. In the absence of social supports for gender-based violence and the acceptance of gender-based violence as a form of discipline, there are constraints on public participation for women. The role of gender-based violence highlights the complexity of looking at women's participation in decision-making and the limits of using only legal reform to pursue social change. This attention to violence also underscores the importance of considering marital status in understanding land governance and decision-making and suggests ways in which we need to consider where women and vulnerable people might be exposed to violence through intimate relationships, family dynamics, and the broader community.

The dynamics surrounding family and kinship relations and control reveal how important it is to consider various sites of power and governance in the context of land access, control, and decision-making. As we have seen above, global dynamics, national laws, and local governance are all relevant to understanding patterns of land governance. However, the role of family and kinship dynamics also needs to be remembered as we seek to understand patterns of land governance and the limits of legal and individual rights-based reforms. Without due consideration of the family dynamics that shape inheritance patterns, the importance of marital relationships (or the lack thereof), and recognition of the threat of domestic violence, government reforms are unlikely to address many of the informal modes of governance that shape land and decision-making.

In the context of Tanzania, and the implementation of land reforms that are designed to both address gender inequality and recognize customary land tenure, we can see many of these tensions at work. Both are laudable goals, but they may conflict in some local contexts, leading to little substantive change in how women access land or participate in decision-making. This is critical to understand: even though government-led reforms create opportunities for change, a full appreciation of how communities are governed and how gender roles discipline behaviours reveals that such efforts alone are insufficient. Once we consider land as being governed through multiple levels of rules and practices, including those that happen within families and kinship relations, we can see how complex reform might be.

Conclusion

There is much at stake when land is sought for large-scale investment or speculation. Both successful and failed land deals can have lasting impacts on rural populations. Although there are many factors that shape such outcomes, land governance and local decision-making are key components in shaping the outcomes of a land deal. Legal requirements to consult with local populations to complete a land deal have the potential to give tremendous power to local decision-makers, whether they are chiefs, elders, or elected representatives. At the same time, secure and recognized customary or individual rights might serve to empower local land users to control their own lands, or to claim an important space in community-based decision-making.

Yet within these governance processes are many modes of power and forms of inequality. State-based rules may exclude certain populations from access to rights. Local governance is often not a harmonious process, and can exclude people of various ethnic, religious, or gender identities. Moreover, norms about who rightfully makes decisions can exclude people and viewpoints whose input might be vital. In addition, within households there are differences regarding who has the right to land and who is suitable to inherit such land.

This chapter has illustrated how considering these levels of analysis reveals the complexity of enacting land reform with the goals of recognizing customary land rights, protecting women's rights to land, and ensuring large-scale land deals are undertaken in a fair and transparent manner. The Tanzanian case is a rich case study, as it reveals the challenges of a state-led effort to address domestic land governance issues at the same time as it pursues an agricultural development strategy that has been dependent on attracting large-scale investments in land.

Together, global, national, local, and family-based modes of governance – formal and informal laws and rules – all shape the outcomes of land governance. Moreover, the governance of communities – specifically the norms and rules around gender-appropriate behaviours – have an impact on how land is governed. The Tanzanian case demonstrates an instance wherein traditional and family modes of land governance are enmeshed with formal political governance via the institutionalization of customary governance. Yet this case also illustrates how laws that are supposed to balance women's rights with the recognition of customary practices are difficult to implement. Enacting legal reforms without full support for implementation means that change may be desperately slow. Although gender quotas exist, women are often still not active participants in local decision-making. Despite legal provisions to protect women's access to land, the reliance on custom in adjudicating disputes reinforces existing practices.

The multi-level governance framework used in this chapter helps to provide this deeper understanding of land governance, but also highlights potential sites for gender-transformative change. By understanding these various sites of power and decision-making, we can also consider strategies wherein positive change can occur and where existing policies or practices might support land security and gender equity. It is essential that our assessment of global land governance efforts include this broader understanding of the real-world dynamics of land policy change and implementation, as well as the broader social norms that influence rules and governance, especially those that pertain to gender.

What are the relevant lessons here in addressing gender inequality in the governance of land and land deals? First, there must be recognition of the possibility of tensions between customary authority and promotion of gender equality, especially where efforts are made to devolve authority to communities. Local contexts vary, but often patriarchal traditional, customary, and/or religious practices may exclude women. On the other hand, recognizing traditional land rights is critically important in protecting rural lands from encroachment (Collins 2019). Efforts to reform land governance by devolving authority to local people thus need to take into consideration local hierarchies and not presume that local governance is equitable. As a result, where both of these goals exist at once, there must be greater recognition of these potential tensions and an identification of strategies that can work to achieve both goals.

Second, there needs to be an awareness that efforts to govern land solely through the recognition of individual (not community) land rights and the expansion of land markets are likewise unlikely to fully support women's equal rights or participation. Again, contexts matter, but often women lack the financial means to acquire land independent from spouses or families. Even if this is feasible, the acquisition of individual rights might alienate them from families and communities. As noted above, it is typically only women without husbands who pursue formal legal solutions to land rights issues, as they are less likely to worry about estrangement.

Finally, lasting, progressive land reform needs to be accompanied by a commitment to implementation. But this commitment is likely to be expensive and long-term, since it may require the establishment of new infrastructure, the training of front-line implementers, and an engagement with leaders and community members. Such costly and likely slow-moving change may well have difficulty keeping pace with broader social and economic changes brought about by agricultural investment practices. Countries that are serious about responsible land investment need to take steps to ensure land reforms are undertaken carefully, and in advance of land investments.

These lessons are essential for understanding the limits of a technocratic understanding of land reform and women's-rights initiatives. The following chapters return to the important role of global actors in establishing narratives and policies for land governance and defining best practices. The rest of the book engages with these global-level efforts to set standards by assessing the extent to which they capture the dynamics that occur at other levels of governance. There are clear opportunities in some global spaces to expand the appreciation of gendered land dynamics and provide support for changes at multiple levels of land governance.

Yet, as we will see in subsequent chapters, nuanced understanding of the complexity of gender relations in land governance are often not the focus of global efforts to improve land governance. Instead of an appreciation of the complex ways in which inheritance patterns, systematic gender-based exclusion, legal obstacles, and other modes of governance intersect to create hierarchies in land governance, international efforts often focus on different priorities.

By focusing on efficiency, market access, and technical fixes to gender equality, global land governance initiatives that do recognize gender equality ultimately elide the deeply contested and political realities of how gender inequality is manifested in various formal and informal institutions.

The following chapters will demonstrate the gaps in several global land governance initiatives, particularly where they emphasize these technical fixes in place of a more complex appreciation of gender and land governance. The effect is to further delay the kinds of research and reforms necessary to push for more gender-equitable land governance reforms at all levels of political activity. At the same time, however, a closer analysis of governance at the global level can reveal opportunities to advance new agendas.

4 "EMPOWERMENT" AS EFFICIENCY: GENDER AND RESPONSIBLE AGRICULTURAL INVESTMENT

Making agricultural investment "responsible" has emerged as a popular focus for international organizations such as the FAO, the World Bank, UNCTAD, and others in the wake of concerns over large-scale land deals.[1] By framing the problems associated with such land deals – forced displacement, inadequate compensation, and loss of access to water and resources – as the result of agricultural investment gone awry, these organizations have tried to portray agricultural investment as having a positive and promising role in agricultural development. Despite recognizing the negative effects of large-scale land deals, the World Bank nonetheless endorses the need for more agricultural investment, pointing to the need for investments in technology and infrastructure, and highlighting poor land governance as the problem (Deininger et al. 2011). The World Bank and the United Nations Conference on Trade and Development (2014, xvi) report that "win-win" situations between "investment performance and their wider positive economic, social, and environmental impact *is* achievable."

Appropriately, the sets of responsible investment principles that have emerged share a similar optimism about the role of investment in improving food security and people's day-to-day lives. The Principles for Responsible Agricultural Investment (PRAI) developed by the World Bank, FAO, IFAD, and UNCTAD, which were launched in 2010, recommend several steps to recognize land rights quickly and efficiently, reduce government interference, and include women in land markets. On the other hand, several INGOs and the UN Special Rapporteur on the Right to Food questioned whether such investment could in fact be responsible (De Schutter 2011). The United Nations Committee on Food Security (CFS) likewise rejected the PRAI, voting against endorsing them, and began negotiations on a new set of investment principles in response. While offering more substance than the PRAI, the similarly named Principles for Responsible Agricultural Investment (henceforth, Rai Principles)[2] did not mark a significant departure in terms of its recommendations. Despite efforts to draft a set of principles in line with the needs of civil society, the Rai Principles nonetheless share a similar focus with the PRAI and have earned the ire of civil society organizations for similar reasons.

This chapter highlights the recommendations of the PRAI as well as the subsequent Rai Principles, revealing how an investment-centred appropriation of the term "empowerment" in both documents leads to an emphasis on efficiency and productivity, rather than a systemic understanding of gender relations, land, and agricultural governance. Moreover, both sets of principles highlight gender, indigeneity, traditional practices, and age as necessary considerations in agricultural investment, but each delineate these concerns in narrow terms. As both the broader literature and empirical evidence suggest, gender inequalities in agricultural production and the functioning of land and labour markets are complex, often tied to cultural practices and beliefs about gender roles and responsibilities. The tendency for international organizations to make the case for women's "empowerment" in local markets overlooks broader trends of gender discrimination and divisions of labour.

Below, this chapter examines the PRAI and argues that narrow economistic and trade-based considerations of land and agriculture continue to overlook the broader context within which gender inequalities are embedded and reproduced. By analyzing the PRAI's synoptic note[3] as well as the CFS Rai Principles, this chapter highlights the lack of detailed consideration of gender in these sets of principles, both in their efforts to incorporate considerations of gender, but also by their silence on gender issues on several key issues. I conducted a content analysis of both documents with reference to key themes related to gender, land governance, and rural agricultural practices, drawing from the literature on gender, land governance, and political economy detailed in chapter 2 and the gender-based challenges of land reform learned from the

Tanzanian context in chapter 3. Specifically, I looked for the extent to which each document considered:

- The roles of women, girls, men, boys, or other references to gender roles or relations related to land, land markets, or agricultural markets;
- The role of marital status or other gendered relations (i.e., parenthood) in land access or ownership;
- Gender and inheritance practices;
- Barriers to women's political representation and participation;
- Barriers to formal legal remedies or judicial review;
- Gender and the division of productive or reproductive roles in agriculture, such as whether women's domestic work or subsistence agricultural workloads were considered;
- The importance of customary tenure in rural land governance and the role of gender therein.

Through this examination of the documents, and with reference to the previous two chapters, we can see the disconnection between the local realities of land governance and the global-level initiatives designed to improve land governance and agricultural investment in response to large-scale land acquisitions. Ultimately, both sets of principles view gender and agricultural investment largely in terms of empowerment *as* market participation by women. I find that, although gender equality and women are mentioned in both sets of principles, neither document meaningfully grapples with structures of gender inequality in land governance, land markets, or agricultural investment.

Instead, as we will see further below, efforts to make land markets more "efficient" and to make market participation more inclusive are not universally empowering for women or other vulnerable groups, nor are efforts to liberalize trade and remove perceived trade barriers. These sets of responsible agricultural investment principles illustrate the limited ways gender and empowerment have been understood by policymakers, removing the political and social aspects of empowerment, and shifting further toward understandings of gender inequality as something requiring a "technical fix" (Parpart 2009). Social transformation requires long-term commitments to social change, not just legislative reform (Tsikata 2003; McAuslan 2010). By making speed, cost, and efficiency priorities of land and agricultural governance reform, these sets of principles overlook the realities of systemic gender-based discrimination. As demonstrated in the previous two chapters, patterns of gendered relations are not easily remedied with a policy fix – policy-makers need to consider the ways in which community-based practices and expectations around gender shape the land governance context.

From "Power" to "Participation" in Development Discourses

"Women's empowerment" has become a key concept integrated into development discourses and global economic policies more broadly. Once considered a transformational and radical approach to questions of gender and development, the language of empowerment used today by the UN, development agencies, and international institutions have been emptied of most of its once-revolutionary content (Cornwall and Rivas 2015). "Women's empowerment" as currently used by most multinational corporations, international organizations, non-governmental organizations, and state development agencies has become oversimplified, and is now typically used as a buzzword denoting women's empowerment within the economic realm. As Cornwall and Rivas (2015, 406) argue, "women's empowerment" has become a discourse whose central belief is that "women's business success is enough to overcome all other barriers to equality." Indeed, one need not look far to see such languages employed by the World Bank, Oxfam, and Nike (Roberts 2014).

This most recent shift in global discourses on gender and development follows a lengthy history of dialogue among activists, scholars, and policy-makers about how best to incorporate considerations of gender into policy-making. Arguably, the contemporary shift from the use of "empowerment" to challenge social and political hierarchies to a means to include women in markets as business actors, loan recipients, and labourers reflects a return to the Women in Development (WID) literatures of the 1970s (Cornwall and Rivas 2015). At that time, work inspired by the scholarship of Ester Boserup (1970) sought to include gender-disaggregated data and consider women's economic roles that had otherwise not been considered in economic-development policies. While transformative for the analysis of development policies, the WID paradigm viewed gender in narrow terms, looking primarily at women and their productive and reproductive roles. The result was a set of policies that, while beneficial, typically reinforced existing gendered divisions of labour and did not question unequal gender relations or "modernization" projects (Brown 2006).

The Gender and Development (GAD) literature that emerged as a reaction to the WID paradigm sought to emphasize how gendered relations and hierarchies structure economies and often restrict the recognition of women's contributions. The GAD scholars implored development scholars and activists to rethink gender relations. Development policies formulated under the GAD paradigm challenge systemic gender inequalities instead of just providing women-centric supports that might reinforce the status quo. Under the GAD paradigm, scholars also problematized "development" as a concept and contested Western conceptions of feminism. This scholarship challenges victimization narratives about "Third World" women and looked at gender ideologies more broadly (Peterson 2010).

Within this context, feminist scholars began adopting "empowerment" as a key term for grassroots movements, especially those resisting top-down state-led development reforms. This is a term with a storied and complex past and no single definition (Parpart 2009). Yet perhaps the most commonly used definition is that proposed by Naila Kabeer. Kabeer (1994; 1999) argues that empowerment should be viewed as a *process of change* that enables one to make choices, which is itself where power comes from. Empowerment is thus viewed by feminist scholars and activists as a process of self-expression and self-understanding; legal reforms and access to resources may help in the process, but are not in and of themselves "empowerment" end points (Cornwall and Rivas 2015). Analyzing empowerment thus requires attention to the order of choices being made, the agency of actors, and resources. A full discussion of these components is beyond this discussion, but suffice it to say that empowerment as envisioned by Kabeer and like-minded scholars is one that is rooted in specific contexts and social structures and as a process that occurs over time, rather than as a quantifiable result.

However, this has not prevented either scholars or policy-makers from employing narrow definitions of empowerment or instrumentalizing gender content in development policies. Instead of pushing an agenda that empowers women to self-actualize and challenge existing hierarchies according to their own needs, in some academic literature and much development practice "women's empowerment" has become synonymous with lowering gendered barriers to the marketplace. Marchand (1996) criticizes the narrow economism and efficiency focus that emerged in some GAD scholarship in the 1990s, denying the socio-political factors of empowerment. The GAD approach within the World Bank has had limited effect, for instance using an understanding of gender relations to focus on micro-social relations between individual men and women instead of looking at broader social structures (Bedford 2007). World Bank studies elsewhere have argued that the incorporation of women into labour markets will help to eliminate gender-based discrimination, without paying attention to gendered divisions of labour and inequality facilitated by neo-liberal capitalism and Western development projects (Bergeron 2003). The United Nations Millennium Development Goals have also been criticized for having a limited focus on women's empowerment, defining it as the ability to participate in labour markets (Kabeer 2005). Efforts to "empower" women through access to microcredit loans have likewise been critiqued for deepening gender processes of accumulation (Keating et al. 2010). More recently, Roberts (2012; 2014) has traced the rise of "transnational business feminism," which makes the case for the gains in profitability and stability to be had through eliminating gender discrimination in labour markets, political leadership, and access to credit. Yet, as Roberts (2014) warns, these essentialized ideas of women and the focus on equal representation also obscure broader structural inequalities, including class divisions and the increasing precariousness of labour around the world.

These empowerment languages thus frequently ignore the many social and political obstacles gender-empowerment policies encounter in practice (Parpart 2009). The shift toward viewing women's empowerment strictly through the lenses of economic efficiency and market participation has undermined the original concept of empowerment as a process of change. Indeed, the effect is to equate equal rights to participate in markets with empowerment. Such a conception is inherently limiting; as we have seen in earlier chapters, gender bias and discrimination runs much deeper throughout societies, and are not easily remedied by statutory reform or access to financial or agricultural inputs. Moreover, the ways in which contemporary investors view empowerment and gender are highly restrictive, which results in social-responsibility programs that fall more squarely in the traditional WID paradigm, serving the needs of women and children in conventional ways (Tsikata and Yaro 2014). Benefits accrued to women in such situations revolve around their reproductive responsibilities. Thus, we not only have a rather limited view of gender discrimination in practice, but also evidence of the limited ways in which firms view gender inequality and meeting the needs of community members.

These trends in contemporary development thinking suggest important areas of focus for global recommendations on land and agriculture. Scholarship suggests that attention needs to be paid to the societal obstacles to gender-equality measures. Yet, as we will see below, the most recent efforts to address agricultural investment fall prey to the same assumptions about gender, markets, and empowerment expressed by institutions like the World Bank. The PRAI, and the Rai Principles that followed, both view gender in isolation from broader societal dynamics of bias and discrimination, focusing on women as untapped resources for the more efficient operation of markets. Rather than asking more difficult questions about the role of gender relations in agricultural production and land access, both sets of principles offer primarily legal solutions to the matter of gender inequality in land and agriculture. The effect is to further reinforce common assumptions about women's economic empowerment via access to resources, formal land rights, and labour-market participation, without a more comprehensive understanding of the socio-cultural restrictions to achieving gender equality.

The Principles for Responsible Agricultural Investment (PRAI)

Despite the extensive scholarly publications on both gender and development policies and gender and land rights (e.g., Razavi 2002), the responsible agricultural investment initiatives endorsed to date do not heed many of their warnings. Though gender equality often appears top of mind in these initiatives – receiving attention in specific sections or subsections – the recommendations tend to demonstrate limited thinking about the role of gender in agriculture and land governance. Though the PRAI purportedly build upon ongoing research by the World Bank and others, a research agenda that includes attention to gender equality and development (World Bank 2012), very few connections are made between gender discrimination and the practices of land governance. As we will see, given the concerns about deep-seated resistance to gender-equal land rights in some customary practices discussed in the previous chapter, the lack of attention to gender and land governance is not a minor oversight in how land is governed. Rather, both sets of principles sidestep the full complexity of land governance and the intersections of community and political governance. Instead, these recommendations tend to focus primarily on how to efficiently bring women into land and labour markets as equal participants, without more critical attention to the ways in which land is used, owned, transferred, and governed and the gendered inequalities associated with liberalized land and labour markets.

The PRAI respond to the wave of large-scale land deals in sub-Saharan Africa and elsewhere in the period after 2007–08. A collaboration between the International Fund for Agricultural Development (IFAD), the United Nations Conference on Trade and Development (UNCTAD), the United Nations Food and Agriculture Organization (FAO), and, most notably, the World Bank Group, the PRAI were developed based on ongoing research about large-scale land acquisitions conducted by these organizations (FAO et al. 2010). As suggested by its title, the PRAI present a global code of conduct focused primarily on providing a non-binding set of guidelines for agricultural investment, emphasizing the perils associated with "weak governance," lack of land rights, and the lack of a "voice" for those affected (FAO et al. 2010). As such, the PRAI address both investor practices and the role of governments in providing oversight and clear legal mechanisms, and facilitating consultations with affected populations (see table 4.1). And although the code of conduct is in part for the use of investors, investors were not directly involved in its design. Many of the recommendations are instead targeted toward state governments, and are specifically related to land rights, the availability of information, monitoring, enforcement, and to a lesser extent, public consultations.

Since being introduced in January 2010, the PRAI have been endorsed by the G8 and the G20 and rejected by a number of NGOs and

Table 4.1 The principles for responsible agricultural investment

Principle 1:	Existing rights to land and associated natural resources are recognized and respected.
Principle 2:	Investments do not jeopardize food security but rather strengthen it.
Principle 3:	Processes for accessing land and other resources and then making associated investments are transparent, monitored, and ensure accountability by all stakeholders, within a proper business, legal, and regulatory environment.
Principle 4:	All those materially affected are consulted, and agreements from consultations are recorded and enforced.
Principle 5:	Investors ensure that projects respect the rule of law, reflect industry best practice, are viable economically, and result in durable shared value.
Principle 6:	Investments generate desirable social and distributional impacts and do not increase vulnerability.
Principle 7:	Environmental impacts due to a project are quantified and measures taken to encourage sustainable resource use while minimizing the risk/magnitude of negative impacts and mitigating them.

Source: FAO et al. 2010.

activist organizations such as GRAIN and La Via Campesina (CECCAM et al. 2011). These organizations and others argue that the effort to make agricultural investment appear responsible and transparent "is an attempt to cover up power imbalances so that the land grabbers and state authorities who make the deals can get what they want," without seriously investing in food sovereignty for small-scale farmers and fisherfolk (CECCAM et al. 2011, 5). Following these themes, this analysis looks more closely at the gender imbalances that go unaddressed by the PRAI. Below, this section analyses the themes within the PRAI synoptic note that are most relevant to addressing gender inequality in land and agriculture: the recognition of rights, food security, the creation of a favourable business climate, and the social impacts of consultations and investments. In doing so, we can see how the PRAI's view of gender equality reflects its focus on business improvement and economic efficiency instead of a more complex understanding of gender relations.

The PRAI use the language of empowerment while making the case for ensuring the protection of land rights for rural populations and vulnerable communities, though their recommendations suggest the priority lies with the facilitation of land sales. The recommendations of the PRAI and the synoptic note generally focus on how states can best facilitate commercial land transactions through demarcating local land rights, streamlining procedures, enhancing transparency, and restricting state involvement, suggesting that equitable participation among marginalized communities is at best a secondary consideration. For instance, the note accompanying Principle 1 – "Existing rights to land and associated natural resources are recognized and respected" (FAO et al. 2010, 2) – gives a nod to the importance of recognizing the myriad forms of land use or ownership rights: "statutory or customary, primary or secondary, formal or informal, group or individual." It acknowledges the importance of investigating "marginal" lands for actual local use and not undermining local livelihoods for the sake of investment (FAO et al. 2010, 2). The note also highlights the vulnerabilities created when the state owns all land and can transfer "unused" land for other uses.

Yet, within the context of the other Principles, the primary objective of establishing such rights is not just to enhance tenure security for marginalized populations – such as rural women – but to ease the process of transfer and exchange of land rights. Indeed, beginning from the premise that all investment is desirable, the stated purpose of Principle 1 is to establish land rights for the purposes of negotiation with investors. "Recognition of rights to land and associated natural resources, together with the power to negotiate their uses, can greatly *empower* local communities and such recognition should be viewed as a precondition for *direct negotiation* with investors" (FAO et al. 2010, 2, emphasis added). This stands in contrast to those who view land rights as an intrinsic good, a means to improve the welfare of smallholder farmers, or to remedy social inequalities, all of which are important benefits of land rights (Jacobs 2009). The "empowerment" associated with the recognition of local land rights in the context of the PRAI is thus desirable insofar as it is a precondition for negotiation with investors and facilitates direct investments unfettered by customary practices or the state. Again, "empowerment" here connotes the ability to participate in business transactions, a far cry from the terms originally employed by feminist activists and scholars. This definition of empowerment sidesteps the social obstacles to equal market participation and does not reckon with the social dynamics that establish and maintain appropriate gender roles.

Thus, although the PRAI synoptic note draws attention to traditionally excluded groups, including herders, women, and Indigenous groups, the measures that are proposed are unlikely to "empower" individuals and communities to bolster their social, political, and/or economic position relative to family or community members, local elites, government officials, or foreign investors beyond the land transaction itself. For instance, the PRAI nod to efforts to register and recognize customary forms of tenure, in particular "to make lesser (oral) forms of evidence admissible, to strengthen women's land rights, and to establish decentralized land institutions," but they note that implementation has been slow (FAO et al. 2010, 4). Indeed, the experiences explored in earlier chapters reflect this reality. But the proposed solution within the PRAI is to "demarcate the rights to community land in a participatory and low-cost way that can be implemented quickly" (FAO et al. 2010, 4). Examples that are provided from Mexico, Peru, and Ethiopia suggest mechanisms to grant rights to the community at large, with the community tasked with demarcating individual rights at a later time.

Such measures share similarities with those already established in several countries, such as Tanzania's Land Acts discussed in chapter 3, where Village Councils and Land Councils oversee the issuing of individual Certificates of Customary Rights of Occupancy (CCROs). But to suggest that such measures can be "low-cost" and "implemented quickly" does not reflect the realities of such implementation measures. The experiences of the World Bank–supported Business Environment Strengthening for Tanzania (BEST) program in Tanzania illustrate the challenges of attempting to issue large numbers of CCROs efficiently and with attention to gender equality. To assist with the implementation of the Land Acts, the World Bank supported the BEST Program, a continuation of the Strategic Plan for the Implementation of the Land Laws (SPILL) undertaken by the Ministry of Land and Human Settlement Development. SPILL had previously been criticized for "[idealizing] the democratic nature of village governance for the sake of cost-cutting and rapid implementation"' (Pallotti 2008, 231). The BEST program suffered similar criticisms, including its failure to prioritize gender-equality measures. Indeed, with gender as an afterthought in the process, implementers resisted an order to add more women to the registration effort. Pedersen and Haule (2013) report that the World Bank made gender-equality measures a focal point only after the program was already under way, earning the scorn of government officials (Pedersen and Haule 2013).

Thus, the authors of the PRAI advance an idea that appears to be common sense: demarcate land rights quickly and efficiently, so that everyone can enjoy the benefits of investment. Yet this oversimplifies the dynamics of local governance and overlooks gender-based inequalities that can hamper implementation. Given the obstacles to including rural women in the processes of land allocation, governance, and ownership explored in earlier chapters, a quick and low-cost way to administer land rights is simply not reflective of the realities on the ground. Even the World Bank notes that their costs in certain land registration schemes in sub-Saharan Africa are much higher than expected (Byamugisha 2013).

By expediting land governance reforms through a reliance on existing rules and practices, such reforms reinforce existing structures rather than challenging them, directly undermining "empowerment" as envisioned by scholars such as Kabeer (1994). Gender-equal participation in governance cannot be assumed to be a given, nor can gender-sensitive implementation of land rights and ownership schemes be an addendum to existing programs. Truly addressing these gender imbalances in land governance requires a deeper understanding of gender inequalities and discriminatory practices that are not resolved by a narrow understanding of "empowerment" as strictly economic. Here, adherence to efficiency as a key value is antithetical to feminist conceptions of empowerment. By relying on existing authorities, a *process of change* is not initiated. Moreover, as we will see in more detail below, the PRAI's reliance on markets as a site of empowerment – that landowners will be "empowered" to sell their land directly to buyers or investors without state interference – neglects the power imbalances that exist between land buyers and sellers. Again, these conceptions of empowerment do not engage with the gendered power structures in local forms of land governance or in transnational structures of agricultural trade and investment. As we have seen in previous chapters, the barriers to land ownership and access are not due to structural economic inequalities alone, but are also due to the social norms and expectations that keep rural women from being able to access and control land.

Food Security as Labour-Market Participation

In addition to the focus on demarcating land rights to improve efficiencies and facilitate equal entry into land markets, the PRAI also endorse the supposed benefits of women's greater participation within land and labour markets as a means of improving food security and household incomes. For instance, as part of the note on Principle 2 – "Investments do not jeopardize food security but rather strengthen it" – *the* PRAI synoptic note highlights a farming model used in both Mali and Tanzania that employed women, "thus providing them with cash to improve their livelihood" (FAO et al. 2010, 7). Consequently, the note recommends the development of projects that provide new cash flows and employment for local communities, especially for women and other economically vulnerable populations. Employment and income are illustrated as unproblematically meshing with the existing economy, reflecting a common view that employment income is in itself liberating for women – without a broader view of the sexual division of labour or the dependencies that structure household relations (Elson 1991b). Indeed, time spent on producing new cash flows often means that there is less time available for household tasks, subsistence farming, and other reproductive tasks that are needed to maintain and care for people.

This view of food security constructed within the PRAI fails to acknowledge the productive or reproductive economic roles that exist prior to the arrival of an agricultural investor and the social limitations that prevent women from being employed in high-value work. Research from Ghana points to trends in which women take on precarious plantation work as less-skilled labourers. They are often paid less and are underrepresented in permanent, office-based work (Tsikata and Yaro

2014). Moreover, social norms restricting speaking in public, or in front of men, makes women less likely to complain about working conditions or the heavy use of pesticides to which they are exposed.

The principles articulated within the PRAI endorse the use of markets to "empower" marginalized populations through employment or individual land rights. Yet the creation of agricultural employment alone does not typically address broader socio-economic factors that restrict the full and equal participation of marginalized groups within land and labour markets. Rural peasant women with few other income options may have to take on precarious and dangerous farm work. When paired with the ability to demarcate and transfer land through the individualization of land rights, economic pressures may lead women to sell plots of land used for subsistence, thus undermining food security.

The economic disruptions that are created by large-scale agricultural investments thus need to be viewed in light of the gendered expectations and social relationships that govern behaviour and restrict women's options. Scholars of feminist political economy and land rights have long noted how these dynamics operate across regional contexts (Elson 1991; Beneria 2007; Jacobs 2009). Where the World Bank and its partners fail to consider the broader context of gendered productive and reproductive relations within the PRAI, their efforts to create employment opportunities for rural women reveal a lack of involvement with scholarship that has long indicated inequalities in the functioning of land and labour markets. The expectation that labour-market participation can solve food insecurity without reference to the actual means of food production for small-scale and subsistence farmers ignores the gendered divisions of labour that exist in local contexts. The expansion of labour opportunities for paid work does not address existing gendered expectations about divisions of labour, including domestic work and subsistence agriculture.

"Constructing the Business Environment": Free Trade as Empowerment?

The PRAI also include several measures to improve the attractiveness of the business environment for foreign investors, though the relationship of such recommendations to the protection of vulnerable communities and their land is unclear. The recommendations accompanying

Principle 3 include responsibilities for investors and governments alike: processes to access land and resources need to be transparent and monitored, as does the investment process. Moreover, these processes need to take place within "a proper business, legal, and regulatory environment" (FAO et al. 2010, 8). The responsibility for ensuring such an environment clearly falls to the state, as the accompanying note advises the availability of information about vacant lands and the presence of an "independent system to monitor progress towards a better investment climate" (FAO et al. 2010, 8). This includes state incentives for domestic and foreign investment and the public disclosure of available land via digitized land registries. These general efforts are all viewed as positive steps to improving the ease and efficiency of doing business. Though the note on Principle 3 mentions that transparency can help communities hold investors and states accountable, and that strong business environments can improve the skills of labourers, there is little consideration of rural populations and their needs. Improving the business environment, in the parlance of the PRAI, is strictly geared toward attracting and retaining investment through streamlining land acquisitions and investment.

It is not self-evident that creating an *efficient* business environment and facilitating a transparent land management system are necessarily in the interests of rural smallholders of land, and rural women in particular. Steps taken to facilitate land transactions and improve the business environment in several African states have not prevented alleged land grabs from occurring. Though Mozambique boasts some of Africa's most progressive land laws, the state's welcoming of foreign investment has resulted in the violation or "bending" of state laws on eviction and compensation (Verma 2014). Several sub-Saharan African countries have likewise sought to attract foreign agricultural investment, revising investment rules, improving business climates, and providing tax incentives accordingly. The G8 New Alliance for Food Security and Nutrition is one such initiative under which ten African states committed to reforms to attract large-scale investment (Badiane et al. 2018).

No space is given in the recommendations of Principle 3 to considerations of gender or other inequalities in the facilitation of more efficient market exchanges and the attraction of foreign investment. Given past scholarship on the impact of neo-liberalization on agricultural economies, and on women in particular, scholars and activists express hesitation about trade incentives for foreign investors (Mbilinyi 1988; Baha 2011; Mbilinyi 2012). Rural women often shouldered the productive and reproductive burdens created by the withdrawal of state supports for agricultural inputs in the 1980s and 1990s. While the PRAI focus on state incentives for investors, there is no comparable recommendation to provide supports for local smaller-scale producers that might alleviate the burdens shouldered by households. Indeed, the expansion of agricultural production for export alone is unlikely to have a net positive effect on women insofar as a focus on export-led growth is unlikely to challenge broader structural problems of gender inequality (Roberts 2014). Thus, although there is attention to gender inequality siloed elsewhere within the PRAI, gender inequality within the context of further liberalized agricultural markets goes unacknowledged.

Moreover, within an expanded commercial land market, smallholders stand to be further marginalized. De Schutter (2011) notes that, although the PRAI are predicated on a notion of co-existence between large- and small-scale farmers in land markets, this model is inherently unstable. "[I]n the real world, land sales do not favor those who need land the most, nor do they lead to land being allocated to those who can use it most efficiently: instead, they favor those who have access to capital and whose ability to purchase the land is greatest" (De Schutter 2011, 270). As illustrated in the previous chapter and in much research on the role of women in such development contexts, rural women are the most unlikely to have access to such capital (Elson 1991a). Jacobs (2009) concurs, noting how women lose out in marketized land systems, as they tend to be poorer and unable to command and pay for labour.

Thus, though states may fulfill or aspire to fulfill many of the desired pro-business mechanisms articulated by the World Bank and its partners through the PRAI, current priorities undermine the abilities of smallholder farmers and the general public to access information or incentives. As earlier chapters have suggested, lack of knowledge, training, and implementation has proven to be a stumbling block for land governance more generally. Lack of awareness about the land available, the processes by which land is acquired by foreign investors, and the ways in which land is transferred to foreign investors has resulted in vulnerabilities for rural populations, particularly rural women, pastoralists, and youth, who are excluded from decision-making. As the discussion below regarding social impacts reveals, this lack of knowledge about how land is governed becomes clear once consultations begin.

The Social Impacts of Negotiations and Investments vs Efficiency Imperatives

Despite the negative attention the PRAI have received, they do not completely ignore social inequalities. However, the attention to inequalities appears insufficient and out of place when considered alongside the efficiency imperative and the realities of land governance. Admirably, Principle 4 – "All those materially affected are consulted, and agreements from consultations are recorded and enforced" (FAO et al. 2010, 10) – and Principle 6 – "Investments generate desirable social and distributional impacts and do not increase vulnerability" (FAO et al. 2010, 16) – both provide some general guidelines for conducting transparent and inclusive consultations for land deals. The recommendations advise syncing development plans with local land use planning, leading "meaningful" consultations and negotiations, monitoring and enforcement of the deals, and fair compensation to all groups, including "secondary" rights holders, such as women (FAO et al. 2010, 17).

Predictably, responsibility for protecting "vulnerable groups" falls to the state: "Since vulnerable groups and the poor generally lack information, voice and influence, they should be protected by government" (FAO et al. 2010, 11). If these vulnerable groups will be affected by a proposed project, "adequate mechanisms for inclusion of these groups as well as women in decision-making should be adopted" (FAO et al. 2010, 11), though it is unclear who should be responsible for ensuring such equality in decision-making. As a principle, this addresses important considerations about who is responsible for protecting vulnerable people who might be affected by a deal. However, given the interest that many host states have in attracting such deals, the legacies of colonization that recognize only some kinds of land rights, and the concentration of power over land governance in state governments, there are potentially many competing pressures on states. Legitimate questions thus might be raised about the likelihood of states having the capacity or political will to protect the most vulnerable in this context. Indeed, as we have seen in the Tanzanian case, both resources and capacity are often lacking, and some of the most vulnerable groups have already experienced displacement, even under a land governance structure that devolves land governance to local communities.

However, if the recommendations of Principle 4 are implemented with the speed and efficiency suggested above by Principle 1, they are unlikely to address matters of inequality in consultation processes. Participatory methods of consultation that fail to recognize social norms and relations or existing local hierarchies are unlikely to capture the far-reaching material impacts of a land deal. Moreover, as I have noted, rural women in many parts of the world tend not to be able to attend public meetings, either because of conflicting productive and reproductive duties that need to be taken care of at the same time, or because of public stigma about attending and participating in public meetings. Societal expectations tend to keep women outside of these realms of decision-making, especially if local officials are not familiar with – or disagree with – the legal requirements for gender quotas in certain forums. Even in those instances where women are elected to such forums, there are still questions about the extent to which women participate in decision-making. As with many men representatives, women representatives in most local administrations lack training on the functioning of the committee, and questions abound about whether they are meaningful contributors to the decision-making process (Yngstrom 2002). As discussed in chapter 3, reliance on customary practices as an efficient means to undertake land reform can retrench patriarchal practices.

In addition, where land deal consultations do occur with the broader community, evidence suggests that investors also fail to consult with women. Whether this is because of the nature of who holds land rights, gendered power relations in the villages, or a broader failure to appreciate gender dynamics on the part of the investors will depend on local dynamics and specifics, but as Behrman, Meinzen-Dick, and Quisumbing (2012) argue, all these elements can shape the consultation processes. The lack of awareness of differing gender roles, responsibilities, and relations leads to consultations that ultimately do not capture the needs of all community members. Investors tend to speak only with men, not involving women in their decision-making, which can result in women losing access to basic household necessities or materials for income-generating activities. Patriarchal norms regarding the appropriate roles of women in public forums and in local decision-making bodies can thus limit the scope of discussion. But the exclusion of women from these decisions can result in the exclusion of critical viewpoints and a full assessment of how communities rely on land and resources. Without deeper considerations of how women use land, the community may find itself without access to important water, food, and fuel sources. Such scarcity risks driving up the costs of household goods, thus increasing pressures on women to provide for their families and communities (ActionAid 2010). Understanding the possible repercussions of a land deal requires meaningful consultations with marginalized groups, including rural women who may not own land but who use it to support themselves, their families, and their communities, and have specific gendered socio-cultural connections to the land (Chung 2017).

Efforts to move quickly to implement land rights and expedite agricultural investment also involve attempts to resolve conflicts quickly and efficiently. But like local consultations, the solutions put forth in the PRAI suggest embracing existing modes of conflict resolution, without paying attention to the power dynamics at work. Principle 4 simultaneously calls for state monitoring and enforcement of land deals, as well as the establishment of alternative dispute mechanisms. Leaving aside the possibility that states might be reluctant to interfere with highly coveted foreign investments, as well as the presumption that recipient states have the technical capacity to monitor and enforce the terms of such deals, the PRAI note suggests that the high cost of resolving disputes through judiciaries increases the need to use "accessible and legitimate fora to resolve conflicts before they escalate" (FAO et al. 2010, 12). The note proceeds to suggest the "establishment of alternative dispute resolution mechanisms that offer recognition of solutions arrived at by local informal bodies provided they follow principles of accountability, equity, and due diligence" (FAO et al. 2010, 12–13).

The suggestion that investors should favour local informal bodies over judicial institutions again raises questions about the extent to which the authors of the PRAI value efficiency and speed over protecting vulnerable and marginalized groups. Although local informal bodies may well be capable of achieving fair outcomes, the existing evidence suggests that relying on local bodies could further exclude certain marginalized groups, as in the cases of widowed and separated women in rural Tanzania who pursue legal remedies beyond their local communities (Koda 2000; Dancer 2015). This is not to suggest that formal judicial institutions are ideal either. Costs and distances can be prohibitive for people in rural communities and, where courts are directed to govern according to local custom, this may not overcome gendered barriers to justice (Dancer 2015). Regardless, this recommendation needs to be considered within the context of how local land governance is shaped by gendered social relations. Moreover, such suggestions need to be considered alongside the colonial attitudes that romanticize local informal modes of governance as inherently fair (Khadiagala 2001). The presumption that alternative dispute resolutions are inherently fair is a risky one for people who are not already protected by local practices.

Thus, in spite of governance mechanisms to ensure that consultations and democratic decision-making occur at the village level, we can see how shortcomings in implementation can undercut these processes if attention to gendered power relations has not been a priority. Expectations that the state will protect vulnerable groups, especially those without available public resources to support the necessary training for field workers and front-line implementers, need to be matched with both resources and attention to the marginalized position of such groups. Moreover, the discrimination in existing state practices needs to be studied and comprehensively addressed. Without close scrutiny of how community governance overlays political governance, little progress can be expected to occur. Consultations that focus on speed and efficiency rather than on understanding local power dynamics will be more likely to exclude vulnerable populations and entrench the position of elites.

In advocating for the rapid securing of land rights for the purpose of conducting more efficient negotiations, the PRAI thus underestimate the resilience of local norms that govern gender roles and the capacity of local authorities to adapt to formal legal change, all of which are dynamics that can and do restrict the full participation of marginalized groups. Moreover, the PRAI leave themselves exposed to similar criticisms faced by advocates for formal land rights: the facilitation of land transactions alone is typically incapable of addressing broader socio-economic factors that will continue to restrict the participation of marginalized groups, especially rural women who lack access to capital inputs and may be restricted by patriarchal social norms. Indeed, as we have seen in previous chapters, there is resistance to women registering land or participating in decision-making, among both men and women. In some cases, this resistance manifests as public and private threats of violence. Thus, despite enshrining principles of equality and protection for local populations, the content of the PRAI does not reflect an understanding of the ways in which social exclusion is manifested in forums of local governance. The efficiency-driven focus of the PRAI leaves little room for meaningful reflection on how foreign investments truly affect local populations. Marginalized groups are mentioned only sporadically, typically with reference to ensuring consultations are fair, but without attention to how the broader dynamics will shape specific experiences and the subsequent outcomes. In this way, the PRAI display limited attention to gender inequalities in land governance and land market participation, and instead favour policies designed to improve the markets for agricultural investments rather than the terms and conditions of investment for rural populations.

The CFS Rai Principles

Following its recent reform and several subsequent successful and widely celebrated negotiations (see chapter 5), the CFS moved to create a new set of principles that would focus primarily on questions of agricultural investment and would serve as an alternative to the PRAI. The CFS's passage of the Voluntary Guidelines on the Responsible Governance of Tenure of Land, Fisheries and Forests in the Context of National Food Security (VGGT) in 2012 addressed many questions of land rights and governance on which the new set of responsible agricultural investment principles would be built. As explained in greater detail in the next chapter, scholars and activists praised the CFS's inclusion of civil society groups in developing the VGGT, as well as its passing of a set of guidelines that aligned with the principle of Free, Prior, and Informed Consent (FPIC) and mainstreamed gender-equality provisions as well (McKeon 2015). Indeed, following on the heels of the successful

Table 4.2 **FAO-CFS Principles for responsible investment in agriculture and food systems**

1. Contribute to food security and nutrition.
2. Contribute to sustainable and inclusive economic development and the eradication of poverty.
3. Foster gender equality and women's empowerment.
4. Engage and empower youth.
5. Respect tenure of land, fisheries, and forests, and access to water.
6. Conserve and sustainably manage natural resources, increase resilience, and reduce disaster risks.
7. Respect cultural heritage and traditional knowledge, and support diversity and innovation.
8. Promote safe and healthy agriculture and food systems.
9. Incorporate inclusive and transparent governance structures, processes, and grievance mechanisms.
10. Assess and address impacts and promote accountability.

Source: CFS 2014.

negotiations of the VGGT, the CFS was well-positioned to begin a new set of consultations with member states, civil society groups, corporations, and observers. Beginning in 2012, the CFS began a series of consultations that would culminate in the passage of the Rai Principles in October 2014. The CFS invited states, corporations, and civil society groups to provide input and feedback.

Yet, in contrast to the celebratory tone that followed the passage of the VGGT, several civil society groups criticized the final version of the Rai Principles. Despite the involvement of civil society groups in the CFS negotiations of the Rai Principles, the independent Civil Society Mechanism (CSM) and several high-profile civil society organizations registered their disapproval with the final set of principles passed by the CFS. Pesticide Action Network Asia Pacific (PAN AP) described the Rai Principles as a "confused" document because of the CFS's simultaneous endorsement of human rights languages while reaffirming the centrality of binding trade regulations. "At worst," according to PAN AP consultant Gilbert Sape, "the Rai Principles is designed to contradict itself in order to legitimize the flawed policies on agricultural investments that are biased against small food producers and favorable to large corporate investors" (Pesticide Action Network Asia Pacific 2014). Similar arguments were made by Oxfam, noting that, in addition to the contradictions between protecting rights and promoting trade rules, the Rai Principles overall were vague and permit stakeholders to pick and choose the provisions they prefer to pursue (Oxfam 2014).

Interestingly, civil society groups were divided on the topic of gender equality in the Rai Principles. The CSM noted that it was "pleased" that the Rai Principles recognized the importance of overcoming discrimination against women, though notes elsewhere that the commitment to trade liberalization often affects women most negatively (Sánchez 2014). Oxfam, despite its broader commitments to gender and food security, offered no commentary regarding gender and the Rai Principles in its initial press release (Oxfam 2014). La Via Campesina (2014) noted that no real progress on discrimination against women was made by the Rai Principles. Perhaps most forcefully, PAN AP noted that the broader failure of the CFS to distinguish between smallholder farmers and small-scale producers could have a particularly negative impact on landless farmers, including women: "Women tend to be more marginalised in terms of access to land and other productive resources. The exclusion of the landless in the rai Principles [*sic*] thus has deep implications for rural women" (Pesticide Action Network Asia Pacific 2014, quoting Rengam). Despite these critiques, however, the focus of civil society groups has been on discrimination against women rather than the broader gender hierarchies at work in land and labour markets, as well as in global trade liberalization more broadly.

Below, this section highlights the ways in which the final negotiated text of the Rai Principles perpetuates much of the same gender and economic empowerment language used by the PRAI, focusing on two major recommendations of the Rai Principles: "Foster Gender Equality and Women's Empowerment," and "Contribute to Sustainable and Inclusive Economic Development and the Eradication of Poverty." Though the CFS sought to address the question of agricultural investment in a manner distinct from the PRAI, the Rai Principles nonetheless bear a striking similarity to its predecessor on the matter of gender. The Rai Principles similarly silo gender-equality measures from other social inequalities and view market participation as a key marker of empowerment. At the same time, gender relations between men and women are repeatedly reduced to matters of the family or household, foreclosing on broader structural issues at work. As we have seen in earlier chapters, gender issues in land and agriculture are not easily separated from other areas of concern, and the languages employed within the Rai Principles are telling of a narrow view of gender equality and empowerment.

"Foster Gender Equality and Women's Empowerment"

Though the Rai Principles do not establish a set of principles of implementation that might lay out adherence to gender-equality measures or explicitly prohibit forms of discrimination, the CFS did dedicate Principle 3 to "[f]oster gender equality and women's empowerment" (see table 4.3). In contrast to the PRAI, this set of principles does include a more detailed approach to the question of gender and agricultural investment. Here, the stakeholders in responsible agricultural investment are asked to eliminate discriminatory practices, and also make efforts to improve women's access to resources to remedy the gender imbalances that might exist in decision-making, though explicit appeals about gender and political participation are not addressed. Given the broader obstacles to discussing women's rights within the CFS (Collins 2022), it is perhaps not a surprise that a negotiated text like the Rai Principles does not engage more deeply on the question of women's political rights.

The general effect of including a token gender-equality measure is that gender equality becomes siloed from other considerations of social inequality and associated primarily with "women's empowerment" as defined in this single principle. The limits of this siloed approach are evident when we consider the obstacles to land security detailed in previous chapters. Aside from this one dedicated section on gender equality, there is little additional mention of gender inequality elsewhere in the Rai Principles. "Women" are mentioned only as "family farmers" elsewhere in the Rai Principles, and though there are several mentions of "smallholders," women are not explicitly mentioned as part of this category of farmer. As suggested by the critiques above, the focus on smallholders does not recognize women that use but do not own or hold land themselves. Indeed, as addressed further below, the Rai Principles include far more discussion of the need to respect traditional knowledges and practices, with no reference to gendered divisions of labour or patriarchal norms and practices within communities.

Table 4.3 FAO-CFS Rai Principle 3 – Gender equality and women's empowerment

i.	Ensuring that all women are treated fairly, recognizing their respective situations, needs, constraints, and the vital role played by women.
ii.	Eliminating all measures and practices that discriminate or violate rights on the basis of gender.
iii.	Advancing women's equal tenure rights, and their equal access to and control over productive land, natural resources, inputs, productive tools; and promoting access to extension, advisory, and financial services, education, training, markets, and information.
iv.	Adopting innovative and/or proactive approaches, measures, and processes to enhance women's meaningful participation in partnerships, decision-making, leadership roles, and the equitable sharing of benefits.

Source: CFS 2014, 13.

Importantly, the four components of responsible investment articulated in Principle 3 all echo the tenets of transnational business feminism highlighted above. Of course, eliminating discriminatory practices and recognizing the needs and constraints imposed by gender roles are critical first steps, but this set of principles does not engage with structures of gender inequality beyond that which occurs within the marketplace. Indeed, many states experiencing large-scale land deals have already passed land reforms and constitutional amendments promoting gender equality in land ownership and political participation; the challenges lie in implementation and addressing cultural biases and customary practice (Daley and Englert 2010). Moreover, the "vital role played by women" is not specified. Though recognizing women's roles in agriculture is an important step, the language here is limited to including women in the agricultural economy and outlining efforts to unleash their economic potential. This focus again overlooks the broader challenges of eliminating discriminatory practices and advancing women's social and political rights, in addition to their economic rights.

These ideas are most evident in two subclauses, which offer the most specific steps to address gender equality in all of the Rai Principles. The first is clearly dedicated to remedying gender inequalities in land markets and agricultural production. It states that women need equal "access to productive land" as well as a range of services provided by financial institutions and agricultural firms, including extension services and training. Here we see a reinforcement of the idea that the primary obstacle to gender inequality is an imbalance in access to resource inputs, and thus greater productivity. Though the Rai Principles advise improving access to such resources, however, there is no broader recognition of the social dynamics that work in tandem with these economic inequalities. If we look more closely at the dynamics of rural gendered divisions of labour, resource control, and gender roles, we can see how expectations about women's productive and reproductive duties come into play, as do societal expectations about the appropriateness of women entering the agricultural labour markets as equals with men.

The second clause addresses the question of participation in "partnerships, decision-making, leadership roles, and the equitable sharing of benefits" (CFS 2014, 13). Interestingly, this does not include explicit references to political involvement or community-specific forms of deliberation, though it does include decision-making. As already highlighted above and in the previous chapters, the participation of rural women in public forums is contingent upon several factors, which vary from one cultural and political context to another. For instance, depending on the local context, even though women may be present at a meeting, they may be less willing to participate due to lower levels of literacy, less experience with public speaking, lack of supportive community members, or even threats from their male relatives or the broader community. Moreover, decision-making over land remains a contentious area for legal reform. Tensions between pushes for individual rights versus existing community practices create broader political and legal challenges (Alden Wily 2014). As the following chapter will explore in detail, even more sensitive efforts to address the challenges of gender and participation in land governance continue to fall short insofar as they do not recognize the broader social dynamics that restrict equal participation by women.

As such, the Rai Principles negotiated within the CFS have limited engagement with the ways in which gender structures land governance and its relevance for agricultural investment. While aligned with principles of inclusion, these recommendations alone do not grapple with the complexity of gender, land, and governance. More importantly, when viewed alongside the remaining recommendations, the isolation of gender equality and "empowerment" from other themes of economic development, conservation, and traditional practices highlights the need for global policy-makers to engage with the realities of gender relations.

"Contribute to Sustainable and Inclusive Economic Development and the Eradication of Poverty"

Given the emphasis on gender and empowerment, it is worth considering where else these concepts are invoked in the Rai Principles. Economic development is the focus of the second Rai Principle, describing responsible agricultural investment as respecting and supporting international labour standards, creating jobs, developing public infrastructure, fostering market opportunities, and implementing policies aimed at "empowering and improving human resource capacity" (CFS 2014, 12). Indeed, the Rai Principles are undoubtedly optimistic about the role of agricultural investment in economic development and the potential for *empowering* farmers. Yet by siloing gender concerns into its own category, the CFS precludes a deeper consideration of gender and labour issues.

Though these recommendations are not accompanied by more specific recognition of social inequalities and their role in uneven rural development, they nonetheless claim to address the problems faced by agricultural labourers and rural populations. However, there remain silences in these recommendations, not the least of which is the vulnerability created when people transition from subsistence or small-scale agriculture into the agricultural labour market, and the precariousness of labour on agricultural plantations. As seen repeatedly in large-scale agricultural projects, agricultural projects often arrive in rural areas with great promises of job creation. Yet many projects hire unskilled labour in the short-term or not at all, and import "more reliable" migrant labourers and/or skilled labour for longer-term managerial positions. As Li (2011) notes, such practices have been common in colonial and post-colonial Southeast Asia, where large-scale projects in rural areas displace locals and favour migrant labour. Yet there are gendered dimensions to this story as well. Large-scale agricultural projects also disproportionately hire local women into short-term, unskilled labour with little room for advancement. Barrientos (1997) has highlighted the invisible gendered labour in the Chilean fruit-export sector, where women working on a temporary basis have been essential to the success of the sector. Tsikata and Yaro (2013) have recently shown that, even under "ideal-type" agricultural investment schemes in Ghana, women tend to be underrepresented in stable, high-paid positions. In Tanzania, though local media still report that many rural populations welcome job creation through agricultural investment (Songa 2015), local activists and legal advocates note that the jobs created are often temporary, do not translate into the transfer of knowledge, and often funnel women into low-paid and precarious work (interview with INGO coordinator, Dar es Salaam, 9 July 2013). Thus, looking at labour without a consideration of gender-based differences and treatment of women does not address systemic problems of gender discrimination and inequality that manifest in labour markets.

Protecting workers and enforcing labour standards place high on the list of responsibilities listed under Principle 2, and include several considerations, such as ending child labour. The Rai Principles do also note the need to "empower" farmers through the implementation of new policies "particularly for smallholders, including those that are family farmers – women and men" (CFS 2014, 12). As noted by PAN AP, the preference for the term "smallholder" rather than small food producers further excludes considerations of gender in promoting access and inputs. By considering only the legal owners of land – of which women remain a very small percentage worldwide – the recommendations of the Rai Principles overlook the complex realities of gender relations, land access, and small-scale farming. As seen in the previous chapters, although rural women in many parts of the world are often able to secure land access through their relations with men, they are often not formal landowners. As articulated here, "empowerment" depends on the individualization of land rights and improved productivity. Yet individual notions of empowerment can be limiting when trying to address gender inequalities in rural areas, especially where connections to community and family members are essential. Indeed, the original feminist concept of empowerment is a structural one that considers an individual's capacity to make choices in each context. This requires considering the community within which someone lives.

The appeal to "family farmers – women and men" stands out under the recommendations of Principle 2. Not only is it the only mention of gender differentiation in this subset of recommendations, but it raises several questions about what the CFS means by "family farmers" and the set of relations to which it refers. Again, the term empowering is used, recommending that policies be developed to build human resource capacity among these smallholder and family famers. Though "empowerment" remains undefined, appeals to developing "human resource capacity" and "promoting their access to resources and inputs" strongly suggest a conception of empowerment closely tied to the ability to participate in markets as a producer or labourer. Thus, these recommendations connote a narrow idea of economic empowerment and offer little recognition of the constraints imposed by either economic liberalization or family discipline.

Indeed, feminist critics have pilloried arguments that favour the use of family farm labour over contract labour as being more efficient. The World Bank's 2003 Policy Research Report advanced the argument that family farms are more cost-efficient producers of goods than farms that hired external local labour (Deininger 2003). The reasoning was that family farmers are more invested in their own success as a household, and thus are more likely to be effective and productive farmers. Yet, as articulated by Manji (2003), such a conception of family farming has to ignore the gender- and age-related hierarchies that often compel family members into family farm labour. Moreover, such farms will always be more cost efficient insofar as they rarely pay family members, including women and children, for their labour. Indeed, under neo-liberal models that have reduced state supports to farms, there is greater incentive to return to exploitative practices that do not compensate family farm workers.

Interestingly, by evoking the language of the family farm here, the CFS raises more questions about how to promote "empowerment" in any meaningful way. Without describing the "family farm" in more specific terms – including whether such family farming is for subsistence or enterprise – and only briefly nodding to the reality of different gender identities within the family, the CFS has clearly sought to avoid any complex understandings of gender relations in these recommendations. Families are sites of complex and uneven gender relations, intersected by the interests and biases of the broader socio-cultural communities within which they are situated. This is no less true in terms of land and agricultural politics, where family practices structure gender roles and responsibilities and often dictate the rules of inheritance and ownership. The liberalization of land reform and agricultural trade has resulted in a tremendous shift of labour onto households, and rural women in particular (Razavi 2003).

Indeed, despite the lack of attention to gender relations in the Rai Principles, gender relations are key to shaping productive and reproductive roles and are influenced by cultural heritage and traditional practices. Other sections in the Rai Principles addressing traditional knowledge, conservation, and inclusive governance do not address gender inequality in customary practices, productive and reproductive roles, or political participation. As we will see in the next chapter, the failure to consider gender in these areas may lead to the further marginalization of women within agricultural investments and land reforms. Without closer attention to the role of gender relations in agriculture and land governance, these principles risk perpetuating patriarchal practices that have already created deep societal divisions and inequalities.

Conclusion

Both the PRAI and the Rai Principles illustrate how the language of empowerment has been appropriated and transformed to mean economic participation rather than the disruption of social relations. Any close examination of the gender dynamics of agricultural economies reveals the ways in which gender shapes productive relationships and the power dynamics therein (for example, Razavi 2003). Moreover, scholarship has repeatedly shown the ways in which incursions by agricultural investors and developers not only build upon existing power relationships, but can also inadvertently introduce new power asymmetries (Behrman, Meinzen-Dick, and Quisumbing 2012; Tsikata and Yaro 2013).

There are notable differences between the two sets of principles. The PRAI, having been developed by officials with the World Bank, IFAD, UNCTAD, and the FAO, has less standing with the international community. The CFS Rai Principles have their origins in a collaborative consultative process held with civil society groups, a claim the drafters of the PRAI cannot make. Both sets of principles note gender inequality as something to be considered, though only the Rai Principles include provisions referring to gender and age differences, environmental impacts, and conservation, though its word choices have created concerns. The Rai Principles also include important notes on inclusive governance that the PRAI do not and, appropriately, build upon the governance principles articulated by the VGGT, which will be discussed in more detail in the next chapter. Finally, both sets of principles refer to the need for improved governance, with the PRAI calling for devolution to existing customary practices in order to do so quickly and "efficiently." As highlighted above, such cost savings come at the expense of addressing entrenched gender inequalities that are pervasive within patriarchal customary practices of inheritance and land ownership.

By reproducing a neo-liberal conception of empowerment that is synonymous with economic participation, both sets of principles overlook the broader obstacles to gender inequality in land tenure and agriculture. As detailed in chapters 2 and 3, the challenges to gender equality are not just economic in nature but are tied to social norms and gendered divisions of labour. Moreover, in favouring efficiency narratives and market participation, they fail to foster community-based ideas of empowerment and social change that might assist in remedying gender imbalances in agriculture and land governance. As feminist scholars such as Chandra Mohanty (1988; 2003) have long argued, Western feminists and development practitioners have tended to view "Third World Women" as undifferentiated and disempowered subjects. Within the context of responsible agricultural investment guidelines, these views of women as disempowered economic agents lead to policy recommendations that do not engage with the complex context of gendered relations in land and agriculture. Without a more comprehensive understanding of gender relations and empowerment, such recommendations are unlikely to unsettle the status quo.

However, there is genuine potential for change when we consider the various socio-political contexts – including gendered hierarchies of power – within which people live. By looking at tensions between existing customary practices and gender equality as opportunities for change, and not as chasms between "tradition" and "modernity," it is possible to see ways in which policy reforms might be able to support grassroots social change. If policy-makers move away from a reliance on market-based goal setting and toward attention to the promotion and protection of both community and individual rights, there is room to consider more revolutionary social change. As suggested by a number of scholars, more thoughtful attention to the flexibility and negotiability of local practices can lead to the promotion of gender equality in land rights and local governance more generally (Daley and Englert 2010; Peters 2010; Mbilinyi 2009).

The next chapter addresses these challenges in greater detail. The CFS's VGGT integrated considerations of customary practices and Indigenous rights as well as references to gender equality throughout its recommendations. In this way, the VGGT stand in contrast to the PRAI and the Rai Principles for their attention to how governance is informed by traditional practices and gender inequality. Though the VGGT do demonstrate some important contradictions, they nonetheless appear to embody a commitment by the CFS to address inequality in land and food security at the global level. Yet by attempting to promote these two goals of gender equality and the protection of customary practices and Indigenous rights independent of each other, the drafters of the VGGT overlook other issues in gender and land governance.

5 CONTESTED CONCEPTS: GENDER IN THE UNITED NATIONS COMMITTEE FOR WORLD FOOD SECURITY

Establishing principles for good land governance at the global level is a challenge. Given the diversity of land governance practices around the world, as explored in earlier chapters, a solution that creates common principles that respond to key concerns in a suitably complex manner has been elusive. The most significant achievement to date, from both the perspective of food-security governance and land tenure governance, has been the reform of the United Nations Committee on World Food Security (CFS) and its subsequent establishment of the Voluntary Guidelines on the Responsible Governance of Tenure of Land, Fisheries and Forests in the Context of National Food Security (VGGT). The CFS was reformed in 2009, amidst concerns about the fragmentation of food-security governance. The goal was to develop a central forum for global policy-making on food-security issues. As a result of open discussions with stakeholders, the reforms adopted in 2009 established the CFS as the foremost forum for food security, with a clear role for both civil society and private sector participation.

For these reasons, the CFS is a fascinating and contested site of global governance. The active and ongoing participation of non-state delegations institutionalizes the role of civil society and private sector actors in shaping global policy. Both the private sector and the civil society mechanisms comprise a diverse array of members. The Private Sector Mechanism (PSM) includes both multinational corporations and farmer's organizations, whose operations range in size. The Civil Society Mechanism (CSM), renamed the Civil Society and Indigenous Peoples' Mechanism (CSIPM) in 2019, includes representation from eleven different constituency groups, such as Indigenous peoples, non-governmental organizations, youth, women, fisherfolk, and smallholder farmers. There is thus a diversity of perspectives that could be represented at the CFS, though additional considerations need to be made about who is able to participate, which of many concerns become priorities for each constituency group, and the method by which competing viewpoints are reconciled.

It is within this context that is worthwhile to consider the CFS as a space that provides key opportunities for civil society actors to challenge the status quo of land and food governance and establish new standards for responsible governance. As Prügl (2014) advises, it is particularly critical for gender-equality advocates to consider spaces within existing – often neo-liberal – institutions and to establish counter-narratives in policy development. In this chapter, I illustrate how the CFS has afforded such opportunities since its reform. The CFS has established space for civil society movements to raise issues related to gender and land governance, as well as food sovereignty and justice issues more broadly. Though member states retained central decision-making responsibility, the initial creation of both a Civil Society Mechanism (CSM) and a Private Sector Mechanism (PSM) enabled these two constituencies to participate within the policy-development processes of the CFS. This means that, instead of simply being observers, civil society and private sector organizations – as well as UN agencies, the WTO, and agricultural research institutes – all participate in the development of policy, up until the point of adoption (McKeon 2015). At that point, only states make the final decisions at the annual plenary, which is usually held in Rome each October.

A shorter version of this story might accept the CFS as a key site for progressive land governance and its advocates. As we will see below, the CFS successfully mainstreamed gender into the VGGT and encouraged policy-makers and local communities to do the same. This means that the negotiators of the text took efforts to incorporate gender considerations throughout the document, rather than siloing gender concerns in one section or overlooking gender inequality and gender-based issues altogether. The VGGT likewise contextualize land governance within social, political, and economic relations and recognize the potential for power imbalances.

However, there nonetheless remain deficits in conceptualizing tensions between traditional and/or customary governance and the strengthening of women's land tenure security, and considering how state governments might navigate these tensions. Given how the governance of communities and the governance of polities intersect to increase vulnerabilities for certain groups, as explored in previous chapters, to what extent do the VGGT address these tensions in governance? Gender is relevant at multiple levels of land governance: in national reforms and implementation, in local land administration, whether customary or statutory, and within families and communities. Understanding the ways in which both formal political rules and gendered assumptions and norms in community modes of governance shape land governance are thus critical for global policy-making. Moreover, given the challenges of implementation that we have seen in previous chapters, what are the practical limits to implementing these reforms in other resource-strapped states, including those that lack political stability and/or state-led reforms that strengthen women's political representation at multiple levels?

Thus, key challenges remain. The VGGT itself, though comprehensive, address gender and other forms of inequality broadly, and in a technical, uniform way. At the same time, the VGGT likewise advise the protection of customary and informal modes of tenure, and the protection of Indigenous rights. This is likewise a laudable goal, but one that is also fraught with complex politics. As we have seen in earlier chapters, gender and land issues are political and deeply entrenched in social, cultural, and political histories. Indeed, pursuing both the promotion of gender equality and protection of customary tenure has historically been an uneven process, as experiences across Sub-Saharan Africa (see chapters 2 and 3) and around the world (e.g., Agarwal 1994; Deere and Léon 2001a) have demonstrated.

Thus, pursuing both goals – protecting customary practice and promoting gender equality – under the VGGT, CFS members have established a worthwhile yet politically fraught task: promoting the adoption of *voluntary* land governance guidelines that simultaneously protect the rights of women, Indigenous peoples, and other informal and customary users of land. The usefulness of a technical approach to gender and governance – that is, one that simply tries to add women to existing structures – is somewhat limited once we consider the possible tensions between these goals of the VGGT. As we will see, reconciling such tensions is not impossible, but requires a less technocratic approach to understanding governance processes and instead grapples with community norms and governance. Without dedicated institutional support, funding, and national government commitments, combined with an understanding of the complexity of the social dimensions of land governance, successful land reform outcomes become improbable.

Below, I elaborate further on the development of the VGGT and why they have been viewed as the CFS's landmark achievement to date. From there, I assess the VGGT using content analysis, specifically considering how the VGGT address gender inequality as well as customary tenure and Indigenous rights, illustrating the technical approach to these two deeply political questions in this negotiated text. This analysis builds on the lessons from the previous chapters that consider the ways in which land governance is shaped by gender relations and examines the VGGT for how it conceptualizes gender in this context. Finally, I delve into the broader implications of VGGT implementation – namely, that despite the important achievement of the VGGT themselves and the commitments made by the FAO to implement them, the realities of global environmental governance means that the burden of responsibility may fall heavily on civil society (Duncan 2015). To date, these actors have done a laudable job. However, the fluid nature of global economic influences, competing state priorities, and the ongoing realities of land acquisition mean that these successes could be short-lived without the ongoing activism and oversight provided by civil society organizations.

The Development of the VGGT

The expressed intent of the formation of the VGGT was "to assist countries wishing to develop a formal policy response to problems of weak land governance and corruption" (McKeon 2013, quoting April 2008 Invitation). Although the VGGT emerged in the aftermath of the 2007–08 food crises and the ensuing concerns about global land deals, the development of the VGGT had its origins in the final declaration of the

International Conference on Agrarian Reform and Rural Development (ICARRD), adopted by ninety-two countries in 2006 (Seufert 2013). The ICARRD declaration noted the importance of "secure and sustainable access to land, water, and other natural resources and of agrarian reform for hunger and poverty eradication" (Seufert 2013, 282). Building from these statements, the initiative to develop the guidelines was launched in 2009, led by the newly reformed CFS.[1]

The development of the VGGT involved a series of regional and topical consultations, in addition to state-to-state negotiations within the CFS itself, and the participation of academics, private sector representatives, and civil society organizations (CSOs), including some of the most marginalized groups affected by land tenure insecurity (McKeon 2013). Promoted by civil society organizations, the process to establish the VGGT took over three years, involved local consultations in several regions around the world, and received input online as well (Seufert 2013). Though a number of states were at one time hesitant to participate, major players in global agricultural trade – including Brazil, China, and a contingent of African states led by Zimbabwe – were active in the process, with the United States acting as chair (Seufert 2013). A zero draft of the Guidelines was made publicly available in April 2011 for Web-based consultation with the general public. Following a first draft based on these inputs and several rounds of consultations in early 2012, the VGGT were endorsed by the CFS in May 2012.

The establishment of the VGGT was a notable first success story for the reformed CFS. The VGGT earned considerable praise from international observers, both for the content as well as the inclusive decision-making process. Scholars have characterized the process of establishing the VGGT as best practice for the development of global guidelines (Duncan 2015). Importantly, the VGGT passed in 2012 included considerations of gender equality and Indigenous rights within the context of land tenure. The final document is comprehensive, providing a broad scope on issues related to land rights and governance, and includes provisions for advancing gender equality as well as protecting customary and traditional practices. Compared to the PRAI and the Rai Principles detailed in the previous chapter, the text of the VGGT sees the formal recognition of existing customary authorities as important for protecting the rights of rural populations, peasants, and Indigenous peoples, rather than as a means to achieve efficiencies in land management. Similarly, inclusions of gender in the VGGT appear less concerned with accessing untapped productive resources and are more focused on bringing women into land ownership and land governance. Indeed, what sets the text of the VGGT apart is its commitment to existing human rights obligations, firmly rooted in the broader CFS commitment to the human right to food.

In many ways, the CFS's development of the VGGT fulfills important criteria for inclusive global decision-making. A common refrain on the part of scholars is that global governance initiatives often fall short of liberal democratic ideals of legitimacy and transparency, failing to listen to key stakeholders, providing too prominent a role for powerful multinational corporations, and reducing opportunities for accountability (Bexell et al. 2010). Yet the CFS consultations on the VGGT were praised as inclusive and transparent, with experts providing topic-specific input on issues such as gender equality and Indigenous rights. The consultative framework has been celebrated as highly democratic for an international initiative, earning it a high level of legitimacy among academics and international NGOs such as FIAN International and Oxfam (Duncan 2015; Seufert 2013). Other organizations, such as GRAIN, praised the process that developed the VGGT, but continue to raise questions about content and implementation (GRAIN 2012).

The results of such an inclusive consultative process are evident both in the document itself and in its public reception. As a negotiated text in the CFS, which typically governs by consensus and aims for unanimous agreement on texts, the VGGT ultimately had broad appeal. The final product echoes other initiatives that have sought to strengthen governance of land through the recognition of existing rights and/or usage. As section 1.2.4, the Objectives of the VGGT (see table 5.1) demonstrates, this strengthening should occur across multiple levels, paying attention to a number of actors and authorities, including farmers, small-scale producers, Indigenous peoples, pastoralists, and "all persons concerned with tenure governance." These objectives include appeals to the obligations of states under international law and human rights agreements and for the fulfillment of the right food among many other human rights.

Table 5.1 Objective 1 of the Voluntary Guidelines on the Responsible Governance of Tenure (VGGT)

Objectives

1.1. These Voluntary Guidelines seek to improve governance of tenure of land, fisheries, and forests. They seek to do so for the benefit of all, with an emphasis on vulnerable and marginalized people, with the goals of food security and progressive realization of the right to adequate food, poverty eradication, sustainable livelihoods, social stability, housing security, rural development, environmental protection, and sustainable social and economic development. All programmes, policies, and technical assistance to improve governance of tenure through the implementation of these Guidelines should be consistent with States' existing obligations under international law, including the Universal Declaration of Human Rights and other international human rights instruments.

1.2. These Guidelines seek to:

1. improve tenure governance by providing guidance and information on internationally accepted practices for systems that deal with the rights to use, manage, and control land, fisheries, and forests.
2. contribute to the improvement and development of the policy, legal and organizational frameworks regulating the range of tenure rights that exist over these resources.
3. enhance the transparency and improve the functioning of tenure systems.
4. strengthen the capacities and operations of implementing agencies; judicial authorities; local governments; organizations of farmers and small-scale producers, of fishers, and of forest users; pastoralists; indigenous peoples and other communities; civil society; private sector; academia; and all persons concerned with tenure governance as well as to promote the cooperation between the actors mentioned.

Source: FAO 2012, 1.

Conflicting Themes in the VGGT

Despite widespread praise for how comprehensive and detailed the VGGT are, the breadth of issues addressed in a negotiated text ultimately requires the sacrifice of analytical depth. As a result, although the Guidelines demonstrate a much broader view of the challenges of gender-based inequalities in land governance, they also produce some conflicting recommendations on key issues. Spanning twenty-six sections, each with several clauses, the VGGT cover issues ranging from general principles of fairness in land tenure security to considerations of land rights under the pressures of climate change and emergencies. Certain recommendations sometimes appear to be at odds with others. For instance, clauses in section 11 illustrate tensions between facilitating land markets and market participation. First, the poor and vulnerable are not to be discouraged from participating in markets (FAO 2012 sec. 11.3). Yet, at the same time, the subclause that follows seeks to protect such vulnerable populations from the negative effects of market dynamics: "States should take measures to prevent undesirable impacts on local communities, indigenous peoples and vulnerable groups that may arise from, inter alia, land speculation, land concentration and abuse of customary forms of tenure" (FAO 2012 sec. 11.2). Thus, in spite of the seemingly clear objectives offered in section 1 (see table 5.1), the VGGT are sometimes tonally uneven, and reflect the various competing interests of those who negotiated the text of the agreement.

For instance, in addition to clauses promoting gender equality and the protection of Indigenous land rights and the rights of customary tenure holders, there are also clauses on the role of land markets and investment. Even though the origins and development of the VGGT predate the land deal phenomenon of the period after 2007–08, the Guidelines include several clauses regarding land markets and investment, reflecting competing attitudes toward such investments. Sections 11 and 12 deal with the responsibilities of states in facilitating land markets in some detail, noting that markets can have negative social impacts. Investments, generally stated, are "essential to improve food security" (section 12.1), but safeguards need to be in place to negate the risks of "large-scale transactions in tenure rights" (section 12.6). "Responsible investments" must meet a wide range of criteria, including meeting objectives such as sustainable land usage and diversification of livelihoods, while meeting the requirements of national and international law (sec. 12.4). For these reasons, though the VGGT do respond to many issues regarding land tenure, forests, and fisheries, they also speak strongly to matters of global land deals and land tenure rights and the global interest in agricultural investment.

That the guidelines include some language indicating different perspectives on the place of land markets and investment is indicative of the kinds of compromises and negotiations that must be made within multilateral agreements. The CFS, as a consensus-driven, political body, commonly seeks to have broad agreement on approved texts. And because the VGGT is a negotiated text, it does mean that there are potentially fewer opportunities for a more nuanced discussion of what the achievement of gender equality and women's rights means in practice, and the compromises that must be made in the process (Hall and Scoones 2016). What is noteworthy here, and explored below, is the extent to which gender equality, women's rights, and human rights more broadly *are* mainstreamed in the text and with reference to important considerations like marital status. This is a significant achievement for a text like this, especially given the subsequent opposition to rights-based language in the CFS (Collins 2022). That being said, however, there are still limits to the extent to which such an agreement might be able to reckon with more complex issues, such as how to grapple with gender equality and protect customary practice at once.

Assessing the VGGT

Mainstreaming Gender

The VGGT are illustrative of some of the advantages and drawbacks of gender mainstreaming in global policies. Gender mainstreaming in global policy-making was popularized in the 1990s. Building from earlier discourses about the role of women and gender in development, the UN Beijing Declaration of 1995 encouraged states and international bodies to "mainstream" gender into policy-making. Rather than set aside singular policies to address women's issues, gender mainstreaming invites policy-makers to consider how gender shapes and is shaped by the issues in question, and to incorporate these considerations into the policy itself. Although pushes for gender mainstreaming have made an impact as global institutions such as the United Nations, the International Monetary Fund (IMF), and the World Bank continue to undertake such initiatives, the inclusion of gender has rarely transformed policies or their implementation. Rather, as many scholars note, the integration of gender analysis into the policy-making and practices of international organizations is often appropriated in an incomplete and piecemeal fashion (Griffin 2010a; Bergeron 2011). Thus, scholars have been increasingly skeptical about the effectiveness of gender mainstreaming to improve gender equality by thoroughly addressing issues with reference to broader gender relations, and not just by including women (Moser 2005; Parpart 2009).

The VGGT do appear to approach gender in a systemic way, by including gender equality as one of the central principles of implementation, all of which reflect various international norms on human dignity, non-discrimination, consultation and participation, sustainability, and transparency (FAO 2012, sec. 3B). Implementers are implored to "(e)nsure the equal right of women and men to the enjoyment of all human rights, while acknowledging differences between women and men and taking specific measures aimed at accelerating de facto equality when necessary" (FAO 2012, sec. 3B.4). States are likewise directed to "ensure that women and girls have equal tenure rights and access to land ... independent of their civil and marital status" (FAO 2012, sec. 3B.4). Importantly, these principles go beyond merely demanding blanket legal equality for men and women, but offer some specific instances of sex- and gender-based discrimination. By acknowledging women's needs independent of their civil and marital status, these principles give explicit attention to how land rights are often bound to women's relationships with men and their broader community. Within the context of other principles of non-discrimination, equity, and justice, this specific attention to the role of women's social status in determining land access is a critical step. As we have seen in previous chapters, understanding the relational element of land access and land rights through a gender lens is essential.

References to gender inequality and gender sensitivity are included throughout the VGGT. The phrase "non-discriminatory and gender-sensitive" appears often; "gender-sensitive" and "gender sensitive" are used a total of seventeen times throughout the twenty-six sections of the VGGT. Attention is paid to where gender inequality might be manifested in various aspects of land governance and where efforts can be made to remedy such inequalities. This includes areas of market participation, governance, and inheritance. Sec. 4.6 promotes land tenure security for vulnerable groups, and women in particular, and expands beyond the definition of rights holders to include those – particularly women – who might not have widely recognized "legitimate" claims to land under the customary practices and social relationships in a specific context:

> States should remove and prohibit all forms of discrimination related to tenure rights, including those resulting from *change of marital status, lack of legal capacity, and lack of access to economic resources.* In particular, States should ensure equal tenure rights for women and men, including the right to inherit and bequeath these rights. (FAO 2012, sec. 4.6, emphasis added)

Sec. 5.4 goes further to specifically encourage states to "consider" the obstacles faced by women and girls and ensure legal equality between men and women to enter contracts. Importantly, these efforts encompass ensuring formal legal equality for women, but also encourage gender-sensitivity across a range of measures, including policy design, implementation, and the recognition of informal tenure.

These clauses illustrate some of the important statements the Guidelines make regarding gendered vulnerabilities surrounding land rights and demonstrate sensitivity to the social obstacles that women might encounter in claiming land rights. Moreover, given the global scope of the VGGT, it is imperative that these statements remain generalized statements to broaden their applicability. In this way, the VGGT exemplify what gender mainstreaming might look like in practice: here gender is not considered independently, but as a factor that implementers should be considering at every turn. In this regard, the VGGT illustrate how gender is relevant to land tenure governance and reform.

However, as we will see further illustrated below, the VGGT understate the connection between instances of gender-based discrimination and the facilitation and recognition of customary forms of governance. Indeed, though the VGGT briefly allude to the social origins of gender discrimination, there is limited consideration of the tensions between customary land governance, local traditions, and gender equality in practice and how stakeholders might begin to constructively address these tensions. Given the obstacles outlined in previous chapters, as well as the broader academic literatures addressing complex relationships between women's rights and customary practices, there is certainly much to be addressed. Thus, although the VGGT include plenty of references to where to eradicate gender discrimination in land tenure, they also demonstrate the limitations of mainstreaming gender without a more complex analysis of how inequality operates in practice.

Recognizing Customary Tenure

Alongside the gender-equality provisions mainstreamed throughout the VGGT, customary tenure holders are likewise described as legitimate holders of land, though they often lack legal recognition. As in the PRAI, several sections and clauses in the VGGT advise the recognition of local modes of authority and land organization, though here these terms are not couched in languages of efficiency or productivity. The VGGT advise states to safeguard the rights of all tenure holders, with specific attention to Indigenous peoples and customary tenure. Wherever states endeavour to provide legal recognition for land holdings, they are advised to "first identify all existing tenure rights and right holders, whether recorded or not. Indigenous peoples and other communities with customary tenure systems, smallholders and anyone else who could be affected" need to be consulted (FAO 2012, sec. 7.3).

The negotiators of the VGGT very consciously made efforts to recognize land, fisheries, and forests as sources of "social, cultural, spiritual, economic, environmental and political value to indigenous peoples and other communities with customary tenure systems" (FAO 2012, sec. 9.1). This recognition acts as a preface to the rights and responsibilities of Indigenous peoples and customary tenure holders, as well as the responsibilities of states to ensure that communities abide by rules related to good governance, specifically transparency and democratic practices. States must recognize and protect the rights of Indigenous peoples and those with customary tenure, and are encouraged to adapt their own policy, legal, and organizational frameworks to recognize these communities. These policies should take into account the views of affected communities, especially vulnerable people within those communities (FAO 2012, sec. 9.4, sec. 9.6, sec. 9.7, sec. 9.9). Moreover, states are encouraged to "respect and promote" customary approaches to resolving tenure-related conflicts (FAO 2012, sec. 9.11).[2]

In order to recognize customary forms of tenure, states are advised to develop recording systems that fit their needs and capabilities while respecting the practices of such communities: "Socio-culturally appropriate ways of recording rights of indigenous peoples and other communities with customary tenure systems should be developed and used" (FAO 2012, sec. 17.2). States are encouraged to "strive to ensure" that everyone is able to record their rights and access information without discrimination (FAO 2012, sec. 17.3). Finally, though states are encouraged to develop their own administrative and legal channels for land tenure dispute resolution, they are likewise encouraged to rely on alternative dispute-resolution mechanisms, particularly at the local level: "Where customary or other established forms of dispute settlement exist they should provide for fair, reliable, accessible and non-discriminatory ways of promptly resolving disputes over tenure rights" (FAO 2012, sec. 21.3).

Considerations of customary tenure thus run deeply throughout the VGGT and reflect a desire to protect customary users of land in the context of new commercial pressures. Similar to the calls for gender sensitivity, references to Indigenous peoples and customary forms of tenure are included in several clauses, and receive dedicated attention in a number of sections. Customary tenure systems, including governance and dispute resolution, are given high priority as a means of recognizing the legitimate rights of land users and respecting non-state or informal forms of land governance. The VGGT highlight customary governance practices as a potentially democratic means to ensure rights in the context of greater international commercial pressures on land. This is not to say that the VGGT seek to prevent the growth of liberalized land markets – that is decidedly not the case – but the focus on recognizing customary land rights and providing fair and transparent exchanges of land rights, including fair valuations on land, provide guidance to states on how to pursue comprehensive land rights for customary rights holders.

Gender and Custom in Practice

The full recognition of land tenure rights for Indigenous and rural populations with customary tenure remains a global struggle, as does the elimination of gender discrimination. As such, the VGGT can be read as an aspirational document toward such ends, providing guidance to states, civil society organizations, multinational corporations, private business, and activists on how to approach land tenure reform. However, this does not preclude an evaluation of the extent to which these recommendations reflect the complex realities of land reform and tenure security. Though no state has ideal land distribution, significant land reforms across several states since the mid-1990s offer glimpses into the challenges associated with recognizing customary tenure, promoting gender equality, and protecting land rights. The seriousness of these struggles indicate that this is no minor issue, but rather one that is indicative of the seeming incompatibility of introducing liberal rights reforms while simultaneously supporting modes of governance that may violate such rights, such as patriarchal customs that discriminate against women.

Feminist scholars of land governance have long debated the potential for tensions between these goals: that to enhance the authority of customs and traditions may mean reinforcing existing patriarchal practices. While some feminist scholars have argued that customary practices and gender equality are incompatible, others argue that customary laws can be flexible, adaptive, and progressive, even though they are increasingly restricted in the face of commercial land pressures (Agarwal 1994; Agarwal 2014; Koda 2000; Mbilinyi 2012). Though these debates on how best to manage this paradox persist, the VGGT are relatively silent on how to navigate these immensely important issues. And as we have seen in earlier chapters, the divide between gender equality and customary tenure, when overlooked, can lead to the retrenchment of existing power dynamics.

When it comes to gender and land reforms, there are clear intersections between the governance of polities – those political forums of governance, including local bodies – and the governance of communities, the disciplining discourses and practices within a community that govern behaviours. As we have seen in earlier chapters, this intersection shapes the realities of land governance. In attempting to improve local governance of land, governmental, international institutional, and civil society projects alike have encountered customary conceptions of land rights that discriminate against women, both in terms of ownership and of governance. Understanding those languages and practices that discipline governance at the local level is critical for anticipating how land governance reforms may be adopted or rejected at the local level.

In Tanzania, for instance, we can see these processes at work across the key measures designed to reconcile tensions between customary practices and gender equality. Tanzania's 1999 Land Acts made efforts to improve the gender balance in land governance and dispute-resolution forums and systematize the registration of customary tenure through the enactment of Certificates of Customary Rights of Occupancy (CCROs). As discussed in chapter 3, CCROs were designed not only to recognize customary tenure, but also to improve the recognition of spousal land rights. Yet these measures are unevenly implemented and face serious socio-cultural obstacles at the village level. Local attitudes about co-registration and the appropriateness of women owning land and property on the part of community members, those implementing reforms, and government officials all shape the extent to which more gender-equitable land ownership might occur. Because village authorities still issue CCROs according to custom, obtaining a CCRO remains tied to accepted local practices. In the rural Tanzanian context, this means that patriarchal customary practices that govern inheritance and marital property will still shape how women acquire land. In spite of co-registration laws for CCROs, the combination of administrative practices and gender bias often keep women's names off CCROs. Moreover, some women hesitate to register land due to distrust of the government, fear of taxation, or a lack of desire to access credit (Englert 2008). Women who seek land ownership are viewed as a threat in places where patrilocal practices dictate that women marry into other clans (Isinika and Mutabazi 2010). These realities keep women from claiming the land rights available to them.

At the same time, global recommendations made by bodies like the CFS must be careful not to essentialize conceptions of local communities as inclusive, fair arbiters of the public interest, but as political bodies in their own right, with competing interests and power relations (Khadiagala 2001; Peters 2009; Sikor and Müller 2009). Languages and practices that discipline behaviours within communities can likewise act to marginalize groups other than women. Devolving responsibilities for land governance can be fraught with problems, particularly regarding how to remedy structural limitations on participation, education, and access to resources. Age, political affiliation, and farming practices have also proven to be divisive in local governance and land access. Indeed, the frequency of mentions of gender in documents like the VGGT without consideration of these other important social and cultural factors reflects a lack of understanding about – or an unwillingness to recognize – how social identities intersect to create both vulnerabilities and opportunities. For instance, Chung (2021) documents the ways in which three male elders in Tanzania dominated opposition to a large-scale land acquisition, excluding legitimate landholders and women from the process. Such cases demonstrate how critical it is to appreciate how local inequality shapes governance as well.

Finally, the experiences of land reform around the world have revealed the centrality of implementation in determining whether the land laws will have any effect. World Bank land reform projects frequently report that projects run longer and cost more than initially planned (Collins and Mitchell 2018). NGOs pursuing their own land registration schemes report that progress can be made when there is time spent on changing attitudes, with dedicated attention to social norms and customs (Collins 2014b). By investing in both land registration schemes as well as sustained public education, attitudes about women's rights to land and land access are more likely to shift. However, there are often insufficient resources for infrastructure development, training, and capacity-building. Though government officials and civil society groups concur that implementation generally remains a problem, they also acknowledge the paucity of gender-sensitive implementation schemes. The failure to provide local leaders and administrators with training leads to a reliance on past practices that privilege local elites and officials while marginalizing other groups. As a result, forms of discrimination that were rooted in customary practices and hierarchies risk being perpetuated, even if such practices have been deemed unlawful.

In attempting to balance the tensions between the recognition of customary tenure and the promotion of gender equality, Whitehead and Tsikata (2003) arrive at the conclusion that overcoming obstacles to participation is key for promoting women's equality within customary governance. They argue it is insufficient to rely on systems of customary governance when it comes to land, and they advise democratic reform and urge resistance to a "flight into the customary" (Whitehead and Tsikata 2003, 103). Instead, Whitehead and Tsikata (2003) emphasize recognizing the social embeddedness of land in the creation of appropriate policy tools and reforms. The passage of legal reforms without attention to the social embeddedness of land relations is unlikely to challenge long-standing cultural norms.

In a working paper developed as part of the VGGT process, Daley and Park (2011) likewise highlight these social dimensions of land and the socio-cultural obstacles that prevent women's participation in land governance. They argue that "sustained high-level political support is likely to be needed to combat often deeply-held perceptions in many cultures and societies that land matters are a male sphere" (Daley and Park 2011, 10). They further note the ineffectiveness of legal reforms if they are not supported by comprehensive multi-level support for gender-sensitive reforms. Given the gender discrimination based on customary norms and practices that occurs around world, Daley and Park argue that gender sensitivity in land governance needs to go beyond formal legal equality and "also address underlying perceptions of gendered relations and power structures, which will require a very long-term perspective and much patience to deal with" (Daley and Park 2011, 16).

Daley and Park's recognition of the tensions between customary governance and gender equality is a critical one, but it is not widely reflected in the final version of the VGGT. An important exception is a brief mention in Sec. 9.6, which encourages states to adapt frameworks to recognize the tenure systems of Indigenous peoples and other communities with customary tenure systems: "Where constitutional or legal reforms strengthen the rights of women and place them in conflict with custom, all parties should cooperate to accommodate such changes in the customary tenure systems" (FAO 2012, sec. 9.6). This clause highlights a critically important tension in the efforts to advance gender equality while also recognizing various modes of land tenure and governance. However, as described throughout this book, this is an enormous challenge requiring consistent political will and appreciation of local contexts.

Despite this brief mention of a very complex problem in the VGGT, there is still cause for optimism in addressing this challenge. As noted above, the VGGT recommendations must necessarily generalize, and this avoids the obvious pitfall of offering specific prescriptions on what land reform should look like. Importantly, the VGGT has broader support from the FAO, which has committed resources to implementing the VGGT. For instance, *Governing Land for Women and Men*, a technical guide that was released following the approval of the VGGT, suggests the depth of expertise and knowledge available to address problems of implementation and reconcile seemingly competing priorities. Although the guide lacks the explicit endorsement of the CFS, it does fill several substantive gaps in the VGGT. Specifically, it shows how the problem of gender inequality in land governance is often tied to the absence of political will and resource commitments at all levels of governance (Collins 2016). While the skills and funding to undertake such tasks is elusive, the existence of the guide suggests the potential that exists within the CFS and the FAO more broadly, provided there is sustained pressure for better gender-aware policy development. As we will see in the section below, implementation remains a key component to the success or failures of these global recommendations.

Implementing the VGGT

Navigating these challenges is not impossible, but past efforts to reconcile gender-equality measures with protection for customary tenure systems illustrates how complex this task truly is. Effective implementation of the VGGT will thus require long-term financial and political commitments by states, institutions, civil society organizations, and front-line implementers. Moreover, as we consider the *voluntary* nature of the VGGT, we must also consider who is willing and able to shoulder responsibility for implementation. Institutional backing from the UN system speaks to the willingness of several agencies to support the CFS and its products, like the VGGT. However, the broader realities of global environmental governance and the global political economy suggest an uphill battle for land reform that effectively promotes gender equality and protection for customary tenure simultaneously.

A key advantage the CFS has is the support that it receives from the Rome-based agencies of the United Nations, most notably the FAO. In addition to various commitments to the VGGT by UN agencies, member states, and corporate initiatives, the FAO has been a key resource in ensuring that the VGGT could have a lasting impact. The FAO has provided important supports for implementing the VGGT, including drafting technical guides in support of the VGGT, producing several training modules, and providing local support for the implementation of VGGT pilot projects. Importantly, the aforementioned *Governing Land for Women and Men: A Technical Guide to Support the Achievement of Responsible Gender-Equitable Governance of Land Tenure* (FAO 2013), henceforth referred to as the "Technical Guide," offers key strategies to be considered in the implementation of gender-equitable land reforms. The 120-page guide acknowledges the complexity of local land reform and the challenges of reconciling gender equality with customary practices. The Technical Guide outlines the many dimensions of creating a gender-sensitive land tenure framework and provides specific steps for implementation. It offers a more complex and complete approach to land governance reform, and also illustrates why political and financial commitments are a necessary condition for success (Collins 2016).

The Technical Guide clearly describes how gender relations shape access to land under different conditions. Critically, its key contributions to discussions of land governance are to distill the complexities of the challenges discussed in previous chapters into specific strategies for policy-makers, legal advocates, the media, and civil society. These include recommendations for public-awareness campaigns using plays, music, radios, or other available media, and highlight the importance of local leaders. Moreover, rather than just a technocratic strategy of "add women and stir," the recommendations develop strategies that respect customary modes of governance, while also looking for ways to enhance gender equality in context-appropriate ways. This entails providing support for customary leaders, as well as sensitization training for a wide array of populations.

For example, the Guide begins by focusing on gender-equitable participation in policy-making and acknowledges the social obstacles to such participation. As we have seen in previous chapters, efforts to improve gender equality in local participation are often constrained by long-standing social practices. Everything from the timing and organization of meetings to possible threats of violence shape the experiences of those participating in meetings, and power hierarchies often fall squarely along gender lines (see chapter 3). In order to understand and address these challenges, the Technical Guide recommends an approach to policy-making that involves a thorough understanding of these local contexts – such as the role of family laws in controlling land, gender inequalities in knowledge or resource access, and colonial legacies – and advocacy and training to address these issues.

The Technical Guide also provides a substantive discussion of legal pluralism and its prevalence in several regions throughout the world, as well as a clear-but-nuanced approach to navigating legal pluralism with an eye to promoting gender equality. The Guide advises an incremental and collaborative approach to reforming customary institutions within the context of decentralizing land governance and encourages legal advocates to provide awareness-raising sessions for the public, including community discussions on marriage and inheritance, training for customary authorities on statutory laws, and help for women negotiating their land rights using customary laws (FAO 2013, 32). The Guide further advises sensitizing both men and women to changes in land governance, providing training to the media, and using "culturally appropriate mechanisms" in order to identify and resolve conflicts (FAO 2013, 92). These recommendations move beyond the dichotomous view that gender equality and customary tenure must be in tension with each other. By viewing customary governance as fluid and looking for customary rules that promote gender equality, the Technical Guide offers an important perspective on the opportunities for change.

At the same time, however, the scope of the challenge that the Technical Guide lays out also speaks to the challenges of gender-equitable land reform. To undertake this training and gain community support requires an immense amount of both consistent political will and financial commitment, neither of which may be in great supply, particularly under existing commercial land pressures. Indeed, there are many other commitments underscored in the VGGT – such as land registration – that may be viewed as being of more immediate importance than gender equality. However, a focus on land registration without a concurrent examination of how gender factors into land registration efforts may result in a repetition of the errors recounted in chapters 2 and 3. For instance, without considering the reasons why women may be excluded from land registration, even opting out themselves, it will be difficult to overcome gendered barriers to gender-equal land registration.

Resources such as the Technical Guide and online training modules for implementing the VGGT illustrate the advantages of having the FAO support the CFS. These efforts have ensured that the VGGT made several key achievements in the early years following its adoption by the CFS, including the adoption of reforms or VGGT strategies in Kenya, Colombia, Sierra Leone, and Senegal (FAO 2017a). VGGT principles have also been supported by INGOs and private corporations like Coca-Cola and PepsiCo (PepsiCo 2014). Thus, in terms of the opportunities afforded by the CFS, by virtue of ongoing support from the FAO, there are clear advantages for civil society movements, including feminist movements, concerned with land rights and food security.

Realities of Implementation and Global Environmental Governance

Despite the opportunities that the FAO and CFS afford for pushing a more progressive land reform agenda, there are still several challenges related to global governance and policy-making that need to be considered. First and foremost is that the Guidelines are voluntary. This is not a unique feature of the VGGT or other CFS recommendations. Although there are still significant legally binding agreements in international human rights law and some significant environmental achievements, such as the 2015 Paris Agreement, the realities of enforcement for international multilateral agreements means that most agreements will necessarily be voluntary. Thus, the fact that the VGGT – and indeed, other CFS recommendations – are voluntary should not be dismissed. There is increasing evidence that legally binding agreements are likely to be thinner or more flexible in their substance, that legally binding mechanisms may ultimately have reduced buy-in from key governments, or that legally binding instruments will ultimately see potential violators drop out (Falkner, Stephan, and Vogler 2010). For example, the withdrawal of Canada from the Kyoto Protocol, Russia's refusal to meet Kyoto's targets, and the United States's refusal to ratify Kyoto at all speak to the limitations of introducing stringent and binding environmental governance.

So, if voluntary guidelines are the norm, can they still be effective as a mode of governance? Indeed, some advocates suggest that they will be. Proponents of the VGGT note that the establishment of voluntary guidelines provides key materials for civil society organizations to use in their advocacy, either by building public pressure on governments to fulfill their international commitments, or as a document that helps focus and prioritize civil society advocacy. According to an FAO publication on land tenure reform, "[t]he real implementers of FAO's soft law instruments are the partners and stakeholders involved" (Arial et al. 2012, 75). This attitude was clearly on display as the VGGT were accepted: key observers viewed the success of the VGGT as ultimately a success for the civil society organizations that will use them (Duncan 2015). For these observers, instruments like the VGGT are best viewed as a document from which local advocates and policy-makers can select measures suited to local contexts and needs (Arial et al. 2012).

Yet there are still issues with these assumptions. While the VGGT and similar instruments may be useful in terms of civil society advocacy around land rights and food security, putting full responsibility for changes in land governance on CSOs instead of on states comes with certain risks. As Duncan (2015) has argued, to be effective, the VGGT must be taken up by governments and implemented carefully. The measures recommended within the VGGT and in supplementary documents like the Technical Guide all point to legal and regulatory changes that are typically the sole domain of state governments. The kinds of reforms envisioned by these documents often require both legal reform and wholesale cultural changes. These tasks absolutely require state commitments to reform.

There are also issues in expecting that CSOs can undertake the kinds of societal changes and shifts in thinking that are required to adapt more gender-equitable modes of land governance, whether statutory or customary. This is both a question of resources and capacity. The availability of funding for CSOs is a concern. Neither local nor international NGOs have the same resource availability as states or international institutions such as the World Bank, which has also found land reform efforts costly (Byamugisha 2013). Sustained funding for multi-year projects may not be an option for many civil society groups, even if they would like to make such commitments.

In addition, not all CSOs interested in land reform will have commitments to gender-inclusive land reform, or even land reform that is inclusive of different Indigenous groups, ethnic groups, migrants, or otherwise marginalized groups. The priorities of CSOs may or may not pay attention to the kinds of concerns highlighted above. Even where CSOs have these commitments, it may not be guaranteed that they have the resources or can provide training for effective implementation. We know that developing plans for land reform that are gender-inclusive and respectful of customary and informal tenure are likely to be complex. Yet relying heavily on CSOs for advocacy and implementation means that we must also recognize that possible limitations in terms of capacity, funding, and expertise may result in the exclusion of key measures. Indeed, this has also been a problem for World Bank–led land reforms done in partnership with state governments, despite the availability of resources and multi-year commitments (Collins and Mitchell 2018). Key goals – such as more land registration for women – have become afterthoughts in some cases (Pedersen and Haule 2013).

Finally, without state commitments to implementing the VGGT, states may ultimately choose development paths and investment strategies that serve to undermine the values of the VGGT. Considering the VGGT alongside measures designed to attract foreign investment in land and agriculture reveal the ways in which competing state agendas on human rights and agricultural investment may ultimately serve to undermine efforts to protect land tenure rights. It would not be surprising to see the more immediate and quantifiable benefits of land investment winning out over the slower-moving social change that accompanies more equitable land reform.

Addressing the complex social structures that have been identified will require comprehensive technical and financial support and keen attention to the possibility that protections for customary practice and promoting gender-equity measures are not inherently compatible. Thus, in order to be an effective instrument, the VGGT require interested parties and policy-makers to assess the current state of land governance in targeted regions, implement suitable reforms, and monitor the outcomes with specific focus on marginalized populations. This requires, in no small part, dedicated attention to the ways in which gender roles and inequality shape land governance and policy prescriptions alike. However, this further raises questions about the viability of such change, given limited capacities for implementation in many countries, even where legal changes might seem poised to usher in important reforms.

Conclusion

The reformed CFS provides clear opportunities for civil society to participate in the shaping of the global food policies and for several organizations to advocate on behalf of underrepresented groups, such as women and small-scale farmers. The most celebrated contribution of the CFS to the global food policy landscape to date is the VGGT. By mainstreaming gender considerations throughout, the VGGT have helped to expand policy discussions about gender equality in land tenure and clearly illustrate the sort of opportunities that the CFS provides for global-level discussions on women's rights, gender equality, and land reform. The FAO's Technical Guide *Governing Land for Women and Men* introduces important ideas and suggestions to translate the broad principles of the VGGT into practical strategies for reform of a contentious social and political nature. Other training and policy support efforts likewise emphasize the need to pay closer attention to gender relations beyond an "add women and stir" approach. Indeed, although the VGGT itself remains quiet on potentially contentious issues relating to gender and custom and mainstreams gender and inequality concerns in a rather technical manner, the FAO's institutional efforts that support the VGGT have a clear understanding of the complexity of reforming both social and political modes of governance. Building from the understanding of gender and land governance established in the earlier chapters of this book, it appears that this is the kind of policy-making that is needed to address the complex multi-level challenge of gender-equitable land reform.

Whether or not the CFS will continue to be the foremost global forum for the development of global food policy remains to be seen. As McKeon (2015) notes, the early successes of the CFS in addressing social and economic inequalities and the creation of effective tools for civil society to use to apply pressure on governments led to more active engagement on the part of governments and private sector actors that resisted such new obligations. As a result, there were contentious debates about the Principles for Responsible Agricultural Investment (Rai) that were passed in 2014, and which several observers characterize as rushed and ultimately lacking in the legitimacy and quality of the VGGT (McKeon 2015; see chapter 4 for more detail). Such concerns about the lack of sufficient time to develop guidelines and consult with key constituencies remains a problem within the CFS, at least from the perspective of some members and participants. In the years since, efforts to create a new science-policy interface for global food policy has drawn significant criticism from those who have been involved in the CFS. Critics argue that these efforts, the most significant being the UN Food Systems Summit (UNFSS) in 2021, undermine the participatory process that has been established. At the same time, the usefulness of the CFS in providing ongoing opportunities for advocacy groups and civil society to engage with global policy development also remains an open question. The opportunity to participate rests on the continued ability of CSOs to engage with the year-long processes of negotiation on multiple fronts. Brem-Wilson (2015) notes that there are key questions to be asked about which individuals and organizations are ultimately able to participate in the CFS in meaningful ways.

Yet, in the most practical terms, the implementation of comprehensive gender-sensitive land reforms such as those recommended by the CFS in the VGGT also requires high-level political commitment on the part of state leaders. The VGGT are strictly voluntary. This means that states are under no obligation to follow the guidelines, despite the formal endorsement of the VGGT by a number of UN bodies. The result is that the burden of advocacy for national land reform falls largely on civil society actors (Duncan 2015), though the FAO has provided policy support. The work of CSOs may be effective in pushing for change, but these organizations often lack the financial resources of states and international institutions to enact and sustain social and political reforms. Equitable land reform is necessarily a long-term project, one that requires political commitment and adequate financial resources. Without changing mindsets at the state level of policy-making, the well-crafted messaging and strategies of the VGGT, the Technical Guide, and other supports from the FAO may be lost.

Without the political – and financial – commitments of political leaders and state governments, implementation efforts will either be short-lived or punted to CSOs to take on. Measures to protect local land rights, strengthen democratic practices, and promote gender equality are not necessarily going to be high priorities for states that are dependent on their commercial agricultural output. Many countries can attract investment based on the ease with which arable land can be alienated for commercial use. State officials may speak about the need for gender equality, but they must also demonstrate clear commitment to implementation. If front-line officials responsible for implementation lack the resources and skills needed to receive or provide comprehensive training, there is little reason to expect substantive changes in land governance. And of course, if the choice is made to default to customary practices without thinking critically about how inequality might operate within customary land practice, we might not expect much change at all. We have already seen how such ideas are prevalent in global discussions about what responsible agricultural investment would look like, and the limited attention to gender inequality therein. If states opt to simply recognize existing customary land governance practices, because they are regarded as more efficient, there is a risk of further entrenching men's land rights over women's land rights, or excluding other marginalized groups such as migrants.

Despite these critiques, the CFS, the VGGT, and the support from the FAO and other UN institutions nonetheless form an important starting point for global policy-making on land governance reform. As far as process goes, the development of the VGGT was widely celebrated by participants and observers. The ongoing participation of both civil society and private sector participants in the policy development and negotiation processes is a remarkable shift in global policy-making and remains rare within the broader scope of global governance practices. Yet as the following chapter explains, understanding the viability of such governance reforms in terms of lasting political and social change also requires a broader understanding of the global political economy within which these reforms must ultimately take place.

6 PROSPECTS FOR FEMINIST GLOBAL LAND GOVERNANCE

As previous chapters have shown, understanding the nature of gender inequality in land governance requires a multi-level approach. Chapters 2 and 3 detail the complexity of gendered land relations and the ways in which political and community governance intersect to discipline how land is managed. Chapters 4 and 5 use those lessons to evaluate the quality of global land governance initiatives and highlight the governance gaps in these transnational initiatives. As a result of efforts to design universal principles for land governance – and in the case of the CFS-created VGGT and Rai Principles, also navigating political debate, negotiation, and compromise – I illustrate how these efforts often overlook the diversity of land governance practices and the role of gendered power relations. Although all the global initiatives evaluated in this book promote gender equality and/or women's empowerment as key values, these efforts often overlook the complexity of gendered power relations and the difficulties of pushing for meaningful change.

Given the shortcomings in these global initiatives, this chapter addresses the question of whether global land governance is worthwhile, and evaluates the prospects for feminist global land governance. One of the fundamental critiques of global governance is the very nature of voluntary rules and guidelines themselves. As with all international law and global governance initiatives, successful implementation in the domestic context is often the key means by which global-level recommendations take force, whether as state law or as other modes of regulation and policy development. When it comes to assessing the potential effectiveness of international law, observers often consider whether there are any requirements to report to an international body, and thus ensure some mode of enforcement.

Human rights instruments such as the Convention on the Elimination of Discrimination against Women (CEDAW) and some agreements under the United Nations Framework Convention on Climate Change (UNFCCC) are legally binding initiatives that require both domestic ratification and regular reporting on the part of states.

In the case of soft-law instruments like the voluntary guidelines and principles discussed in this book, there is no such enforcement or ratification. Although voluntary guidelines might be passed by consensus in bodies such as the CFS, there are no clear legal channels through which implementation can be monitored and states required to report on progress. And, as detailed in previous chapters, these guidelines and principles don't always offer specific guidance on how they should be put into practice. Moreover, given that states are likely to pursue their own economic interests and expand foreign agricultural investment, perhaps at a speed that outpaces land reform, how can we expect states to abide by such voluntary guidelines?

I argue that there is still good reason to support voluntary guidelines to improve land tenure and the rights of local populations, particularly with reference to gender inequality. It is useful to consider the contributions of feminist scholars, who, despite their pointed critiques of patriarchal institutions, still find reason for optimism in the niches where substantive change may occur. While states are still largely oriented toward an agenda of resource development and export, often without attention to the gendered impacts of these practices, understanding the broader scope of political activism and influence highlights the ways in which voluntary guidelines and principles can provide support to local and transnational activists. Moreover, having a policy space like the CFS that includes various interest groups is an important innovation in global governance.

In this chapter, I briefly review the emerging research on how the VGGT have been put into practice since they were adopted by the CFS in 2013 – and the obstacles to their implementation. This research suggests both the limitations of the VGGT to guide policy, but also the ways in which global economic pressures and local political and community dynamics, including elite control, shape the extent to which the VGGT might be adopted. Yet despite these obstacles, I argue that there are still good reasons to support the creation of voluntary global governance in forums like the CFS. As a body that brings together an array of stakeholders and is supported by independent research and expertise, it represents a critical opportunity to negotiate complex social, political, and economic terrain to establish best practices for equity and justice in the global food system.

What Have Global Land Governance Initiatives Achieved?

Given the shortcomings of voluntary global standards and guidelines for the securing of land or agricultural investment discussed throughout this book, it is worth reviewing what these initiatives have achieved to date. Reviewing voluntary global land governance standards and institutions has revealed several key gaps, particularly where we consider the needs and interests of marginalized people, such as women and the holders of customary tenure. And, in addition to the ways in which these mechanisms overlook matters of gender inequality, there are key questions about their usefulness in the context of the broader global economy. Critical scholars of global governance note how "commonsense" discourses of good governance and business practices perpetuate notions of neo-liberal development and deepen global inequalities (Overbeek 2005; Soederberg 2006).

These are important considerations, especially as we can see how certain initiatives attempt to reframe key issues: the PRAI in particular are viewed as depoliticizing transnational land deals and recasting them as necessary for rural development (GRAIN 2008; Chu 2011). In the years since their creation, these principles have not been widely embraced or endorsed by the international community. Widespread criticism of the PRAI and the refusal of the CFS to endorse them illustrate the importance of having broader support if guidelines are to be adopted.

In contrast, the VGGT have been more widely accepted, sometimes with reference to the CFS Rai Principles (which also refer to the VGGT). Both the VGGT and the CFS Rai Principles have been used together in several different country contexts to guide land transactions and tenure reform (Myers and Sanjak 2022). For this reason, this assessment focuses primarily on what the VGGT have been able to achieve, although the Rai Principles are sometimes introduced at the same time. The FAO (2017a) reports that major legal changes in several countries echo the

VGGT principles, and in some cases governments are explicitly using the VGGT to guide the implementation of key policy changes, such as in Colombia's rural reform program, Sierra Leone's National Land Policy Implementation Plan, and Senegal's Land Policy Document (FAO 2017a). In the first five years since the VGGT were endorsed by the CFS, the FAO held national and regional workshops in seventy-eight countries (FAO 2017a). *Governing Land for Women and Men*, the FAO technical guide discussed in chapter 5, has been developed into a program to support capacity development and strengthen the gender-equitable implementation of the VGGT by training a wide range of stakeholders, including policy-makers, CSOs, and private enterprises (FAO 2017b).

The VGGT are still held in high regard by many researchers, activists, and CSOs as important guidelines for land governance (Dieterle 2023; Lay et al. 2021), but many note that they have not yet met expectations. A comprehensive assessment of the translation of the VGGT into state law, policy, or practices is elusive due to the absence of baseline data and the challenges associated with collecting new quantitative and qualitative data. However, Myers and Sanjak (2022) attempt to assess the impact to date based on available data. They argue that, despite uptake in a few countries, there has not been a significant improvement in land tenure security in sub-Saharan Africa. At the core of Myers and Sanjak's (2022) assessment is that the VGGT haven't had an impact "at scale": that there is not widespread evidence of adoption or impact. Indeed, although the number of large-scale land deals have levelled off in the past few years, this seems not to be the result of the implementation of the VGGT, but of various factors, such as state moratoria on foreign land investments following the land rush and declining interest in biofuels like jatropha (Lay et al. 2021).

There are many reasons why the VGGT have not yet achieved a broad, scalar impact. From an international relations perspective, it stands to reason that the voluntary nature of the guidelines is at least one factor. The VGGT are not binding, and there is no global mechanism to ensure that states enforce these rules or accountability for how they will be enacted. Without accountability mechanisms, and with states having competing economic interests and obligations under international trade law, it is challenging to see how such guidelines would be effective if left for states alone to enforce (Tzouvla 2019). While countries may be signing on to a more progressive land reform agenda through initiatives like the CFS-Rai Principles and the VGGT, they are also often designing and implementing agricultural development policies and programs that favour large-scale agricultural investment, reduced trade barriers, and, importantly, better access to arable land and easier access for land purchases and rentals (Lavers 2012, Lay et al. 2021). Meanwhile, fertile land and sub-surface minerals could prove to be a boon to state coffers if governments facilitate more foreign investment in agribusiness and extractive industries and make such lands and resources available.

It is within this context that agriculturally dependent and less industrialized states are still likely to seek foreign investments in agriculture and natural-resource extraction, even when signatories to the VGGT. These governments increasingly face global pressures to facilitate investment in local industries to improve the business environment and attract and retain investors (World Bank 2019). State governments further demonstrate their openness to foreign investment via tax relief and exemptions for foreign investors. And states are increasingly taking proactive measures to improve the ease of doing business. In Tanzania, Mozambique, Cameroon, and elsewhere across sub-Saharan Africa, state-created one-stop investment centres and agencies increasingly work to facilitate land acquisition, streamline permit processes, and/or assist with business registration to further entice foreign investors in key agricultural sectors (Bélair 2018). These structural factors all work to limit the potential of achieving change at scale.

However, there is also the question of whether the VGGT have been effective in case-specific instances. Again, there is limited data available to date, but there are reasons for both optimism and caution when assessing the implementation of the VGGT in practice. Many scholars point to Sierra Leone as an illustrative case, given the incorporation of the VGGT into its National Land Policy implementation plan (Tzvoula 2019; Myers and Sanjak 2022; Dieterle 2023). Sierra Leone followed a multi-stakeholder process to develop a new land policy and draft new land legislation over several years (Myers and Sanjak 2022). While it is too soon to conclude what the impacts of that new legislation will be, Dieterle (2023) compares the differences in outcomes in several cases in Sierra Leone, where land deals made under the revised National Land Policy and with reference to the VGGT have starkly different outcomes based on the role of local practices. Specifically, Dieterle (2023) finds that the difference comes down to the role of local paramount chiefs: where chiefs exercised the most control, global governance norms like the VGGT tended to be absent. In cases where decision-making power was distributed to families, Dieterle finds that there was more likely to be uptake of the VGGT. Here, understanding the unevenness in the implementation of the VGGT in practice comes down to "the interplay between land deals, global norms, and the local land tenure institutions" (Dieterle 2023, 3). Indeed, as we have seen throughout this book, it is imperative that land governance account for the various levels of authority and governance through which land is managed. To overlook local dynamics, including the role of customary or chiefly authorities, would be a significant gap in policy design and practice.

There is an important thread running through these assessments of how the VGGT were designed, adopted, and put into practice: the need for attention to specific details and local contexts in policy design and implementation. Myers and Sanjak (2022, 4) take issue with the VGGT as a negotiated text and its consequences for efficient land reform: "If lessons [from specific examples of land reform] had been taken into consideration, some provisions of the VGGT might have been more technical and strategic rather than political or aspirational, and consequently more effective." Tzouvala (2019) argues that the false promise of the VGGT was that states would bear responsibility for implementing land reform when they have competing obligations and interests in the international sphere, such as obligations under international trade and investment law. Moreover, Tzouvala (2019, 252) argues that a model that assumes the state is unitary overlooks the realities of the post-colonial world: "Indeed, the post-colonial state in Africa is characterized by the ongoing relevance of ethnicized customs that was historically a necessary component of 'indirect rule'" (Tzouvala 2019, 252). And finally, Dieterle (2023) argues that the specific form of local land tenure governance is a critical component in understanding whether global norms will shape local outcomes.

All these studies speak to the importance of understanding local contexts in the effective implementation of the VGGT and CFS-Rai principles. As this book argues, land governance must be regarded as multilevel and grounded in specific local contexts. Global land policy will be limited in its effectiveness if it cannot grapple with the complexities of multiple forms of authority and governance, particularly where there are many competing authorities.

But in addition to these early, largely gender-neutral, assessments of the VGGT and CFS-Rai, we also must be aware of the gender dimensions of all these modes of governance. As Ryan (2018) argues, there are clearly gendered impacts of land deals in places like Sierra Leone, but these need to be understood with reference to local land politics. "It is through looking at the 'messy' politics on the ground that we begin to see how gender, lineage, age, and patronage all interact to determine who benefits from large-scale land deals and who doesn't" (Ryan 2018, 190). Elite control over the distribution of land – or even compensation when land deals occur – can reinforce existing inequalities, excluding women and other marginalized groups.

Thus, while I concur with the scholars above who argue that global land policy needs to be more specific in its recommendations, I would expand that to include more attention to the actual functioning of gendered norms and assumptions in governing land. To make sense of the VGGT recommendations on how to govern land more equitably, there must be clearer understanding of the role of gender relations and how they connect to both customary practice and the design and implementation of statutory land laws. Specific examples and details of what these might look like in practice are also absent in the VGGT, but it is imperative that those working on land reform grapple with these challenges as well. Further evaluation and assessment is needed to understand both the gendered effects of land deals and the ways in which gender inequality is addressed – or not addressed – when new land policies are designed and put into practice. As we have seen throughout this book, meaningful gender-sensitive policy implementation is likely to be its own challenge, a challenge made only more difficult when local gender norms and expectations are not considered.

Is Global Land Governance Worthwhile? A Hesitant "Yes"

Given the voluntary quality of these instruments and the flaws therein, is global governance for land deals and agricultural investment worthwhile? I offer a hesitant "yes." There are several formidable obstacles to enacting gender-equitable land reform on a global scale, as enumerated above. The incentives for low-income and agriculturally dependent economies to liberalize land markets to attract foreign investment in agriculture cannot be dismissed. Local elite control and land conflicts still need to be navigated, even where there are commitments to implementing global recommendations. And finally, gender gaps in land governance initiatives across levels of policy-making cannot be overlooked. Expecting that voluntary initiatives could resolve such issues and result in inclusive land governance without accounting for multi-layered and multi-level gendered power relations would be naive.

Yet, despite these challenges, voluntary global guidelines like the VGGT have had some positive effects. Although voluntary instruments alone are not likely to resolve key tensions in the global economy, overcome elite power, or address structural issues related to poverty or gender inequality, this does not mean that they are not worthwhile. These structural features are not likely to change under new governance rules without concerted, coordinated efforts by a range of key actors. However, global governance initiatives *can* create important opportunities within these power structures and guide the way to activities that are already spurring changes in land governance. Although the structures of the global economy may offer few obvious opportunities for substantive change, global voluntary guidelines may be useful even beyond the scope of implementation in specific contexts like those highlighted above. As argued by O'Neill (2017), assessing the full scope of the effectiveness of global rules and guidelines can go beyond agreement and compliance to include the broader social influence of global governance. When states sign onto such agreements, participate in their negotiation, and remain as members of decision-making bodies, they are still brought into discussion and dialogue on these issues, which can create ideational change over time.

From a feminist perspective, it is also useful to consider the ways in which institutional spaces might provide important new venues to address gendered power imbalances, create more nuanced policy instruments, and facilitate multi-stakeholder governance. Feminist scholars have advocated for finding the spaces in which meaningful change might occur in political and economic forums. Nancy Fraser, though very famously noting how feminism has become capitalism's "handmaiden" (Fraser 2013b), nonetheless argues that the expansion of women's access to markets and economic opportunities can be beneficial. In some circumstances and under certain conditions, spaces for economic opportunity can bring meaningful empowerment to women's lives (Fraser 2013a). Similarly, though she notes the ways in which neo-liberal reforms can create risks for women, Prügl (2014) likewise argues that neo-liberal spaces can bring opportunities for women's empowerment in unexpected ways. This includes investigating various policy spaces to see the ways in which gender equality might be pushed further. For these reasons, these scholars note that we need to examine political and economic initiatives for potential opportunities, even where the conditions may not seem ideal. While it is imperative that we be critical of certain institutions and ideas, they may also offer strategic opportunities for feminist activism and change.

Thus, while we can and should recognize the limitations of voluntary guidelines and institutions like the CFS, there are some reasons for optimism. I posit three justifications for the continued negotiation and establishment of global guidelines, even if only voluntary: (1) when done in a consultative and inclusive way, they may establish an important normative baseline for global institutions to support land reforms in domestic contexts; (2) the creation of global guidelines via forums like the CFS may help to foster collaboration between civil society actors and other groups; and (3) the guidelines can be used in domestic efforts to pressure governments and corporate actors into reform.

These initiatives reflect a seemingly minor but meaningful change in the ways in which global institutions approach questions of land governance in voluntary standards and principles. Across all the principles and guidelines studied in this book, there are calls for states and investors to respect rural residents, to undertake participatory and transparent investment practices in accordance with local laws, and to improve the representation of marginalized people. Even though such rules are not binding, these remain important shifts in terms of how global policy-makers regard the role of land in development, and could be the basis on which advocacy groups – including feminist advocacy groups – build their work.

Creating a Baseline for Institutions Undertaking Land Reform

The VGGT seem likely to remain the global standard in terms of land governance and reform recommendations, and with good reason. The VGGT are a comprehensive set of guidelines for more equitable land governance, designed to reflect the priorities of a wide range of stakeholder groups. The VGGT reinforce key priorities around the protection of customary tenure, the promotion of free, prior, and informed consent (FPIC) in land governance, and women's rights. And the VGGT are not single-mindedly market-oriented in their design. Indeed, the recommendations to secure land tenure for vulnerable populations, especially pastoralist communities and women, are important, if somewhat underdeveloped, in the final text. Although there is a lack of nuance in the VGGT regarding gender relations, especially relating to custom, the general effort to mainstream gender throughout the text with ongoing input and support from civil society illustrates the importance of civil society's input and the potential such processes might have in the future. The VGGT reflect the contentious nature of debates about agricultural investment and the conflicts that shaped their writing, which might be regarded as both a necessity of global negotiation but also a limitation in terms of articulating a clear agenda for land reform (Myers and Sanjak 2022).

Regardless, we have seen the uptake of the VGGT in several state contexts in different forms, such as a broad set of principles to organize land reform policies (Myers and Sanjak 2022) or in the design of land deal agreements (Dieterle 2023). The scale of the uptake of the VGGT is still small. Regardless, organizations like Land Matrix argue in favour of their implementation, stating in 2021 that their number-one recommendation to improve land governance is the implementation and enforcement of the VGGT (Lay et al. 2021).

To overcome the limitations of the document, there are also supplemental documents to close the gap. Many of the issues related to gender and custom that are not fully addressed in the VGGT are addressed in the accompanying FAO Technical Guide, *Governing Land for Women and Men: A Technical Guide to Support the Achievement of Responsible Gender-Equitable Governance of Land Tenure* (FAO 2013), which offers concrete proposals for implementation. As we saw in chapters 2 and 3, the relationship between customary practices and gender equality is neither straightforwardly progressive nor regressive, but always embedded in specific local contexts. These are dynamics that require serious attention, and this is where efforts to create common global guidelines like the VGGT sometimes stumble. Yet the FAO Technical Guide offers a thoughtful assessment of these dynamics, with clear strategies for engaging communities, governments, and companies on questions of gender equality. When states push ahead with land reforms that do not recognize the multi-faceted nature of land governance, they risk deepening the exclusion of women and other marginalized groups (Ryan 2018). As a result, clear and straightforward practical guides like *Governing Land for Women and Men* in conjunction with the VGGT may help lay out clearer steps for governments, investors, and civil society organizations to take.

Voluntary Governance as a Tool for Change

With voluntary guidelines, there is no guarantee that land reforms will be enforced by states, local officials, or customary authorities. However, the usefulness of these transnational rules is not limited to state enforcement. The establishment of global rules – even voluntary ones – can provide a tool for land rights activists in their work. The VGGT have been promoted by various political actors, activists, and social movements, particularly those working to reform local governance processes or advocate for change from state governments. NGO and social-movement advocacy on land tenure security and food sovereignty are often at the leading edge of pushes for legal reform.

For instance, Franco and Monsalve Suárez (2017) illustrate how marginalized populations in Mali, Nigeria, Uganda, and South Africa have employed the vision of rights articulated within the VGGT to push for change in land governance in their own communities. These communities have been able to use the VGGT to assess state legal frameworks and activities that undermine land security and food sovereignty. Taking the VGGT as a guide, local civil society organizations have provided communities with knowledge about land governance principles and empowered them to push for change from state governments. Elsewhere, social activism on women's land rights and food sovereignty in

Latin America has also led to significant changes in several countries. As Deere (2017) has found, the presence of robust women's social movements in rural Latin America may be determining the effectiveness of state-led land reforms. In this way, guidelines like the VGGT can assist in the dissemination of these concepts and lead to significant legal and political change through local activism and political pressure.

In addition, although there are clear limits to this approach, the VGGT have also been used by INGOs to pressure multinational corporations on their land and resource practices. Oxfam International's advocacy on responsible land investments used the VGGT to obtain public commitments from Coca-Cola and PepsiCo (Oxfam 2014b). PepsiCo's 2014 Land Policy states that the company will operate in alignment with the principle of free, prior, and informed consent (FPIC), and will advocate for state governments to follow the VGGT (PepsiCo 2014). Oxfam International has continued monitoring both Coca-Cola and PepsiCo's implementation efforts on the VGGT (Christman and Feronni 2016). The effectiveness of this kind of accountability and monitoring is limited, especially for companies that lack the strong public profile like the cola giants (Clapp 2017). However, this kind of pressure on corporate actors can still be considered alongside the other tools and targets of activist pressure.

The few assessments of the VGGT that have emerged speak to the importance of non-state actors in their implementation. In Sierra Leone, the international community, specifically donors and NGOs, are seen as significant players in implementing change using the VGGT. Dieterle (2023, 23) finds that both the land reforms and the donor efforts to test soft laws like the VGGT are "exerting substantial pressure on investors." While land reform policy orchestrated and enforced by states is certainly the preferable course of action, other actors are still able to shape outcomes by insisting on the implementation of soft law. And as we have seen throughout the course of this book, there is a significant role to be played by those who would be the front-line implementers of land reform policies. International organizations like the World Bank have noted the challenges in implementing land reform, including gender-equitable reform. NGOs likewise face challenges in advancing the cause of women's rights, including tenure rights. However, common guidelines can create broader awareness of these challenges and, when supported by specific examples and strategies to address them, may improve land tenure security.

Collaborative Governance with and among Civil Society Organizations

Finally, we can also consider the processes that create voluntary guidelines as a benefit of these guidelines. Initiatives that make concerted efforts to include civil society input often also create key linkages between civil society actors and international institutions, as well as opportunities for civil society groups to network and strategize. Having a central focus – such as tenure guidelines – brings together organizations in a common cause and can link them for several months or years as the terms are being negotiated.

Among existing global institutions, the CFS is perhaps the best poised to incorporate civil society perspectives into the governance of land and the food system more broadly. Duncan (2015) has detailed these processes, revealing the role of civil society in this reformed global policy space. With the formal Civil Society and Indigenous Peoples' Mechanism (CSIPM) as part of the CFS, various movements, including feminist organizations, are already participating in the CFS. These forums, as well as CSIPM meetings held before and during the annual CFS plenary every year in Rome, provide opportunities for civil society members from around the world to communicate about these key issues. It also provides opportunities for engagement with institutional actors. Throughout the year, CFS-negotiated texts keep various actors – from civil society groups, states, and the private sector – in communication. Although these processes certainly tend to privilege certain populations – such as those who speak UN languages and those with the means and time to travel and participate in year-long negotiations (Brem-Wilson 2015) – their normalization in the CFS is noteworthy.

As a result of this inclusion, the CFS is one of a few international forums where the re-politicization of gender and food politics is ongoing (Duncan and Claeys 2018). For instance, in 2017, a forum held in Rome in advance of the 2017 CFS plenary welcomed feminist organizations from around the world to address issues in food and land security.

Many participants directly interrogated and challenged the language of "empowerment" as deployed by the CFS, calling instead for a re-emphasis on women's rights and the obligations of states to not simply enforce women's rights, but to end the assault on women who act as defenders of food security, land, and the environment more broadly (Collins 2022). This re-politicization is important for highlighting the contentious nature of fighting for women's rights and moving away from policy language that compromises on human rights (Duncan and Claeys 2018). Re-politicization is an important step toward recognition of the ways in which women's rights are resisted by various authorities at multiple levels of governance.

These are concerns about gendered power relations within the food system that have received public hearings within the international forum of the CFS. Moreover, the forums demonstrate the disagreements that still exist between institutional actors and civil society organizations, and even between and within civil society organizations themselves. This all shows that these debates and struggles are ongoing, with parties still willing to debate and work toward new efforts to promote gender equality in land governance and the food system more broadly. At the time of writing, the battle to recognize women's rights in this forum continues, with conservative states refusing to recognize intersectionality, women's sexual and reproductive rights, and the presence of sexual and gender-based violence (Welsh 2022). While this is discouraging for activists (CSIPM 2023), it also illustrates the importance of having multi-stakeholder forums within which this activism and politicization occurs.

Conclusion

Voluntary initiatives that push for rights-based visions of land tenure security – and of the food system more broadly – can result in change at multiple levels of political engagement. Doing so requires recognizing the multi-level quality of land governance and the various actors that engage at each level. Importantly, at all these levels, questions of gender inequality must also be addressed. Policy developments and activism that thoughtfully incorporate gender-aware analysis and provide clear guidance on next steps must also be encouraged to respond to the challenges on the ground. This includes using gender-aware analysis to consider the forums, organizations, and actors that are also involved in these processes. This is an important new trajectory for feminist research in global governance, particularly in forums like the CFS. Global forums like the CFS and initiatives like the VGGT offer new opportunities for inclusive decision-making. The CFS is an important site for global policy-making, and the creation of the VGGT was an important moment for feminist policy development. This is in no small part due to the inclusion of civil society organizations and the persistence of NGOs and social movements in pushing for feminist policy language in this context.

Of course, as seen above, any policy changes that might occur in practice are contingent on a number of other factors. The broader global context, including the nature of the global food system and the economic pressures facing state governments, is a limiting factor. Even if the CFS succeeds in passing more gender-equitable guidelines – ideally supported by institutional funding, the private sector, and civil society – state governments must still be willing to make lasting reforms, matched with implementation that meets local needs and overcomes local obstacles. In the case of land governance, this often requires the dedication of public resources to land demarcation and registration, and, in the case of progressive land reforms, also requires social and economic assessments of inequality. At the same time, there may need to be a reckoning with local power struggles and dynamics. These are tall orders to fill, especially when states have competing priorities regarding these resources.

So why should we remain cautiously optimistic about the role of global land governance and voluntary guidelines? Despite the odds against progressive land reforms in the context of a more intensely financialized and concentrated food system (Clapp 2021), social movements promoting equity in land and food systems nonetheless persist. Globally, organizations like the World March for Women and La Via Campesina continue to push for change and look for opportunities to advocate for rights-based approaches to land and food governance. Despite setbacks and the increased participation of private sector actors in the CFS, it remains an important forum for debate. There are likewise genuine opportunities for social movements to shape agendas, including on matters of gender inequality.

As we have seen in this book, feminist analysis of multi-level governance is essential for understanding the multi-dimensional qualities of power relations and the intersection of political and community governance. When embedded in the broader scholarship of feminist economics and agrarian change, it allows us to understand how various forms of social discipline prevent women from achieving the "empowerment" that so many international institutions aspire to create. But feminist analysis in global governance is not useful only for understanding the obstacles to equality. Feminist analysis can also help to point to the spaces in which change might occur by understanding the ways in which power is exercised. Given the multi-level and multi-layered nature of global resource governance, there is much for us to consider as we move forward.

CONCLUSION: AN AGENDA FOR FEMINIST RESEARCH IN GLOBAL GOVERNANCE

The rise of large-scale agricultural land acquisitions over the past two decades raises many questions for those studying global governance, international political economy, global development, and agrarian change. As a result of large-scale land acquisitions, communities have lost access to traditional lands through the failure to recognize traditional practices, corruption of local officials, poor implementation and administration of existing land laws, complicated land governance structures, and so on. Within the context of increased food insecurity, displacement of human populations due to climate change, and further oil and mineral exploration across the globe, pressures on land – both commercial and non-commercial – stand to rise even further. Ecological and climatic changes will also have ripple effects on political, social, and economic structures. Some also speculate that a post-COVID resources boom may drive increased land acquisitions in the years to come (Lay et al. 2021).

Addressing land governance challenges is thus incredibly complex and requires attention to multiple levels of authority. However, any efforts to improve or reform land governance also require careful consideration of gender at all levels of authority. As this book has illustrated, gender inequality in land use, ownership, and control is a worldwide phenomenon. Although the nature of inequality varies from place to place, and even from family to family, gender inequality persists in the management and control of this key resource. Moreover, these inequalities are much more than a local issue: assumptions about gender roles and male biases are embedded in policies locally, nationally, and globally. Effective policy and political responses to large-scale land acquisitions – and to land issues more broadly – must consider the importance of gendered inequalities.

It is to the credit of several global institutions that they organized to address the fundamental challenges of the land rush that accompanied the 2007–08 food price crisis and the issues that continued in its wake. These efforts included voluntary guidelines on land tenure and principles for responsible agricultural investment that sought to guide a fairer path to land deals. Trying to balance the political and economic inequalities between rural peoples, small-scale farmers, fisherfolk, and landless peasants and the investors seeking arable land is a worthwhile goal. Yet, as this book has laid out, these efforts have not fully incorporated considerations of gender inequalities while understanding the various dimensions of land governance.

If such efforts are to address the systemic gender inequality in land governance, they must have a more complete view of what gender inequality looks like, how it is reproduced, and why it matters to the governance of land and other resources. This book has demonstrated the importance of policy design that approaches gender not as an individual identity characteristic, but as a set of social relations. Doing so highlights the ways in which assumptions about gender roles shape governance across multiple levels of policy-making. This is important for global-level governance institutions broadly, but in the case of land, it is vital for understanding the power dynamics around the possession, use, control, and decision-making over land.

It is critical that global land policy-makers incorporate more detailed and thorough consideration of gender relations when advancing new recommendations for land governance and dealing with large-scale land acquisitions. Below, this chapter briefly summarizes the book and its contributions, before laying out some new research questions that may help to guide research on gender and global land and resource policies going forward.

Summary of Book

This book begins with an appreciation for the broader sub-fields of research on gender inequality and land. Although sometimes overlooked in research on land governance, feminist scholars of various stripes and epistemological commitments – including feminist economists, geographers, political ecologists, political scientists, political economists, and so on – have built a body of scholarship that illustrates the gender differences in how land is used and the gender inequalities in how land is owned, managed, and governed. These scholars likewise show us how increased economic pressures on land risk reducing the ability of rural women to support their families and themselves (Daley and Pallas 2013). That rural women are often excluded from local, national, and global discussions of how land transactions may affect their communities needs to become part of our understanding of global land governance.

To understand these layers of exclusion, I advance an analytical framework for gender and land governance (see chapter 1). Fundamental to this multi-level analytical framework is the understanding that the governance of polities intersects with the governance of communities (Rai 2010). As Rai explains, it is insufficient to focus only on the governance of polities, that is, the more formal or conventional forms of institutional governance. Though it is important to understand the rules of international organizations, states, sub-state authorities, and communities, we also need to understand how communities are disciplined and governed by other means. We need to understand the informal rules that govern who is permitted to speak, participate, or otherwise hold or exercise power. This includes gendered hierarchies and relationships, but also exclusionary racist and homophobic language and acts of violence. I would also extend these languages of exclusion to include transphobic language and the exclusion of those who do not fit a gender binary. Such exclusion further reifies divisions based on sex and gender. Thus, social dynamics and languages of discipline govern communities by dictating who the rightful participants are in the exercise of power. These dynamics create gendered and racialized structures that intersect with political governance to create gender-differentiated outcomes.

This framework allows us to conceptualize the multiple levels of governance activity and highlights the ways in which the governance of polities and communities intersect at each level. When conceptualized this way, we see how gender relations and expectations of behaviour inform governance. The framework is employed to examine the multiple levels of governance across several African countries, with an in-depth examination of Tanzania, as Tanzania serves as a particularly useful "most-likely" case to evaluate gender equality under pluralist land reform policy. Many of its land reforms were widely praised and enacted prior to the recent land rush, in which Tanzania was a high-profile target for international investment. However, examining this case illustrates the challenges of grappling with legal pluralism in land governance while also promoting gender equality and promoting agricultural investment.

These cases offer important insights into the multiple levels of land governance within states. Assessments of national-level land laws and constitutional rules are essential to understanding specific legal dynamics around land ownership and transfer. Although there are few states that currently completely prohibit women's property ownership under the law, many states continue to have laws that restrict women's ability to access resources and credit and purchase or sell land (World Bank 2018). Understanding the broader legal context rather than just the presence or absence of legal rights to land is also important. As we see through several examples, the realization of land rights may also depend on the broader legal structure of land control, laws on marital property and divorce, inheritance laws, gender-discrimination laws, and systems of adjudication, including courts and local administration. The wider complex of legislation illustrates the ways in which male bias or gender-neutral approaches to policy-making may reinforce existing gender assumptions or fail to challenge the status quo of gender discrimination.

These gendered norms also shape the ways in which policies are implemented – or not. Even where there may be national-level commitment to gender equality in land rights, the complicated nature of land registration requires mid-level authorities and staff to be well-trained. Failure to effectively train staff who are responsible for land registration has resulted in the failure to use gender-equitable practices, even when those practices were preferred by authorities (Pedersen and Haule 2013). At this level of policy implementation within states, the failure of governments to provide adequate funding and time, combined with the gender biases held by front-line staff, result in the failure to advance gender equity in land governance.

National-level policy also needs to be understood within the context of local land dynamics, including subnational authorities, communities, and families. The specifics of traditional customs, religious values, marital patterns, and gender norms and expectations all shape the specific nature of land governance. As we see in chapters 2 and 3, these dynamics vary between communities based on various characteristics, such as ethnic identity, religion, clan, etc. Land governance is shaped by gendered power relations and can predict some of the contours of those power relations, but the specific manifestations of land governance are always context specific. For example, inheritance practices are often gender-specific, but these practices may be patriarchal or matriarchal depending on the region, ethnicity, and/or religious affiliations of the family or community. Moreover, age or order of birth may also intersect with gender to influence the inheritance of land and resources, demonstrating the need to consider such practices. The diversity of practices around land ownership illustrates the importance of an intersectional understanding of land governance. Paying attention to these details is crucial for understanding how marital relationships and residence practices, patrilineal and matrilineal inheritance practices, the role of religious beliefs, and the customary administration of decision-making and local politics can all influence the control of land.

Using this understanding of the role of gender relations in shaping land governance, I analyze three global guidelines for responsible agricultural investment and land tenure guidelines. Chapter 4 explores how efforts to discipline agricultural investment through the development of responsible agricultural investment principles tend not to approach the question of gender equality through an understanding of various levels of analysis or the nature of gendered structures of power. Instead, these efforts often focus on the vaguely defined notion of women's "empowerment." In doing so, these efforts to govern investment overlook the complex dynamics of land politics and governance, and instead focus on what can be done to make agricultural land markets and production more inclusive of historically marginalized people. As a result, such efforts are often widely criticized by civil society movements advocating for broader recognition of structural inequalities, as well as protection for traditional modes of land governance. Debates about the relationship between gender inequality and customary practices are not new, and yet agricultural investment principles often overlook the social norms and forms of community discipline that shape local politics, governance, and patterns of land ownership, including the gendered power relations therein.

On the other hand, some initiatives have recognized the importance of traditional modes of governance. As discussed in chapter 5, the Committee for World Food Security made critical strides in this direction, with early initiatives recognizing the complex nature of gender and land issues, as well as the positions of various marginalized groups the world over. Efforts to promote the recognition of traditional, customary, and Indigenous modes of land governance mark an important shift away from the presumption that only liberalized land markets and individual land ownership can protect rural populations from land dispossession. Yet the question of customary authorities and practices looms large in discussions of gender and land rights. Given the widespread reliance on customary authorities and the tendency for global governance mechanisms to recommend both devolution of authority and the use of customary governance of land and local politics, more must be done to consider the relationship between customary authorities and gender inequality.

Understanding these power relations and their influence within land governance, land deals, and the design and delivery of land reform is no easy task. While the first five chapters assess the extent to which global governance initiatives considered these challenges, we must also be aware of the challenges of implementation. Even if global guidelines were improved, there are clear obstacles to the effective implementation of voluntary initiatives like these. Chapter 6 considers whether these initiatives are worthwhile within this context. Given the importance of voluntary guidelines as tools for civil society organizations and social movements, as well as the importance of forums like the CFS as a space to re-politicize questions of gender inequality, the chapter concludes that these global initiatives are worth pursuing.

Why Do We Need a Feminist Analytical Framework for Global Governance?

As we have seen throughout this book, changing the formal rules of land governance is only one piece of the puzzle. We need to have a clearer sense of the gender dynamics that create and reinforce gender inequalities and shape policy-making and implementation. Technocratic changes alone do not address the pervasiveness of gendered attitudes and the social structures within which we live. What has often been missing in the study and practice of global governance is an appreciation of the deep-rooted social structures that maintain the status quo of gender inequality. These structures prevent the full participation of women in markets, politics, and society more broadly.

We can see these realities when we look at the global, domestic, and local changes to land governance highlighted in this book. Despite efforts to address gender inequality through the establishment of rules and laws at all these levels, the failure to acknowledge or address broader societal opposition to gender equity means that little change occurs. Global efforts to encourage women's participation in agricultural land markets fail to address other systemic issues such as lack of access to credit or gender discrimination in hiring. National land reforms might nominally give women equal rights to land, but the failure to train or fund the implementation of laws means that the status quo remains. Even local community efforts to include more women in decision-making over land often don't consider the very real barriers to women's equal participation. In addition, family practices of inheritance and marriage often reinforce patriarchal traditions, which can leave women without secure access to land or resources in the event of divorce, separation, or widowhood. However, if a more complete understanding of gendered power relations can be incorporated into both the study and practice of global governance, there may be opportunities for activism and policy change.

This book has shown how a comprehensive feminist approach to global land governance must include an appreciation of how both political governance and community governance intersect across various levels of authority. As the early chapters of the book revealed, understanding land governance as at one and the same time the function of political and community rules presents a richer picture of inequalities in land governance. Yet we also need to consider these intersections across multiple levels of political activity. National laws and public discourses are rooted in local histories, politics, and community practices that are difficult to disentangle. Longer-term projects that aim to achieve gender equality need to be aware of both the formal and informal rules that exist.

However, these lessons apply beyond the politics of land. Gendered power relations are pervasive in the ways in which governments, economies, and communities operate, and fuller understanding of these relations requires an appreciation of the inequalities manifested not only in governance in a formal sense, but in markets, communities, and families as well. The languages and behaviours that discipline gendered expectations and roles need to be investigated everywhere, not least within the halls of policy-making institutions. In this way, this book, alongside other critical feminist global governance analyses (Griffin 2009; Bedford 2008), reminds those studying and practising global policy development that we must continue to critique the "add women and stir" approach. Both scholars of global policy and global policymakers themselves must do more to recognize that gender is more than just a matter of adding another variable or another clause to existing frameworks.

Attention to gendered power relations in both the study of resource governance and in the governance mechanisms designed to address such issues are lacking in the scholarship on international relations. As we have seen throughout this book, agricultural land deals can have a range of gendered impacts, including the potential to disrupt sociopolitical organization associated with land access and land use (Behrman, Meinzen-Dick, and Quisumbing 2012). Scholarship is beginning to address these dynamics in the context of land deals (Behrman, Meinzen-Dick, and Quisumbing 2012; Chu 2011; Daley and Pallas 2014; Ossome 2014; Ryan 2018), though little has been incorporated into the analytical frameworks of international relations, international political economy, global governance scholarship, and other fields concerned with global policy development. There is much work to be done, and this analytical framework is one tool we can use to continue this work.

Applying a Feminist Analytical Framework for Global Governance

The framework developed and used in this book is one tool with which we can understand the power dynamics at multiple levels of political activity and how formal and informal rules intersect to create gender-differentiated outcomes. This approach reveals the need to consider community practices as well as laws understanding the obstacles to designing and enacting gender-equitable policy. By looking at both the political and community-based forms of governance at various levels, we not only see challenges, but also opportunities for dialogue, contestation, and spaces in which to build alliances and partnerships. It also shows that we need to be aware of the broader political and economic realities that are also barriers to change. Below, I map out some potential ways in which this framework might be further applied in the global politics of land, food, and agriculture.

Institutional Reforms

Despite some progressive and inclusive modes of global governance, state interests and the realities of the global economy of food and agriculture mean that meaningful changes to patterns of land governance are likely to be slow. As we saw in the previous chapter, we must balance optimism about the nature of voluntary governance with the realities of state interest in foreign investment. Low-income and rapidly industrializing state governments continue to actively participate in the negotiation of land deals and establish new mechanisms for foreign investment in land and other resources. The speed at which these new strategies for agricultural development are designed and implemented often exceed the pace at which societal shifts in gender relations around land governance occur. Moreover, in many parts of the world, the capacity for and interest in implementing gender-equitable land reform is still lacking. The steps taken by the FAO and other organizations are important starting points in increasing this capacity and shifting how land reforms occur. The extent to which states, social movements, and intergovernmental organizations support these efforts over the long-term will be essential for effective change.

Domestic Politics and Economic Reforms

States are the key actors in the enactment and enforcement of land reforms, as well as in the administration of agricultural trade and investment policies. Though this book has highlighted the differentiated gender outcomes of land deals as well as land governance policies, there are broader issues to be considered as well. As state governments pursue agricultural investment and boost development via shifts to export-led agriculture and the development of other natural resources, the gendered effects of these shifts need to be addressed. Agrarian policies and agricultural development plans have gendered effects, even though policy-makers and scholars might consider them to be gender neutral (Tsikata 2016). Moreover, there is an additional need to study how reforms to seed laws and the rules governing agricultural inputs like herbicides and pesticides have gender-differentiated impacts as well (Shiva 2016). These are essential dynamics to consider as governments pursue food security through various means.

In addition to understanding the various assumptions that underpin the design of policy reforms, we also need to pay careful attention to the attitudes and beliefs of those undertaking the implementation of reforms. As we have seen in the Tanzanian case outlined in chapter 3, although laws may be well designed to balance both local traditions and gender equality, whether those rules are effectively enforced and/or correspond to local practices must be considered as well. When those rules are being enacted, however, there is some early evidence to suggest that Tanzania's land reforms might have some positive – but slow – effects on customary governance (Pedersen 2015). Thus, there are key questions to be asked: What reforms have been proposed or undertaken? Who supports these reforms? What assumptions do reformers make about landholders, markets, and investment? What resources have been allocated to implement and enforce reforms? What is the broader economic and trade policy context and how does it align with reforms of resource governance?

Communities and Families

Understanding that social practices shape land and resource governance in practice provides a greater understanding of the limits of reforms designed to address inequality. Over the past twenty years, global institutions and land governance initiatives have come to embrace community-level governance as both potentially more democratic but also more economically and politically efficient (Deininger and Binswanger 1999). However, proponents of community-based governance sometimes also make unjustified assumptions about a certain level of homogeneity and harmony within communities. Extensive anthropological scholarship on the politics of land and resource conflicts in

Africa has shown that communities are not necessarily harmonious, peaceful, or fully participatory (Khadiagala 2001; Peters 2009; Sikor and Muller 2009). Community-based governance is often structured by histories of clan- and family-based relationships, political alliances and affiliations, age- and gender-based discrimination, and so on, and not by inherently equitable practices.

Land governance is profoundly shaped by community-based land governance practices. While efforts to recognize traditional governance practices are important for protecting Indigenous knowledge and communities, we must also examine these practices for the ways in which they might restrict the participation of some people. This point has often been made by feminist scholars who have warned about some of the risks of relying on traditional practices. However, we must also not dismiss community- and family-based governance as inherently discriminatory. Rather, traditional practices – particularly those that are rooted in flexible customary practices – might be amenable to gender-equitable changes. Analyzing community- and family-based governance practices means looking at where power lies. Who are the decision-makers? What power do they have? How have traditional practices shifted over time? Which rules are flexible or already in a state of flux? What opportunities are there for women or other marginalized groups to advocate for change or resist community- or family-based expectations?

New Questions for Future Research

Taking a multi-level feminist approach to questions of governance has the potential to open up many new lines of inquiry into various aspects of resource governance. Beyond the above questions, however, there are also some areas that require more attention and research. First, as detailed in the previous chapter, there is still a knowledge gap about the impacts and effectiveness of the VGGT. As there are more instances of the VGGT being put into practice, there are more opportunities to evaluate these ideas on the ground. Moreover, for practitioners, there are opportunities to employ tools like the FAO technical guide *Governing Land for Women and Men*.

Second, we need a better understanding of the role of national and sub-national elites in shaping land policy and practice. Legal gaps matter for the realization of equal rights to land, as do broader national narratives about women's roles in society. National-level discourses can reveal elite attitudes toward the extension of rights to women and their participation in decision-making, which may give some idea of the level of national support for the realization of equal access to land in practice. Many powerful figures also continue to hold openly or implicitly hostile views toward gender equality at the global level. A state-level focus that pays attention to the legal frameworks as well as social attitudes about gender and the ways in which both manifest in legislation and other policies is thus vital. Looking at both legal rules and gender norms can help determine whether states are amenable to gender-equity reforms, and the extent to which they are likely to commit resources for their effective implementation in the years to come. There needs to be an understanding of how the rules do or do not align with the values of the political elite.

At the same time, understanding more about the differences in local governance practices and the conditions under which gender equity is embraced or resisted is also needed. Local power relations are also critically important: local authorities – customary and/or governmental – may act in ways that shore up their own wealth or influence at the expense of community members, and this can also have gendered effects (Chung 2021; Mbilinyi 2016). More understanding of the role of elites at various levels of authority would be a worthwhile goal for future research.

Finally, continued collection of data and analysis of large-scale land deals is needed. One of the long-standing issues in the study of land deals has been concerns about the quality of data. While estimates of the number of land deals appear to have levelled off, there are still hundreds of thousands of hectares of arable land slated for development. Tracking and calculating the data around these deals is still useful to understanding investment flows and the impacts of agricultural and mining projects.

However, we must also bring a feminist political analysis to these deals. Who participates, who decides who is compensated, and who is affected? Much existing research on large-scale land acquisitions reveals that gendered power dynamics that shape the governance of land likewise shape how land deals occur. Systematic inequality in terms of political status, land ownership, and educational attainment lead to the exclusion of women and other marginalized groups from forums that may be able to influence the land acquisition process (Behrman, Meinzen-Dick, and Quisumbing 2012; Daley and Pallas 2013). Thus, understanding the process of land grabs and the potential gender implications therein requires an assessment of broader social contexts, and the various modes of governance at work.

Conclusion

The feminist analytical framework developed in this book and the questions above help to create new paths of feminist inquiry in the governance of land and resources. This analysis illustrates the importance of introducing a more specific understanding of gender relations and power dynamics into the creation of global policy. While all contexts will have unique local dynamics, a more meaningful understanding of gender relations requires attention to the social expectations that govern family relations, community practice, and legal statutes. Understanding the interplay of these modes of governance, as well as the role of community-based expectations around gendered behaviours at all these levels, can lead to better policy design, as well as new focal points for activist work. This type of analysis also helps to anticipate points of resistance and to identify new opportunities for change.

However, this work will not be easy, and there are many reasons to be skeptical. A number of policy-makers continue to view economic development and trade policies as gender neutral or gender equal in their impact. More questions need to be raised about the roles of UN agencies, the World Bank, the G7, multinational corporations, international investors, and their relationships with states that seek economic growth and industrialization, including the potential impact on marginalized populations.

Although this work is difficult, it is already being done. Activist groups and civil society organizations have been instrumental in advocating for the VGGT. Civil society organizations were instrumental in shaping the document itself, mainstreaming rights-based visions of food security and gender equality within the context of the reformed CFS. They have also been pivotal actors in pushing for more attention to gender inequality in the governance of land and food.

It is thus critical that we keep using feminist tools to understand and reshape the nature of global politics. This book has illustrated that we can use a feminist framework to better understand the multi-level governance of land, particularly how various forms of power and influence intersect. This book has emphasized the need to understand the role of gendered power relations in the structuring of land governance. It is now time to expand this analysis to consider the broader dynamics of the global economy, and how the processes that scholars are trained to view as global are rooted in the power hierarchies so frequently considered to be local. This understanding can help us to assess global and national policies designed to address land and resource governance and highlight where future efforts can improve on those of the past.

NOTES

Chapter One

1 For the purposes of this book, I will use the terms large-scale land acquisition or large-scale land deals interchangeably. The term "land grab" will largely be used when describing how activists, social movements, or affected peoples use this term.

2 The United Nations defines the least developed countries as having "low levels of income and [facing] severe structural impediments to sustainable development" (United Nations Department of Economic and Social Affairs, 2021).

3 Chimhowu and Woodhouse use the term vernacular land markets to refer to "commoditized transfers of land within the framework of customary tenure" (2006, 348), pointing to how land is transferred between individuals under customary systems without the aid of titles.

4 The Rome-based agencies include the Food and Agriculture Organization of the United Nations (FAO), the International Fund for Agricultural Development (IFAD), and the World Food Programme (WFP).

Chapter Two

1 The global-level institutions are addressed in chapters 4 and 5.

2 Although there is much that could be learned through a systematic comparative analysis as conducted by scholars like Agarwal (1994), here the general intent is to create a sense of how various forms of governance intersect to create unique local contexts. Thus, while the work of scholars that do comparative analysis is useful here, the overall objective is to illustrate the complexity of gender and land issues in order to better assess the global land governance instruments in later chapters.

3 Though customary tenure might be construed or misunderstood as traditional or even pre-colonial, the establishment of customary modes of land governance as distinct from statutory titling throughout much of the African continent need to be understood

within the context of colonial history. What is currently understood as customary law or tenure is often the product of colonial interpretations of local rituals. The establishment of these customary authorities often served to create political alliances between colonial administrators and local elites (Migot-Adholla and Bruce 1994). As Peters explains, "[w]here the colonial rulers could not identify an appropriate 'chief,' they created one" (2004, 272). Consequently, the creation of political units with defined territorial boundaries served particular interests and entrenched particular authorities (Migot-Adholla and Bruce 1994). As such, "tribes," "clans," "chieftaincies," or ethnic groups identified during the colonial era need to be understood as the product of interactions between colonial powers and Indigenous communities. Through the reification of particular authorities and the establishment of territorial boundaries, they retain importance insofar as groups continue to self-identify as various cultural communities with distinct customary practices (Odgaard 2002; Mbilinyi 2003). While there are debates about the extent to which customary authorities were "created" by colonial powers, there is little doubt that the interaction of Indigenous and colonial powers worked to entrench political authorities and social practices in specific ways (Spear 2003).

Chapter Three

1 The Land Act and Village Land Act are commonly referred to as the 1999 Land Acts. I will also refer to the Land Acts together hereafter, except where specific discussion of clauses of a single act are necessary for the discussion.

2 Interview with NGO Executive Director, Dar es Salaam, 17 June 2013.

3 Interview with INGO Land Rights Advisor, Dar es Salaam, 20 June 2013.

4 Chung (2021) has indicated the ways in which local inequalities and elite capture may have shaped this resistance, to the exclusion of non-elite members of the community.

5 In April 2022, the International Centre for Settlement of Investment Disputes (ICSID) decided in favour of Agro EcoEnergy, requiring the Government of Tanzania to pay them $165 million (USD). Although the Government of Tanzania appealed for a stay of execution of the penalty, Agro EcoEnergy has filed counter-arguments to this claim. The conflict made headlines again in late 2022 when an Air Tanzania A220-300 jet was seized in the Netherlands in relation to the case and released back to Tanzania in 2023 (Mushi 2023).

6 Interview with INGO Gender Officer, Dar es Salaam, 25 June 2013.

7 Of note, discrimination against Maasai peoples is particularly pronounced, which was not only articulated by interviewees, but witnessed in

day-to-day interactions in Tanzania. Maasai and other pastoralist communities are particularly vulnerable as Tanzania shifts toward systematizing land ownership, either through title or customary modes of ownership, and where the government plans to make more land available for foreign investment, mining, or tourism (Cotula 2012; Gardner 2012).

8 In an effort to reorganize the peasant population of Tanzania, Nyerere proposed a process of voluntary relocation to rural villages in order to streamline service delivery. The villages were seen as essential for revolutionizing Tanzania's agricultural production and improving rural livelihoods. In 1973, pressed by members of his political party, the Tanzania African National Union (TANU), to accelerate resettlement, Nyerere began a program of forced resettlement into planned villages (Saul 2012; Scott 1998; Shivji 2012). Scott (1998) groups the Tanzanian villagization scheme alongside brutal socialist relocation schemes that envisioned particular modernist modes of production and development. Indeed, few scholars dispute the negative effects villagization had on rural Tanzanians who were forced to relocate. Both cultivators and pastoralists had developed customs, practices, and patterns of settlement, which were adapted to their environment and were threatened by forced resettlement (Scott 1998; Gastorn 2008). The failure to consider modes of livelihood and environmental impacts resulted in the concentration of human populations and livestock in smaller land units and created resource competition, landlessness, and land degradation (Gastorn 2008).

9 Interview with official in the Ministry of Lands, Housing and Human Settlements Development, Dar es Salaam, 9 July 2013.

10 In addition to the Village Council and Village Assembly, there is also the Welfare and Social Services Committee; the quasi-judicial Land Adjudication Committee; the Land Use Management Committee, which also collaborates with the District Land Use and Management Committee; and the Village Land Council, which manages disputes and conflict resolution.

11 Interview with Research Lead, Legal Aid NGO, Dar es Salaam, 5 June 2013.

12 There are no gender-equality provisions in place for the position of Village Chairperson, but given the authority these leaders wield, it is important to note that women are marginalized from this position as well.

13 Nine different interviewees cited the lack of capacity building for women in public forums as critical issues. At least two INGOs had programming dedicated to improving women's capacity in local decision-making, and many NGOs have advocacy and public-education programs to address the issue.

14 Interview with INGO Program Director, Dar es Salaam, 13 June 2013.

15 Ibid.

16 Interview with NGO Executive Director, Dar es Salaam, 17 June 2013.

17 Inheritance rules in Tanzania are governed by three groups of rules: statutory, customary, and Islamic rules. Though the discussion here focuses largely on customary law in mainland Tanzania, Islamic practices feature predominantly in the coastal regions on the mainland and in Zanzibar. For the purposes of this book, it is worth noting that Islamic rules of inheritance typically disadvantage women as well, granting women smaller shares than male relatives and requiring women to turn over the care of land when marrying a man outside the village (Hilhorst 2000). Similar to patrilineal and patrilocal customary laws throughout the rest of the mainland, there is evidence of family members navigating and negotiating Islamic rules to extend inheritance rights to women. Such practices are not widespread, however, and for the most part Islamic rules that protect village land similarly limit women's land ownership. Though Islamic and customary practices are distinct, most interviewees and organizations were engaged with non-Islamic forms of governance on the mainland, and that is reflected in the discussions here. In the course of research there was no indication that Islamic law for land governance was perceived to be any more detrimental for women's rights than customary practices, and they are treated the same under Tanzanian law.

18 Customary law as described in the Village Land Act is defined by reference to The Interpretation of Laws and General Clauses Act, 1972: "'customary law' means any rule or body of rules whereby rights and duties are acquired or imposed, established by usage in any Tanganyika African Community and accepted by such community in general as having the force of law, including any declaration or modification of customary law made or deemed to have been made under section 9A of the Judicature and Application of Laws Ordinance, 1961 and references to 'native law' or to 'native law and custom' shall be similarly construed" (United Republic of Tanzania 1972, sec. 3).

19 Interview with Agricultural Economist, Morogoro, 28 June 2013.

20 Indeed, such instances of property grabbing from widows has also been studied in Uganda, Kenya, Zambia, and elsewhere in Southern and Eastern Africa (Izumi 2007).

21 Interview with INGO Program Director, Dar es Salaam, 13 June 2013.

Chapter Four

1 Acknowledgment: This chapter is derived from an article published in *International Feminist Journal of Politics* 18, no. 4 (2016): 559–73. Copyright Taylor and Francis, available online: https://www.tandfonline.com/doi/full/10.1080/14616742.2016.1191791 DOI: 10.1080/14616742.2016.1191791

2 In an effort to avoid confusion while still reflecting common acronym usage by policy-makers and scholars, the CFS Principles for Responsible Agricultural Investment (Rai) will be referred to as the Rai Principles, and the World Bank–led set of principles will continued to be referred to as the PRAI.

3 The PRAI and its synoptic note are both analyzed to give a more complete understanding of the justifications for each of the PRAI.

Chapter Five

1 For a detailed discussion of the politics of the reformed CFS and the emergence of the VGGT, see McKeon (2013).

2 The VGGT are also careful to delineate between customary forms of tenure and "informal" tenure, in order to capture informal tenure that might not be rooted in customary practices, and gives specific mention to informal tenure that might arise, for instance, where large-scale migration occurs (FAO 2012, sec.10.1). The responsibilities of states and communities are similar to those under customary tenure, requiring gender sensitivity and promoting legal recognition for informal tenure.

REFERENCES

Ackah-Baidoo, Patricia, Andrea M. Collins, and J. Andrew Grant. 2022. "Gender, Land Grabbing and Glocal Land Governance in Ghana and Uganda." In *Natural Resource-Based Development in Africa: Panacea or Pandora's Box*, edited by Nathan Andrews, J. Andrew Grant, and Jesse Salah Ovadia, 101–22. Toronto: University of Toronto Press.

ActionAid. 2010. *Implications of Biofuels Production on Food Security in Tanzania*. Dar es Salaam: Action Aid Tanzania.

Agarwal, Bina. 1994. *A Field of One's Own: Gender and Land Rights in South Asia*. New York: University of Cambridge Press.

– 2003. "Gender and Land Rights Revisited: Exploring New Prospects via the State, Family, and Market." *Journal of Agrarian Change* 3, no. 1–2: 184–224.

– 2018. "Gender Equality, Food Security, and the Sustainable Development Goals." *Current Opinion in Environmental Sustainability*. Special Issue, *Sustainability Science* 34: 26–32.

Alden Wily, Liz. 2011. "'The Law Is to Blame': The Vulnerable Status of Common Property Rights in Sub-Saharan Africa." *Development and Change* 42, no. 3: 733–57.

– 2014. "The Law and Land Grabbing: Friend or Foe?" *Law and Development Review* 7, no. 2: 207–42.

– 2021. "Transforming Legal Status of Customary Land Rights: What This Means for Women and Men in Rural Africa." In *Land Governance and Gender: The Tenure-Gender Nexus in Land Management and Land Policy*, edited by Uchendu Eugene Chigbu, 169–81. Oxfordshire, UK, and Boston, MA: CABI.

Amanor, Kojo Sebastian. 2010. "Family Values, Land Sales, and Agricultural Commodification in South-Eastern Ghana." *Africa* 80, no. 1: 104–25.

Andersson Djurfeldt, Agnes. 2020. "Gendered Land Rights, Legal Reform, and Social Norms in the Context of Land Fragmentation: A Review of the Literature for Kenya, Rwanda, and Uganda." *Land Use Policy* 90, no. 1: 104305.

Anseeuw, Ward, Liz Alden Wily, Lorenzo Cotula, and Michael Taylor. 2012. *Land Rights and the Rush for Land: Findings of the Global*

Commercial Pressures on Land Research Project. Rome: International Land Coalition.

Archambault, Caroline S. 2015. "Gendered Perspectives on Rangeland Privatization among the Maasai of Southern Kenya." In *Global Trends in Land Tenure Reform: Gender Impacts*, edited by Caroline S. Archambault and Annelies Zoomers, 201–16. Routledge Studies in Gender and Development. New York: Routledge.

Arial, Anni, David Palmer, Margret Vidar, Juan Carlos Garcia Cebolla, Francesca Romano, and Leila Shamsaifar. 2012. "Governance of Tenure: Making It Happen." *Land Tenure Journal* 1: 63–76.

Associated Press. 2012. "ISU Pulls Out as Adviser of Ag Project in Tanzania." 11 February 2012.

Badiane, O., J. Collins, B. Dimaranan, and J. Ulimwengu. 2018. "An Assessment of the New Alliance for Food Security and Nutrition: Synthesis Report." Addis Ababa: African Union Commission. https://au.int/sites/default/files/documents/34472-doc-nafsn20full20report20with20annexes.pdf.

Baha, Bernard. 2011. *The Politics of Investment in Large Scale Agricultural Ventures: Case of Mpanda Rukwa, Tanzania*. Dar es Salaam: Haki Ardhi.

Barrientos, Stephanie. 1997. "The Hidden Ingredient: Female Labour in Chilean Fruit Exports." *Bulletin of Latin American Research* 16, no. 1: 71–81.

BBC News. 2018. "Tanzania's President Magufuli Calls for End to Birth Control." 10 September 2018. https://www.bbc.com/news/world-africa-45474408.

Bedford, Kate. 2007. "The Imperative of Male Inclusion: How Institutional Context Influences World Bank Gender Policy." *International Feminist Journal of Politics* 9, no. 3: 289–311.

– 2008. "Governing Intimacy at the World Bank." In *Global Governance: Feminist Perspectives*, edited by Shirin M. Rai, and Georgina Waylen, 84–106. New York: Palgrave Macmillan.

– 2009. *Developing Partnerships: Gender, Sexuality, and the Reformed World Bank*. Minneapolis: University of Minnesota Press.

Behrman, Julia, Ruth Meinzen-Dick, and Agnes Quisumbing. 2012. "The Gender Implications of Large-Scale Land Deals." *Journal of Peasant Studies* 39, no. 1: 49–79.

Bélair, Joanny. 2018. "Land Investments in Tanzania: Assessing the Role of State Brokers." *Journal of Modern African Studies* 56, no. 3: 371–94.

Beneria, Lourdes. 2007. "Gender and the Social Construction of Markets." In *The Feminist Economics of Trade*, edited by Irene van Staveren, Diane Elson, Caren Grown, and Nilufer Cagatay, 13–32. New York: Routledge.

Bergeron, Suzanne. 2003. "The Post-Washington Consensus and Economic Representations of Women in Development at the World Bank." *International Feminist Journal of Politics* 5, no. 3: 397–419.

– 2011. "Economics, Performativity, and Social Reproduction in Global Development." *Globalizations* 8, no. 2: 151–61.

Bergius, Mikael, Tor A. Benjaminsen, and Mats Widgren. 2018. "Green Economy, Scandinavian Investments, and Agricultural Modernization in Tanzania." *Journal of Peasant Studies* 45, no. 4: 825–52.

Berry, Sara. 2021. "Governing African Land in an Era of Instability." In *Land Governance and Gender: The Tenure-Gender Nexus in Land Management and Land Policy*, edited by Uchendu Eugene Chigbu, 51–62. Oxfordshire, UK, and Boston, MA: CABI.

Bexell, Magdalena, Jonas Tallberg, and Anders Uhlin. 2010. "Democracy in Global Governance: The Promises and Pitfalls of Transnational Actors." *Global Governance: A Review of Multilateralism and International Organizations* 16, no. 1: 81–101.

Beyene, Atakilte, Claude Gasper Mung'ong'o, Aaron Atteridge, and Rasmus Klocker Larsen. 2013. *Biofuel Production and Its Impacts on Local Livelihoods in Tanzania: A Mapping of Stakeholder Concerns and Some Implications for Governance.* Stockholm: Stockholm Environment Institute.

Biddulph, Robin, and Ellen Hillbom. 2020. "Registration of Private Interests in Land in a Community Lands Policy Setting: An Exploratory Study in Meru District, Tanzania." *Land Use Policy* 99 (December): 104830.

Boone, Catherine. 2014. *Property and Political Order in Africa: Land Rights and the Structure of Politics.* New York: Cambridge University Press.

Boserup, Esther. 1970. *Women's Role in Economic Development.* Chicago: George Allen and Unwin.

Brem-Wilson, Josh. 2015. "Towards Food Sovereignty: Interrogating Peasant Voice in the United Nations Committee on World Food Security." *Journal of Peasant Studies* 42, no. 1: 73–95.

Brondo, Keri Vacanti. 2013. *Land Grab: Green Neoliberalism, Gender, and Garifuna Resistance in Honduras.* Tucson: University of Arizona Press.

Brown, Andrea M. 2006. "WID and GAD in Dar Es Salaam, Tanzania: Reappraising Gender Planning Approaches in Theory and Practice." *Journal of Women, Politics and Policy* 28, no. 2: 57–83.

Byamugisha, Frank F.K. 2013. *Securing Africa's Land for Shared Prosperity.* Washington, DC: World Bank.

Calaguas, Mark J., Cristina M. Drost, and Edward R. Fluet. 2007. "Legal Pluralism and Women's Rights: A Study in Postcolonial Tanzania." *Columbia Journal of Gender and Law* 16: 471–550.

Campbell, Horace, and Howard Stein. 1992. *Tanzania and the IMF: The Dynamics of Liberalization.* Boulder, CO: Westview Press.

Caron, Cynthia M. 2021. "Women's Insights on Bargaining for Land in Customary Tenure Systems: Land Access as an Individual and Collective

Issue." In *Land Governance and Gender: The Tenure-Gender Nexus in Land Management and Land Policy*, edited by Uchendu Eugene Chigbu, 80–90. Oxfordshire, UK, and Boston, MA: CABI.

Carrington, Damian. 2011. "UK Firm's Failed Biofuel Dream Wrecks Lives of Tanzania Villages." *The Guardian* (UK), 30 October 2011. https://www.theguardian.com/environment/2011/oct/30/africa-poor-west-biofuel-betrayal.

CECCAM (Centro de Estudios para el Cambio en el Campo Mexicano), FIAN International, Focus on the Global South, Friends of the Earth International, Global Campaign on Agrarian Reform, GRAIN, La Via Campesina, Land Research Action Network, Rede Social de Justiça e Direitos Humanos, World Alliance of Mobile Indigenous Peoples, and World Forum of Fisher Peoples. 2011. "It's Time to Outlaw Land Grabbing, Not to Make It 'Responsible.'" *GRAIN.org*, 17 April 2011. https://grain.org/en/article/4227-it-s-time-to-outlaw-land-grabbing-not-to-make-it-responsible.

CFS. 2014. *Principles for Responsible Investment in Agriculture and Food Systems.* Rome: CFS Secretariat. https://www.fao.org/3/au866e/au866e.pdf.

– 2017. "Background Document: CFS Forum on Women's Empowerment in the Context of Food Security and Nutrition." Rome: CFS Secretariat. https://www.fao.org/3/mu268e/mu268e.pdf.

Chan, Man-Kwun, Grace Kamugisha, Mary Kesi, and Annmarie Mavenjina. 2016. "Strengthening Women's Voices in the Context of Agricultural Investments: Lessons from Tanzania." International Institute for Environment and Development and Tanzania Women Lawyers Association. https://www.iied.org/12593iied.

Chanock, Martin. 1989. "Neither Customary nor Legal: African Customary Law in an Era of Family Law Reform." *International Journal of Law and the Family* 3: 72–88.

Chigbu, Uchendu Eugene. 2019. "Anatomy of Women's Landlessness in the Patrilineal Customary Land Tenure Systems of Sub-Saharan Africa and a Policy Pathway." *Land Use Policy* 86: 126–35.

– 2021. "Introducing Land Governance and Gender in the Context of Land Tenure." In *Land Governance and Gender: The Tenure-Gender Nexus in Land Management and Land Policy*, edited by Uchendu Eugene Chigbu, 1–12. Oxfordshire, UK, and Boston, MA: CABI.

Chimhowu, Admos. 2019. "The 'New' African Customary Land Tenure. Characteristic, Features, and Policy Implications of a New Paradigm." *Land Use Policy* 81: 897–903.

Chimhowu, Admos, and Phil Woodhouse. 2006. "Customary vs Private Property Rights? Dynamics and Trajectories of Vernacular Land Markets in Sub-Saharan Africa." *Journal of Agrarian Change* 6, no. 3: 346–71.

Christman, Chloe, and Gustavo Ferroni. 2016. "Oxfam Briefing Note: Land Rights and Soda Giants: Reviewing Coca-Cola and PepsiCo.'s Land Assessments in Brazil." *Oxfam International.* https://www.oxfam.org/en/research/land-rights-and-soda-giants.

Chu, Jessica. 2011. "Gender and 'Land Grabbing' in Sub-Saharan Africa: Women's Land Rights and Customary Land Tenure." *Development* 54, no. 1: 35–9.

Chung, Youjin Brigitte. 2017. "Engendering the New Enclosures: Development, Involuntary Resettlement and the Struggles for Social Reproduction in Coastal Tanzania." *Development and Change* 48, no. 1: 98–120. https://doi.org/10.1111/dech.12288.

Chung, Youjin B. 2021. "The Curious Case of Three Male Elders: Land Grabbing, Lawfare, and Intersectional Politics of Exclusion in Tanzania." *African Studies Review* 64, no. 3: 605–27. https://doi.org/10.1017/asr.2020.125.

The Citizen. 2013. "Villagers Cry over Land Grabbing." 13 March 2013. https://thecitizen.co.tz/magazines/-/29613-villagers-cry-over-land-grabbing..

Clapp, Jennifer. 2017. "Responsibility to the Rescue? Governing Private Financial Investment in Global Agriculture." *Agriculture and Human Values* 34, no. 1: 223–35.

– 2018. "Mega-Mergers on the Menu: Corporate Concentration and the Politics of Sustainability in the Global Food System." *Global Environmental Politics* 18, no. 2: 12–33.

Clapp, Jennifer, Andrea M. Collins, and Phoebe Stephens. 2021. "How the Legacies of the Last Global Food Crisis Sowed the Seeds for the Next One." In *Critical Perspectives in Food Studies,* edited by Mustafa Koc, Jennifer Sumner, and Anthony Winson, 271–86. Don Mills, ON: Oxford University Press.

Clapp, Jennifer, and Eric Helleiner. 2011. "Troubled Futures? The Global Food Crisis and the Politics of Agricultural Derivatives Regulation." *Review of International Political Economy* 19, no. 2: 181–207.

Clapp, Jennifer, and S. Ryan Isakson. 2018. *Speculative Harvests: Financialization, Food, and Agriculture.* Winnipeg, MB: Fernwood Publishing.

Coldham, Simon. 2000. "Land Reform and Customary Rights: The Case of Uganda." *Journal of African Law* 44, no. 1: 65–77.

Collins, Andrea M. 2014a. "Governing the Global Land Grab: What Role for Gender in the Voluntary Guidelines and the Principles for Responsible Investment?" *Globalizations* 11, no. 2: 189–203.

– 2014b. "Reconsidering Gender in the Multi-Level Governance of Land in East Africa: Governing the 'Global Land Grab'?" PhD diss., Queen's University.

– 2016. "Improving Land Tenure Security for Women: Assessing the Voluntary Guidelines' Technical Guide." In *Women in Agriculture Worldwide: Key Issues and Practical Approaches,* edited by Amber J. Fletcher and Wendee Kubik, 133–46. Oxford, UK, and New York, NY: Routledge.

– 2017. “Goal Setting and Governance: Examining the G8 New Alliance for Food Security and Nutrition with a Gender Lens.” *Global Governance: A Review of Multilateralism and International Organizations* 23, no. 3: 423–41.
– 2019. “Financialization, Resistance, and the Question of Women’s Land Rights.” *International Feminist Journal of Politics* 21, no. 3: 454–76.
– 2022. “Empowerment, Rights, and Global Food Governance: Gender in the UN Committee for World Food Security.” *Globalizations* 19, no. 2: 220–37.
Collins, Andrea M., J. Andrew Grant, and Patricia Ackah-Baidoo. 2019. “The Glocal Dynamics of Land Reform in Natural Resource Sectors: Insights from Tanzania.” *Land Use Policy* 81: 889–96.
Collins, Andrea, and Matthew I. Mitchell. 2018. “Revisiting the World Bank’s Land Law Reform Agenda in Africa: The Promise and Perils of Customary Practices.” *Journal of Agrarian Change* 18, no. 1: 112–31.
Conway, Janet M. 2018. “When Food Becomes a Feminist Issue: Popular Feminism and Subaltern Agency in the World March of Women.” *International Feminist Journal of Politics* 20, no. 2: 188–203.
Cornwall, Andrea, and Althea-Maria Rivas. 2015. “From ‘Gender Equality’ and ‘Women’s Empowerment’ to Global Justice: Reclaiming a Transformative Agenda for Gender and Development.” *Third World Quarterly* 36, no. 2: 396–415.
Cotula, Lorenzo, Sonja Vermeulen, Rebeca Leonard, and James Keeley. 2009. *Land Grab or Development Opportunity? Agricultural Investment and International Land Deals in Africa.* London and Rome: International Institute for Environment and Development, Food and Agricultural Organization of the United Nations, and the International Fund for Agricultural Development. https://www.iied. org/sites/default/files/pdfs/migrate/12561IIED.pdf.
CSIPM (Civil Society and Indigenous Peoples’ Mechanism). 2023. “The UN Committee on World Food Security Must Acknowledge the Intersectionality of Hunger, Sexual and Gender-Based Violence, and Discrimination.” *CSIPM*, 4 March 2023. https://www.csm4cfs.org/the-un-committee-on-world-food-security-must-acknowledge-the-intersectionality-of-hunger-sexual-and-gender-based-violence-and-discrimination/.
Daley, Elizabeth. 2011. *Gendered Impacts of Commercial Pressures on Land.* Rome: International Land Coalition. https://landportal.org/ru/library/resources/isbn-978-92-95093-22-5/gendered-impact-commercial-pressures-land.
Daley, Elizabeth, and Birgit Englert. 2010. “Securing Land Rights for Women.” *Journal of Eastern African Studies* 4, no. 1: 91–113.
Daley, Elizabeth, and Clara Mi-young Park. 2011. *Governing Land for Women and Men: Gender and Voluntary Guidelines on Responsible Governance of Tenure of Land and Other Natural Resources.* Rome: Food and Agriculture Organization

of the United Nations. https://www.fao.org/documents/card/fr/c/d300507a-98ec-58db-912b-298e0d43c135.

Daley, Elizabeth, and Sabine Pallas. 2014. "Women and Land Deals in Africa and Asia: Weighing the Implications and Changing the Game." *Feminist Economics* 20, no. 1: 178–201.

Dancer, Helen. 2015. *Women, Land, and Justice in Tanzania*. Eastern Africa Series. Suffolk, UK: James Currey.

– 2017. "An Equal Right to Inherit? Women's Land Rights, Customary Law, and Constitutional Reform in Tanzania." *Social and Legal Studies* 26, no. 3: 291–310. https://doi.org/10.1177/0964663916677560.

Dancer, Helen, and Emmanuel Sulle. 2015. "Gender Implications of Agricultural Commercialisation: The Case of Sugarecane Production in Kilombero District, Tanzania." *Future Agricultures Consortium Working Papers Series*, Working Paper 118, 1–36. https://www.future-agricultures.org/publications/working-papers-document/gender-implications-of-agricultural-commercialisation-the-case-of-sugarcane-production-in-kilombero-district-tanzania.

Davison, Jean. 1988a. "Land and Women's Agricultural Production: The Context." In *Agriculture, Women, and Land: The African Experience*, edited by Jean Davison, 1–32. Boulder, CO: Westview Press.

– 1988b. "Who Owns What? Land Registration and Tensions in Gender Relations of Production in Kenya." In *Agriculture, Women, and Land: The African Experience*, edited by Jean Davison, 157–76. Boulder: Westview Press.

De Schutter, Olivier. 2011. "How Not to Think of Land-Grabbing: Three Critiques of Large-Scale Investments in Farmland." *Journal of Peasant Studies* 38, no. 2: 249–79.

Deere, Carmen Diana. 2009. "The Feminization of Agriculture? The Impact of Economic Restructuring in Rural Latin America." In *The Gendered Impacts of Liberalization*, edited by Shahra Razavi, 99–127. New York: Routledge.

– 2017. "Women's Land Rights, Rural Social Movements, and the State in the 21st Century Latin American Agrarian Reforms." *Journal of Agrarian Change* 17, no. 2: 258–78.

Deere, Carmen Diana, and Magdalena León. 2001a. *Empowering Women: Land and Property Rights in Latin America*. Pittsburgh, PA: University of Pittsburgh Press.

– 2001b. "Who Owns the Land? Gender and Land-Titling Programmes in Latin America." *Journal of Agrarian Change* 1, no. 3: 440–67.

Deininger, Klaus W. 2003. *Land Policies for Growth and Poverty Reduction*. Washington, DC: A World Bank Publication.

Deininger, Klaus, Derek Byerlee, Jonathan Lindsay, Andrew Norton, Harris Selod, and Mercedes Stickler. 2011. *Rising Global Interest in Farmland: Can It Yield Sustainable and Equitable Benefits?* Washington, DC: World Bank.

Deininger, Klaus, Harris Selod, and Anthony Burns. 2012. *The Land Governance Assessment Framework: Identifying and Monitoring Good Practice in the Land Sector*. Washington, DC: The World Bank.

Dieterle, Carolin. 2023. "Variations of Customary Tenure, Chiefly Power, and Global Norms for Responsible Land Investments in Sierra Leone." *African Affairs* 122, no. 487: 245–67.

Doss, Cheryl, Chiara Kovarik, Amber Peterman, Agnes Quisumbing, and Mara van den Bold. 2015. "Gender Inequalities in Ownership and Control of Land in Africa: Myth and Reality." *Agricultural Economics* 46, no. 3: 403–34.

Duncan, Jessica. 2015. *Global Food Security Governance: Civil Society Engagement in the Reformed Committee on World Food Security*. London and New York: Routledge.

Duncan, Jessica, and Priscilla Claeys. 2018. "Politicizing Food Security Governance through Participation: Opportunities and Opposition." *Food Security* 10, no. 6: 1411–24.

Elmhirst, Rebecca. 2011. "Introducing New Feminist Political Ecologies." *Geoforum* 42, no. 2: 129–32.

Elson, Diane. 1991. "Male Bias in the Development Process: An Overview." In *Male Bias in the Development Process*, edited by Diane Elson, 1–28. Manchester: Manchester University Press.

– 1995. "Gender Awareness in Modeling Structural Adjustment." *World Development* 23, no. 11: 1851–68.

Elson, Diane, Caren Grown, and Irene van Staveren. 2007. "Introduction: Why a Feminist Economics of Trade?" In *The Feminist Economics of Trade*, edited by Irene van Staveren, Diane Elson, Caren Grown, and Nilufer Cagatay, 1–10. New York: Routledge.

Englert, Birgit. 2008. "Changing Land Rights and Gendered Discourses: Examples from the Uluguru Mountains, Tanzania." In *Women's Land Rights and Privatization in Eastern Africa*, edited by Birgit Englert and Elizabeth Daley, 83–101. Suffolk, UK: James Currey.

Ezeuduji, Ikechukwu O., Antonia T. Nzama, Nontuthuzelo N. Mbane, Nompumelelo Nzama. 2022. "Land Tenure and the Nuanced Gender Debates in Sub-Saharan Africa: Realities and Illusions." In *Land Governance and Gender: The Tenure-Gender Nexus in Land Management and Land Policy*, edited by Uchendu Eugene Chigbu, 23-4. Oxfordshire, UK, and Boston, MA: CABI.

Fairbairn, Madeleine. 2013. "Indirect Dispossession: Domestic Power Imbalances and Foreign Access to Land in Mozambique." *Development and Change* 44, no. 2: 335–56.

Falkner, Robert, Hannes Stephan, and John Vogler. 2010. "International Climate Policy after Copenhagen: Towards a 'Building Blocks' Approach." *Global Policy* 1, no. 3: 252–62.

FAO (Food and Agriculture Organization of the United Nations). 2012. *Voluntary Guidelines on the Responsible Governance of Tenure of Land, Fisheries and Forests in the Context of National Food Security.* Rome: Food and Agriculture Organization of the United Nations. https://www.fao.org/policy-support/tools-and-publications/resources-details/en/c/416990/.

– 2013. *Governing Land for Women and Men: A Technical Guide to Support the Achievement of Responsible Gender-Equitable Governance of Land Tenure.* Rome: Food and Agriculture Organization of the United Nations (FAO). https://www.fao.org/3/i3114e/i3114e.pdf.

– 2017. *Commemorating the 5th Anniversary of the Voluntary Guidelines on Tenure.* Rome. https://www.fao.org/3/i7893e/i7893e.pdf.

FAO (Food and Agriculture Organization of the United Nations), IFAD (International Fund for Agricultural Development), UNCTAD (United Nations Conference for Trade and Development), and the World Bank. 2010. *Principles for Responsible Agricultural Investment That Respects Rights, Livelihoods, and Resources.* Rome: United Nations Conference for Trade and Development. https://unctad.org/system/files/official-document/diaemisc2010d2_en.pdf.

Ferguson, James. 2013. "Declarations of Dependence: Labour, Personhood, and Welfare in Southern Africa." *Journal of the Royal Anthropological Institute* 19, no. 2: 223–42.

Franco, Jennifer, Clara Mi Young Park, and Roman Herre. 2017. "Just Standards: International Regulatory Instruments and Social Justice in Complex Resource Conflicts." *Canadian Journal of Development Studies / Revue canadienne d'études du développement* 38, no. 3: 341–59.

Franco, Jennifer, and Sofía Monsalve Suárez. 2018. "Why Wait for the State? Using the CFS Tenure Guidelines to Recalibrate Political-Legal Struggles for Democratic Land Control." *Third World Quarterly* 39, no. 7: 1386–402.

Fraser, Nancy. 2013a. "How Feminism Became Capitalism's Handmaiden – and How to Reclaim it." *The Guardian*, 14 October 2013.

– 2013b. *Fortunes of Feminism: From State-Managed Capitalism to Neoliberal Crisis.* London. Verso.

Freeman, Carla. 2001. "Is Local: Global as Feminine: Masculine? Rethinking the Gender of Globalization." *Signs* 26, no. 4: 1007–37.

Gastorn, Kennedy. 2008. *The Impact of Tanzania's New Land Laws on the Customary Land Right of Pastoralists: A Case Study of the Simanjiro and Bariadi Districts.* Zurich: LIT.

Genicot, Garance, and Maria Hernandez-de-Benito. 2022. "Women's Land Rights and Village Institutions in Tanzania." World Development 153 (May): 105811. https://doi.org/10.1016/j.worlddev.2022.105811.

George, Alexander L., and Andrew Bennett. 2005. *Case Studies and Theory Development in the Social Sciences.* Cambridge, MA: Belfer Center for Science and International Affairs.

Gmür, Désirée. 2019. "Grabbing the Female Commons: Large-Scale Land Acquisitions for Forest Plantations and Impacts on Gender Relations in Kilolo District, Iringa Region, Tanzania." In *The Commons in a Glocal World,* edited by Tobias Haller, Thomas Breu, Christian Rohr, Tine de Moor, and Heinzpeter Znoj, 301–17. London and New York: Routledge.

GRAIN. 2008. "Seized! The 2008 Land Grab for Food and Financial Security." 24 October 2008. https://grain.org/article/entries/93-seized-the-2008-landgrab-for-food-and-financial-security.

– 2012. "Responsible Farmland Investing? Current Efforts to Regulate Land Grabs Will Make Things Worse." 22 August 2012. https://grain.org/en/article/4564-responsible-farmland-investing-current-efforts-to-regulate-land-grabs-will-make-things-worse.

Griffin, Penny. 2009. *Gendering the World Bank: Neoliberalism and the Gendered Foundations of Global Governance.* New York: Palgrave Macmillan.

– 2010a. "Development Institutions and Neoliberal Globalisation." In *Gender Matters in Global Politics: A Feminist Introduction to International Relations,* edited by Laura J. Shepherd, 218–33. New York: Routledge.

– 2010b. "Gender, Governance, and the Global Political Economy." *Australian Journal of International Affairs* 64, no. 1: 86–104.

Hall, Derek. 2013. *Land.* Cambridge, UK: Polity.

Hall, Ruth. 2011. "Land Grabbing in Southern Africa: The Many Faces of the Investor Rush." *Review of African Political Economy* 38, no. 128: 193–214.

Hannay, Leslie, and Elisa Scalise. 2015. "Strengthening Women's Land Rights while Recognizing Customary Tenure in Northern Uganda." In *Global Trends in Land Tenure Reform: Gender Impacts,* edited by Caroline S. Archambault and Annelies Zoomers, 251–67. London and New York: Routledge.

Hilhorst, Thea. 2000. "Women's Land Rights: Current Developments in Sub-Saharan Africa." In *Evolving Land Rights, Policy, and Tenure in Africa,* edited by Camilla Toulmin and Julian Quan, 181–96. London: International Institute for Environment and Development.

Hoffmann, Matthew J., and Alice D. Ba. 2005. "Contending Perspectives on Global Governance." In *Contending Perspectives on Global Governance: Coherence, Contestation, and World Order,* edited by Alice D. Ba and Matthew J. Hoffmann, 249–67. New York: Routledge.

Isinika, Aida C., and Khamaldin Mutabazi. 2010. "Gender Dimensions of Land Conflicts: Examples from Njombe and Maswa Districts in Tanzania." In *Tanzania in Transition: From Nyerere to Mkapa,* edited by Kjell Havnevik and Aida C. Isinika, 131–58. Dar es Salaam: Mkuki na Nyota.

Izumi, Kaori. 2007. "Gender-Based Violence and Property Grabbing in Africa: A Denial of Women's Liberty and Security." *Gender and Development* 15, no. 1: 11–23.

Jackson, Cecile. 2003. "Gender Analysis of Land: Beyond Land Rights for Women?" *Journal of Agrarian Change* 3, no. 4: 453–80.

Jacobs, Susie. 2009. "Gender and Land Reforms: Comparative Perspectives." *Geography Compass* 3, no. 5: 1675–87.

– 2010. *Gender and Agrarian Reforms*. New York: Routledge.

Kabahinda, Jackline. 2017. "Culture and Women's Land Rights on the Ground in Uganda." *Development in Practice* 27, no. 6: 828–38.

Kabeer, Naila. 1994. *Reversed Realities: Gender Hierarchies in Development Thought*. London: Verso.

– 1999. "Resources, Agency, Achievements: Reflections on the Measurement of Women's Empowerment." *Development and Change* 30, no. 3: 435–64.

– 2005. "Gender Equality and Women's Empowerment: A Critical Analysis of the Third Millennium Development Goal." *Gender and Development* 13, no. 1: 13–24.

Kabumbuli, Robert. 2016. "Joint Ownership of Family Land in Uganda: Examining the Responses, Challenges, and Policy Opportunities." *African Sociological Review / Revue Africaine de Sociologie* 20, no. 1: 67–86.

Kamata, Ng'wanza. 2003. "People, State, and Resources." In *Activist Voices: Feminist Struggles for an Alternative World*, edited by Marjorie Mbilinyi, Mary Rusimbi, Chachage S.L. Chachage, and Demere Kitunga, 91–105. Dar es Salaam: TGNP/E&D Limited.

Keating, Christine, Claire Rasmussen, and Pooja Rishi. 2010. "The Rationality of Empowerment: Microcredit, Accumulation by Dispossession, and the Gendered Economy." *Signs* 36, 1: 153–76.

Kessy, Flora, Josaphat Kweka, Robert Makaramba, and Irenei Kiria. 2008. *Vulnerability and Property Rights of Widows and Orphans in the Era of the HIV and AIDS Pandemic: A Case Study of Muleba and Makete Districts, Tanzania*. Rome: Food and Agriculture Organization of the United Nations (FAO).

Khadiagala, Lynn. 2001. "The Failure of Popular Justice in Uganda: Local Councils and Women's Property Rights." *Development and Change* 32, no. 1: 55–76.

Khan, Fatima Noor, Andrea M. Collins, Prateep Kumar Nayak, and Derek Armitage. 2018. "Women's Perspectives of Small-Scale Fisheries and Environmental Change in Chilika Lagoon, India." *Maritime Studies* 17, no. 2: 145–54.

Kihacha. 2002. *Food Is Politics: Struggles over Food, Land, and Democracy*. Dar es Salaam: E&D Limited.

Kisambu, Nasieku. 2016. "Mainstreaming Gender in Tanzania's Local Land Governance." International Institute for Environment and Development. https://www.iied.org/12594iied.

Klopp, Jacqueline. 2000. "Pilfering the Public: The Problem of Land Grabbing in Contemporary Kenya." *Africa Today* 47, no. 1: 7–26.

Koda, Bertha. 2000. "The Gender Dimension of Land Rights: Case Study of Msindo Village, Same District." PhD diss., University of Dar es Salaam.

Krahmann, Elke. 2003. "National, Regional, and Global Governance: One Phenomenon or Many?" *Global Governance* 9, no. 3: 323–46.

La Via Campesina. 2014. "CFS in Rome: The Majority of Governments Remain Blind to the Challenges of Global Food Security." Press Release. 17 October 2014. https://viacampesina.org/en/cfs-in-rome-the-majority-of-governments-remain-blind-to-the-challenges-of-global-food-security.

Lambrecht, Isabel, Monica Schuster, Sarah Asare Samwini, and Laura Pelleriaux. 2018. "Changing Gender Roles in Agriculture? Evidence from 20 Years of Data in Ghana." *Agricultural Economics* 49, no. 6: 691–710.

Land Matrix Global Observatory. 2019. "By Target Country: Tanzania," accessed 15 August 2019. https://landmatrix.org/map.

– 2023. "By Target Country: Tanzania," accessed 4 May 2023. https://landmatrix.org/map.

Lanz, Kristina. 2022. *Large-Scale Land Acquisition in Ghana: Institutional Change, Gender, and Power.* New York: Routledge.

Lanz, Kristina, Elisabeth Prügl, and Jean-David Gerber. 2019. "The Poverty of Neoliberalized Feminism: Gender Equality in a 'Best Practice' Large-Scale Land Investment in Ghana." *Journal of Peasant Studies* 47: 1–19.

Lavers, Tom. 2012. "'Land Grab' as Development Strategy? The Political Economy of Agricultural Investment in Ethiopia." *Journal of Peasant Studies* 39, no. 1: 105–32.

Lay, Jann, Ward Anseeuw, Sandra Eckert, Insa Flachsbarth, Christoph Kubitza, Kerstin Nolte, and Markus Giger. 2021. "Taking Stock of the Global Land Rush: Few Development Benefits, Many Human and Environmental Risks. Analytical Report III." Centre for Development and Environment, University of Bern; Centre de coopération internationale en recherche agronomique pour le développement; German Institute of Global and Area Studies; University of Pretoria: Bern Open Publishing. DOI: 10.48350/156861.

Levien, Michael. 2017. "Gender and Land Dispossession: A Comparative Analysis." *Journal of Peasant Studies* 44, no. 6: 1111–34.

Li, Tania Murray. 2011. "Centering Labor in the Land Grab Debate." *Journal of Peasant Studies* 38, no. 2: 281–98.

Mackenzie, Fiona. 1990. "Gender and Land Rights in Murang'a District, Kenya." *Journal of Peasant Studies* 17, no. 4: 609–43.

– 1993. "'A Piece of Land Never Shrinks': Reconceptualizing Land Tenure in a Smallholding District, Kenya." In *Land in African Agrarian Systems*, edited by Thomas J. Bassett and Donald E. Crummey, 194–221. Madison: University of Wisconsin Press.

– 2010. "Gender, Land Tenure, and Globalisation: Exploring the Conceptual Ground." In *Land Tenure, Gender, and Globalisation: Research and Analysis from Africa, Asia, and Latin America*, edited by Dzodzi Tsikata and Pamela Golah, 35–69. Ottawa: Zubaan and the International Development Research Centre.

Makoye, Kizito. 2016. "Villagers Spared Eviction as Tanzania Halts $500 Million Energy Project to Save Wildlife" *Reuters*. 6 June 2016. https://www.reuters.com/article/us-tanzania-investment-wildlife-idUSKCN0YS20T.

Manji, Ambreena. 2003. "Remortgaging Women's Lives: The World Bank's Land Agenda in Africa." *Feminist Legal Studies* 11, no. 2: 139–62.

Marchand, Marianne. 1996. "Reconceptualising 'Gender and Development' in an Era of 'Globalisation.'" *Millennium – Journal of International Studies* 25, no. 3: 577–603.

Masson, Dominique, Anabel Paulos, and Elsa Beaulieu Bastien. 2017. "Struggling for Food Sovereignty in the World March of Women." *Journal of Peasant Studies* 44, no. 1: 56–77.

Mbilinyi, Marjorie. 1988. "Agribusiness and Women Peasants in Tanzania." *Development and Change* 19, no. 4: 549–83.

– 1991. *Big Slavery: Agribusiness and the Crisis in Women's Employment in Tanzania*. Dar es Salaam: Dar es Salaam University Press.

– 2003. "The Restructuring of Agriculture in Tanzania: Gender and Structural Adjustment." In *Against Neoliberalism: Gender, Democracy, and Development*, edited by S. L. Chachage Chachage and Marjorie Mbilinyi, 116–33. Dar-es-Salaam: E&D Limited.

– 2012. "Struggles over Land and Livelihoods in African Agriculture." *Development* 55, no. 3: 390–92.

– 2016. "Analysing the History of Agrarian Struggles in Tanzania from a Feminist Perspective." *Review of African Political Economy* 43, sup. 1: 115–29.

– 2017. "Debating Land and Agrarian Issues from a Gender Perspective." *Agrarian South: Journal of Political Economy*, 5, no. 2–3: 164–86.

Mbilinyi, Marjorie, and Gloria Shechambo. 2009. "Struggles over Land Reform in Tanzania: Experiences of Tanzania Gender Networking Programme and Feminist Activist Coalition." *Feminist Africa* 12: 95–103.

McAuslan, Patrick. 1998. "Making Law Work: Restructuring Land Relations in Africa." *Development and Change* 29, no. 3: 525–52.

– 2010. "Personal Reflections on Drafting Laws to Improve Women's Access to Land: Is There a Magic Wand?" *Journal of Eastern African Studies* 4, no. 1: 114–30.

– 2013. *Land Law Reform in Eastern Africa: Traditional or Transformative?* New York: Routledge.

McKeon, Nora. 2013. "'One Does Not Sell the Land upon Which the People Walk': Land Grabbing, Transnational Rural Social Movements, and Global Governance." *Globalizations* 10, no. 1: 105–22.

– 2015. *Food Security Governance: Empowering Communities, Regulating Corporations.* New York: Routledge.

McVeigh, Karen. 2018. World Bank Pulls $300m Tanzania Loan over Pregnant Schoolgirl Ban. *The Guardian*, 15 November.

Meyer, Mary K., and Elisabeth Prügl. 1999. *Gender Politics in Global Governance.* Lanham, MD: Rowman and Littlefield.

Migdal, Joel S. 2001. *State in Society: Studying How States and Societies Transform and Constitute Each Other.* Cambridge: Cambridge University Press.

Migot-Adholla, Shem E., and John W. Bruce. 1994. "Introduction: Are Indigenous African Tenure Systems Secure?" In *Searching for Land Tenure Security in Africa*, edited by John W. Bruce and Shem E. Migot-Adholla, 1–14. Dubuque, IA: Kendall/Hunt Publishing.

Misafi, Haidari Pascal. 2014. "Women's Participation in Decentralized Local Governance: The Case of Pastoral and Non-Pastoral Women in Kondoa Local Authority, Tanzania." PhD diss., Universiteit Gent.

Mohanty, Chandra Talpade. 1988. "Under Western Eyes: Feminist Scholarship and Colonial Discourses." *Feminist Review* 30: 61–88.

– 2003. *Feminism without Borders: Decolonizing Theory, Practicing Solidarity.* Durham, NC: Duke University Press.

MoHCDGEC (Ministry of Health, Community Development, Gender, Elderly, and Children), Ministry of Health-Zanzibar, National Bureau of Statistics – Tanzania, Office of Chief Government Statistician – Zanzibar, and ICF. 2016. "Tanzania Demographic and Health Survey and Malaria Indicator Survey, 2015–2016." https://dhsprogram.com/publications/publication-fr321-dhs-final-reports.cfm.

Moser, Caroline. 2005. "Has Gender Mainstreaming Failed?" *International Feminist Journal of Politics* 7, no. 4: 576–90.

Mshana, Rogate R. 2003. "The Impact of Economic, Social, and Political Reforms in Tanzania." In *Against Neoliberalism: Gender, Democracy, and Development*, edited by Chachage S.L. Chachage and Marjorie Mbilinyi, 110–15. Dar-es-Salaam: E & D Limited.

Mushi, Janeth. 2023. "Air Tanzania Plane Seized in the Netherlands Released, Returns Home." *The Citizen*. 9 July 2023. https://www.thecitizen.co.tz/tanzania/news/national/air-tanzania-plane-seized-in-the-netherlands-released-returns-home-4297688.

Mwanza, Kevin. 2018. "Less Than Two Percent of Land in Kenya Issued to Women Despite Legal Gains." *Reuters*. 13 March 2018. https://www.reuters.com/article/us-kenya-landrights-women-idUSKCN1GP22B.

Myers, Gregory, and Jolyne Sanjak. 2022. "Reflections on the Limited Impact of the VGGT in Sub Saharan Africa and Opportunities for Its Future with Lessons from Nigeria and Sierra Leone." *Land Use Policy* 113 (February): 105870. DOI:10.1016/j.landusepol.2021.105870.

Nayak, Prateep Kumar, and Fikret Berkes. 2010. "Whose Marginalisation? Politics around Environmental Injustices in India's Chilika Lagoon." *Local Environment* 15, no. 6: 553–67.

Nightingale, Andrea. 2006. "The Nature of Gender: Work, Gender, and Environment." *Environment and Planning D: Society and Space* 24, no. 2: 165–85.

Nyamu-Musembi, Celestine. 2008. "Breathing Life into Dead Theories about Property Rights in Rural Africa: Lessons from Kenya." In *Women's Land Rights and Privatization in Eastern Africa*, edited by Birgit Englert and Elizabeth Daley, 18–39. Suffolk, UK: James Currey.

Nyantakyi-Frimpong, Hanson, and Rachel Bezner Kerr. 2017. "Land Grabbing, Social Differentiation, Intensified Migration, and Food Security in Northern Ghana." *Journal of Peasant Studies* 44, no. 2: 421–44. DOI:10.1080/03066150.2016.1228629.

Oakland Institute. 2011. "Land Deal Brief: Agrisol Energy and Pharos Global Agriculture Fund's Land Deal in Tanzania." 24 May 2011. https://www.oaklandinstitute.org/land-deal-brief-agrisol-energy-and-pharos-global-agriculture-fund%E2%80%99s-land-deal-tanzania.

– 2012. "Land Deal Brief: Tanzanian Villagers Pay for Sun Biofuels Investment Disaster." 25 September 2012. https://www.oaklandinstitute.org/land-deal-brief-tanzanian-villagers-pay-sun-biofuels-investment-disaster.

Obeng-Odoom, Franklin. 2016. "Understanding Land Reform in Ghana: A Critical Postcolonial Institutional Approach." *Review of Radical Political Economics* 48, no. 4: 661–80. DOI:10.1177/0486613415603161.

O'Brien, Robert, Anne Marie Goetz, Jan Aart Scholte, and Marc Williams. 2000. *Contesting Global Governance: Multilateral Economic Institutions and Global Social Movements*. Cambridge: University of Cambridge Press.

Odgaard, Rie. 2002. "Scrambling for Land in Tanzania: Processes of Formalisation and Legitimisation of Land Rights." *European Journal of Development Research* 14, no. 2: 71–88.

Okoth-Ogendo, H.W.O. 2000. "Legislative Approaches to Customary Tenure and Tenure Reform in East Africa." In *Evolving Land Rights, Policy, and Tenure in Africa*, edited by Camilla Toulmin and Julian Quan, 123–34. London: International Institute for Environment and Development.

O'Neill, Kate. *The Environment and International Relations.* Cambridge: Cambridge University Press, 2009.

Ossome, Lyn. 2014. "Can the Law Secure Women's Rights to Land in Africa? Revisiting Tensions between Culture and Land Commercialization." *Feminist Economics* 20, no. 1: 155–77.

Overbeek, Henk. 2005. "Global Governance, Class, Hegemony: A Historical Materialist Perspective." In *Contending Perspectives on Global Governance: Coherence, Contestation, and World Order,* edited by Alice D. Ba and Matthew J. Hoffmann, 39–56. New York: Routledge.

Oxfam. 2014a. "Oxfam Response to UN Committee on World Food Security Endorsement of Principles." Press Release. 15 October 2014. https://www.oxfam.org/en/press-releases/oxfam-response-un-committee-world-food-security-endorsement-principles.

– 2014b. "PepsiCo Declares 'Zero Tolerance' for Land Grabs in Supply Chain." Oxfam International. 18 May 2014. https://www.oxfam.org/en/press-releases/pepsico-declares-zero-tolerance-land-grabs-supply-chain.

Pallotti, Arrigo. 2008. "Tanzania: Decentralising Power or Spreading Poverty?" *Review of African Political Economy* 35, no. 116: 221–35.

Parpart, Jane. 2009. "Fine Words, Failed Policies: Gender Mainstreaming in an Insecure and Unequal World." In *Development in an Insecure and Gendered World: The Relevance of the Millennium Goals,* edited by Jacqueline Leckie, 51–70. Burlington, VT: Ashgate.

Pearce, Fred. 2012. *The Land Grabbers: The New Fight over Who Owns the Earth.* Boston, MA: Beacon Press.

Pedersen, Rasmus Hundsbaek. 2012. "Decoupled Implementation of New-Wave Land Reforms: Decentralisation and Local Governance of Land in Tanzania." *Journal of Development Studies* 48, no. 2: 268–81.

– 2015. "A Less Gendered Access to Land? The Impact of Tanzania's New Wave of Land Reform." *Development Policy Review* 33, no. 4: 415–32.

Pedersen, Rasmus Hundsbaek, and Scholastica Haule. 2013. *Women, Donors, and Land Administration: The Tanzania Case.* Copenhagen: Danish Institute for International Studies (DIIS).

Perrons, Diane. 2021. *Is Austerity Gendered?* Cambridge, UK: Polity.

Pesticide Action Network Asia Pacific. 2014. "CFS Agri Investment Principles Don't Uphold Food, Land Rights." Press Release. 16 October 2014. http://panap.net/campaigns/land-food-rights/international-advocacy-and-instruments/2497.

Peters, Pauline E. 2010. "'Our Daughters Inherit Our Land, but Our Sons Use Their Wives' Fields': Matrilineal-Matrilocal Land Tenure and the New Land Policy in Malawi." *Journal of Eastern African Studies* 4, no. 1: 179–99.

Peterson, V. Spike. 2010. "International/Global Political Economy." In *Gender Matters in Global Politics: A Feminist Introduction to International Relations*, edited by Laura J. Shepherd, 204–17. New York: Routledge.

Po, June Y.T., and Gordon M. Hickey. 2018. "Local Institutions and Smallholder Women's Access to Land Resources in Semi-Arid Kenya." *Land Use Policy* 76: 252–63.

Prügl, Elisabeth. 2014. "Neoliberalising Feminism." *New Political Economy* 20, no. 4: 614–31.

Prügl, Elisabeth, and Mary K. Meyer. 1999. "Introduction: Gender Politics in Global Governance." In *Gender Politics in Global Governance*, edited by Mary K. Meyer and Elisabeth Prügl, 3–16. Lanham, MD: Rowman and Littlefield.

Quan, Julian, Lora Forsythe, and June Y.T. Po. 2021. "Advancing Women's Position by Recognizing and Strengthening Customary Land Rights: Lessons from Community-Based Land Interventions in Mozambique." In *Land Governance and Gender: The Tenure-Gender Nexus in Land Management and Land Policy*, edited by Uchendu Eugene Chigbu, 65–79. Oxfordshire, UK, and Boston, MA: CABI.

Rai, Shirin M. 2008. "Analysing Global Governance." In *Global Governance: Feminist Perspectives*, edited by Shirin M. Rai and Georgina Waylen, 19–42. New York: Palgrave Macmillan.

Rai, Shirin M., and Georgina Waylen. 2008. "Introduction: Feminist Perspectives on Analysing and Transformng Global Governance." In *Global Governance: Feminist Perspectives*, edited by Shirin M. Rai and Georgina Waylen, 1–18. New York: Palgrave MacMillan.

Rankin, Katharine N. 2001. "Governing Development: Neoliberalism, Microcredit, and Rational Economic Woman." *Economy and Society* 30, no. 1: 18–37.

Rao, Nitya. 2005. "Questioning Women's Solidarity: The Case of Land Rights, Santal Parganas, Jharkhand, India." *Journal of Development Studies* 41, no. 3: 353–75.

Ravnborg, Helle Munk, Rachel Spichiger, Rikke Brandt Broegaard, and Rasmus Hundsbæk Pedersen. 2016. "Land Governance, Gender Equality, and Development: Past Achievements and Remaining Challenges." *Journal of International Development* 28 no. 3: 412–27.

Razavi, Shahra. 2003. "Introduction: Agrarian Change, Gender and Land Rights." *Journal of Agrarian Change* 3, no. 1-2: 2–32.

– 2007. "Liberalisation and the Debates on Women's Access to Land." *Third World Quarterly* 28, no. 8: 1479–500.

– 2009a. "Engendering the Political Economy of Agrarian Change." *Journal of Peasant Studies* 36, no. 1: 197–226.

– 2009b. “The Gendered Impacts of Liberalization: Towards ‘Embedded Liberalism’?” In *The Gendered Impacts of Liberalization: Towards “Embedded Liberalism”?* edited by Shahra Razavi, 1–36. New York: Routledge.

Republic of Kenya. 2010. *Constitution of Kenya 2010*. National Council for Law Reporting.

Rocheleau, Dianne E., Barbara P. Thomas-Slayter, and Esther Wangari. 1996. *Feminist Political Ecology: Global Issues and Local Experiences*. London/New York: Routledge.

Roberts, Adrienne. 2012. “Financial Crisis, Financial Firms ... and Financial Feminism? The Rise of ‘Transnational Business Feminism’ and the Necessity of Marxist-Feminist IPE.” *Socialist Studies* 8, no. 2: 85–108.

– 2014. “The Political Economy of ‘Transnational Business Feminism.’” *International Feminist Journal of Politics* 17, no. 2: 209–31.

Rosenau, James N. 1995. “Governance in the Twenty-First Century.” *Global Governance* 1: 13–43.

Rusimbi, Mary. 2003. “SAPs for Whom? Grassroots Perspectives.” In *Against Neoliberalism: Gender, Democracy, and Development*, edited by Chachage S.L. Chachage and Marjorie Mbilinyi, 99–115. Dar es Salaam: E&D Limited.

Ryan, Caitlin. 2018. “Large-Scale Land Deals in Sierra Leone at the Intersection of Gender and Lineage.” *Third World Quarterly* 39, no. 1: 189–206.

Sánchez, Javier. 2014. “CSM Statement on the Adoption of RAI.” *Civil Society and Indigenous People’s Mechanism for Relations with the UN Committee on World Food Security*. https://www.csm4cfs.org/wp-content/uploads/2016/06/CSM_raiStmt_final_en.pdf.

Sauer, Birgit, and Stefanie Wohl. 2011. “Feminist Perspectives on the Internationalization of the State.” *Antipode* 43, no. 1: 108–28.

Saul, John S. 2012. “Tanzania Fifty Years on (1961–2011): Rethinking Ujamaa, Nyerere, and Socialism in Africa.” *Review of African Political Economy* 39, no. 131: 117–25.

Scott, James C. 1998. *Seeing Like a State: How Certain Schemes to Improve the Human Condition Have Failed*. New Haven, CT, and London: Yale University Press.

Seguino, Stephanie. 2007. “Plus Ça Change? Evidence on Global Trends in Gender Norms and Stereotypes.” *Feminist Economics* 13, no. 2: 1–28.

Seguino, Stephanie, and Caren Grown. 2007. “Gender Equity and Globalization: Macroeconomic Policy for Developing Countries.” In *The Feminist Economics of Trade*, edited by Irene van Staveren, Diane Elson, Caren Grown, and Nilufer Cagatay, 292–315. New York: Routledge.

Seufert, Philip. 2013. “The FAO Voluntary Guidelines on the Responsible Governance of Tenure of Land, Fisheries, and Forests.” *Globalizations* 10, no. 1: 181–6.

Shepherd, Laura J., and Lucy Ferguson. 2011. "Gender, Governance, and Power: Finding the Global at the Local Level." *Globalizations* 8, no. 2: 127–33.
Shiva, Vandana. 2016. *Who Really Feeds the World?* Berkeley, CA: North Atlantic Books.
Shivji, Issa G. 2012. "Nationalism and Pan-Africanism: Decisive Moments in Nyerere's Intellectual and Political Thought." *Review of African Political Economy* 39, no. 131: 103–16.
Sikor, Thomas, and Daniel Müller. 2009. "The Limits of State-led Land Reform: An Introduction." *World Development* 37, no. 8: 1307–16.
Soederberg, Susanne. 2006. *Global Governance in Question: Empire, Class, and the New Common Sense in Managing North-South Relations.* Ann Arbor, MI: Pluto Press.
Songa, Songa wa. 2015. "Special Report: Land Grabbing in Tanzania: The Truth, Fallacies, and Fights – Part 1." *The Citizen*, 24 March 2015. https://www.thecitizen.co.tz/tanzania/news/national/special-report-land-grabbing-in-tanzania-the-truth-fallacies-and-fights-part-1-2523858.
Spear, Thomas. 2003. "Neo-Traditionalism and the Limits of Invention in British Colonial Africa." *Journal of African History* 44, no. 1: 3–27.
Spichiger, Rachel, and Paul Stacey. 2014. "Ghana's Land Reform and Gender Equality." *Danish Institute for International Studies*. 1 January 2014. https://www.jstor.org/stable/resrep13371.
Sud, Nikita. 2014. "The Men in the Middle: A Missing Dimension in Global Land Deals." *Journal of Peasant Studies* 41, no. 4: 593–612.
Sulle, Emmanuel, and Helen Dancer. 2020. "Gender, Politics, and Sugarcane Commercialisation in Tanzania." *Journal of Peasant Studies* 47, no. 5: 973–92.
Sulle, Emmanuel, and Ruth Hall. 2013. *Reframing the New Alliance Agenda: A Critical Assessment Based on Insights from Tanzania.* Brighton, UK: Future Agricultures Consortium and PLAAS Policy Brief. https://www.future-agricultures.org/publications/policy-briefs-document/reframing-the-new-alliance-agenda-a-critical-assessment-based-on-insights-from-tanzania.
Sulle, Emmanuel, and Fred Nelson. 2009. *Biofuels, Land Access, and Rural Livelihoods in Tanzania.* London: International Institute for Environment and Development.
Tanzania Media Women's Association. n.d. *Project Proposal: Increase Women's Participation in Tanzania's 2014 and 2015 Elections.* Dar es Salaam: Tanzania Media Women's Association (TAMWA).
Tanzania Women Lawyers Association. 2013. *Position Paper on Gender Mainstreaming the Constitution Review Process of Tanzania.* Dar es Salaam: Tanzania Women Lawyers Association.
Theting, Hans, and Brita Brekke. 2010. *Land Investments or Land Grab? A Critical View from Tanzania and Mozambique.* Oslo: Spire.

Toulmin, Camilla, and Julian Quan, eds. 2000. *Evolving Land Rights, Policy and Tenure in Africa*. London: International Institute for Environment and Development.

Tripp, Aili Mari. 2004. "Women's Movements, Customary Law, and Land Rights in Africa: The Case of Uganda." *African Studies Quarterly* 7, no. 4: 1–19.

Tsikata, Dzodzi. 2003. "Securing Women's Interests within Land Tenure Reforms: Recent Debates in Tanzania." *Journal of Agrarian Change* 3, no. 1-2: 149–83.

– 2016. "Gender, Land Tenure, and Agrarian Production Systems in Sub-Saharan Africa." *Agrarian South: Journal of Political Economy* 5, no. 1: 1–19.

Tsikata, Dzodzi, and Joseph Awetori Yaro. 2014. "When a Good Business Model Is Not Enough: Land Transactions and Gendered Livelihood Prospects in Rural Ghana." *Feminist Economics* 20, no. 1: 202–26.

Tzouvala, Ntina. 2019. "A False Promise? Regulating Land-Grabbing and the Post-Colonial State." *Leiden Journal of International Law* 32, no. 2: 235–53.

United Nations Department of Economic and Social Affairs. 2021. *Handbook on the Least Developed Country Category: Inclusion, Graduation, and Special Support Measures*, Fourth Edition. https://www.un.org/development/desa/dpad/wp-content/uploads/sites/45/LDC-Handbook-2021.pdf.

United Republic of Tanzania. 1972. *The Interpretation of Laws and General Clauses Act*. Dodoma: Parliament of the United Republic of Tanzania.

– 1994. *Report of the Presidential Commission of Inquiry into Land Matters*. Dar es Salaam: Ministry of Lands, Housing, and Urban Development, Government of the United Republic of Tanzania.

– 1999a. *Land Act, No. 4*. Dodoma: Parliament of the United Republic of Tanzania.

– 1999b. *Village Land Act, No. 5*. Dodoma: Parliament of the United Republic of Tanzania.

– 2002. *The Courts (Land Disputes Settlements) Act*. Dodoma: Parliament of the United Republic of Tanzania.

– 2015. *Integrated Labour Force Survey (ILFS) 2014*. Dar es Salaam: National Bureau of Statistics.

Verma, Ritu. 2014. "Land Grabs, Power, and Gender in East and Southern Africa: So, What's New?" *Feminist Economics* 20, no. 1: 52–75.

Vermeulen, Sonja, and Lorenzo Cotula. 2010. "Over the Heads of Local People: Consultation, Consent, and Recompense in Large-Scale Land Deals for Biofuels Projects in Africa." *Journal of Peasant Studies* 37, no. 4: 899–916.

Walker, Cherryl. 2005. "The Limits to Land Reform: Rethinking 'the Land Question.'" *Journal of Southern African Studies* 31, no. 4: 805–24.

Welsh, Teresa. 2022. "Exclusive: Conservative Nations Block UN Gender and Food Guidelines." *Devex*, 7 October 2022. https://www.devex.com/news/

sponsored/exclusive-conservative-nations-block-un-gender-and-food-guidelines-104151.
Whitehead, Ann, and Dzodzi Tsikata. 2003. "Policy Discourses on Women's Land Rights in Sub-Saharan Africa: The Implications of the Re-Turn to the Customary." *Journal of Agrarian Change* 3, no. 1–2: 67–112.
– 2009. "The Gendered Impacts of Liberalization Policies on African Agricultural Economies and Rural Livelihoods." In *The Gendered Impacts of Liberalization: Towards "Embedded Liberalism"?* edited by Shahra Razavi, 37–62. New York: Routledge.
Whitworth, Sandra. 1994. "Theory as Exclusion: Gender and International Political Economy." In *Political Economy and the Changing World Order*, edited by Richard Stubbs and Geoffery Underhill, 116–29. Toronto: McClelland and Stewart.
Wise, Timothy A. 2014. "Picking Up the Pieces from a Failed Land Grab Project in Tanzania." *The World*, 27 June 2014. https://theworld.org/dispatches/globalpost-blogs/rights/picking-the-pieces-failed-land-grab-project-tanzania.
Women's Legal Aid Centre. 2010. *Assessing Rural Women's Land Ownership Ten Years after the Enactment of the Land Laws.* Dar es Salaam: Women's Legal Aid Centre.
– 2013. "Legal Aid Unit." Web resource. https://www.wlac.or.tz/whatwedo.php?p=233.
World Bank. 2012. *World Development Report 2012: Gender Equality and Development.* Washington, DC. http://hdl.handle.net/10986/4391.
– 2019. *Doing Business 2019.* Washington, DC. https://www.doingbusiness.org/content/dam/doingBusiness/media/Annual-Reports/English/DB2019-report_web-version.pdf.
– 2022. *Tanzania Gender Assessment.* Washington, DC. https://documents1.worldbank.org/curated/en/099155103312251069/pdf/P1760510ca289d0400a40e03f64088 26f07.pdf.
World Bank and United Nations Conference on Trade and Development. 2014. *The Practice of Responsible Investment Principles in Larger-Scale Agricultural Investments: Implications for Corporate Performance and Impact on Local Communities.* Washington, DC: World Bank.
Yngstrom, Ingrid. 2002. "Women, Wives, and Land Rights in Africa: Situating Gender beyond the Household in the Debate over Land Policy and Changing Tenure Systems." *Oxford Development Studies* 30, no. 1: 21–40.
Zoomers, Annelies. 2010. "Globalisation and the Foreignisation of Space: Seven Processes Driving the Current Land Grab." *Journal of Peasant Studies* 37, no. 2: 429–47.

INDEX